NEVER A VIABLE

ALTERNATIVE

BY

RAYMOND J. BARRY

Contents

Preface

Los Angeles, California, December 27, 2013

Acting for me was insanely difficult, but not to say impossible. Self-doubt was often the fountainhead of numerous mishaps along the way. Pride was a large factor in my refusal to surrender, like a rhino charging a truck again and again, not realizing the truck is made of impenetrable steel. One cannot approach the profession "by trying it out for a while to see what happens, before I try something else". Personal pride forced me to fully embrace that original foolhardy decision and bring it to its natural end, perhaps similar to Eve's bite into the forbidden apple in the Garden of Eden. Becoming an actor involved 'free will' to choose a profession and then fully embrace the struggle that lay ahead; all the profession's hazards, its entire package of part time jobs, numerous failures, fear, self-doubt along with moments of absolute joy, blended with sporadic and then finally consistent success. Today, after sixty years of doing it, acting represents *(along with my role as a father and husband)*, the measure of my worth. The profession not only has provided a living enough to send my four children through college but also has endowed me with absolute pride for having survived 'the life' with some measure of dignity.

Fulfilling a dream is part of everyone's make-up, well, not everyone but certainly those willing to battle it out for the sheer love of 'the work'. Foraging for 'food on the table' and 'a roof over one's head' by doing what one loves is not for the faint of heart. In my case, avoidance was never a viable alternative. I was either too stubborn or too naïve to avoid the hazards I would face. Stubbornness characterized who I was at the early stage of my career. Same is true today, although I admit that I've softened a bit. But stubbornness has served me well, insistence upon moving forward, no matter what that original choice entailed. Struggle has become a way of life, my life, yes, all mine, the entire experience in one package and maybe a paradigm for any actor's life.

Writing this book has made me aware of how often my work has been sabotaged by fear. Perhaps this condition is common to all young people, but one fact is clear; the danger of being on stage before a live audience forced me to evolve both as an artist and as a person. The trick was to 'stick it out' and eventually arrive on the other side. As years passed, I was unaware of how frequent that 'anxious visitation' raised its ugly head. The exact source of my fear was always mysterious. Nonetheless, at that early period of my career, tension on stage was common; that is, until my tenure with the *'Open Theater'*, when confidence as a performer gradually established itself, thanks to the company's director, Joseph Chaikin, who, aside from his genius, was sensitive enough to guide me during our creative process. Gradually I realized that confidence has to do with all aspects of life, relationships and offspring, all of the details that surround a man's existence. Life in the theater has been good, yes, regardless of large blunders earlier during the journey. Yes, I have faltered from time to time, but slowly, inch by inch, something good did happen internally, and a viable career did finally take shape.

Professionalism is expected, and I will provide that, regardless of what is required. The theater has expanded me into a conscious being, perhaps even a proud one. Dignity has been salvaged and the beacon still shines in the harbor, guiding me towards the glory of a life well-lived. Endurance has blessed me with a solid foundation, from which I relate both to my profession and to the people in it. My greatest bouts of self-doubt occurred during my youth, thank God, which left time to recover, to reeducate myself, to play parts badly and to learn from my mistakes, to fall on my face repeatedly, to recover and to stand wounded on my feet before finding light at the end of the tunnel. I have few goals left, aside from a desire to complete what I began when I was young man with a cloudy dream of performing roles that fascinated me. I wished to be Marlon Brando then but instead became a true version of me.

Time marches on, events happen, the audience is swayed, and somehow I manage to be on top of things. Today I am a normal person, not on top of the world but 'normal', whatever that word represents, normal, happy, balanced, calm, all those good things that suggest that life is going my way. But whatever comes my way also goes 'its way' independently, often ignoring my needs. Life plods onward without my 'willing it'. One must simply keep one's head up, while moving through time, observing the details of the journey, yes, noticing it all. And if time is available, to record it, to write it down, to act it, to paint it, as an artist would, to record the experience by creating of a work of art, a happy work, a sad work, a work anchored in both life's soft and harsh experiences.

~~~

A memory of two boys lying under a tree on a hot summer day with nothing to do but play. I remember that time of my youth. I had it all then without realizing. I had it all with little means to

3

express it. But today, seventy years later, that time exists in memory only, and what has replaced it is a 'wholeness' that refuses to budge from its base. Today a sense of 'well-being' is born from that foundation with little desire to upset the apple cart. No reason to return to the angst of my youth. Today creativity is derived from pleasure and so very grateful for that.

This book's purpose is not designed to instruct. Pontificating upon the subject of 'how to act' is not my interest here. After six decades in the theater, what I know is purely intuitive. But I do know something. Of this I am sure. The so-called 'life' of an actor and the lessons learned along the way are what most fascinate me; an actor's joy, as well as his or her doubt and anxiety about what comes next. 'Self-worth' too often parallels performing skill, but that is the plight of an actor. What mindset is necessary to survive such a life? Is the struggle worth it? These questions are dealt with 'piecemeal' in this book, as my life's search has also been 'piecemeal'.

Barbara Constance Barry, Last Visit

January 24, 2006, 1:46 pm, Upstate New York

Originally published in the 2019 edition of 'Caveat Lector'

Mist rises from the Hudson River's surface, forming a gossamer cloud that dissolves softly into a gray sky. Ducks fly in the distance, settling in the faraway river bank. The water is placid from the moving train's window, its smooth, shiny surface reminding me of a shimmering looking-glass that reflects the closest bank. I remember myself, as a young boy, playing on a lake. Once playing on lakes was a frequent pastime. Those were carefree times of fishing every day. Nowadays I never fish, and I shall never fish again, have no interest in fishing. When I was a boy, fishing was my first love. The love remained, but fishing gave way to other boyish activities not worth mentioning. Today there are more important things than fishing. I am older now, and it is time to wrap up my life, time to tie loose ends together. One of those loose ends is my ninety-four-year-old mother, saying my final goodbye, speaking a few loving words, telling her that she means a great deal to me. It must be done.

The river is a comforting sight with its placid beauty and flying birds. Mother is unaware that I am coming. I shall surprise her with my unexpected arrival. If I warned her with a call, I might not show up. I cannot trust myself when it comes to showing up. I have been known to change my mind. When that happens, I leave everyone in a lurch. I have been known to disappoint people. In mother's case, disappointment would be too much for her to take. My promises are not always kept, but I do my best.

It's January 24, 2006, 1:46 in the afternoon. I must arrive at mother's doorstep feeling right about myself. She deserves the truth, and the truth is that I do love my mother. She will soon die at the age of ninety-four. I'm making the necessary visit to show I still care. I do care, but I do not care. How easy it is for me to say, "I do not care". During the earlier part of my life, I lived without caring and without loving; that is, until my first daughter was born. Later came two sons and much later another daughter. Gradually I was softened by my love toward my children and my wife, and that has been a small miracle. I appreciate my love for my family. I do love them. Today I know what I mean by the word 'love', when it comes to my wife and children.

But with mother I do not call anymore. She doesn't answer the phone, and I hardly ever visit her. I depended upon her when we worked together in the theater. A strong bond of love still lies between us. We both lent a helping hand when creating plays. But today our relationship involves a few sentimental visits thrown in on holidays and birthdays. This meeting represents one of those visits. This might be my last. It might be awkward being there. But I have said that.

The town is approaching. Our meeting is imminent. Time to prepare myself for my role, the dutiful son paying a visit, the responsible son, showing he cares. Birds fly off in the distance. Mist

6

comes off the river. It is quiet out there; a lovely river, a lovely sight. Outside the air is brisk. I am somewhat chilled by that coolness. The sun is beginning to burn off the mist rising above the river. The train has stopped. I hear birds outside, along the river bank. How fortunate they are with their ability to fly, their simple approach that finds happiness in mere survival. They know what is best for them. Ignorance is bliss. Their mothers have flown away, never to be seen again.

~~~

Upon entering mother's living quarters, her paintings line its walls, as they did our bungalow during my youth. A large one in the living room is composed of bright yellows with a few bold reds that vitalize the somberness of her tiny dwelling. Mother created that painting when she was in her forties, a configuration of blazing color and brazen brush stokes that holds forth an unpredictable maze and teases the viewer's eyes with radiant circles collided against rigid, right angles, each upon another. A dynamic explosion of line, form and color reflects the roadmap of mother's mind, complete with its numerous detours and dead ends that represent her life's complex journey.

~~~

In the beginning, Barbara Constance Barry was satisfied by marriage. Then she had children. Mother never planned that. We were born, that's all. We were born and needs were again temporarily satisfied, as well as created by responsibilities that came from raising us. Screaming infants with outstretched arms demanded undivided attention, while mother dutifully toilet-trained us, delivered us to and from school, washed stains from our underwear and cleaned up our mess when we were sick.

In between filthy diapers and screaming babies, Barbara Constance Barry's passions were satisfied by publishing short stories and exhibiting her paintings in New York City galleries. Numerous New York art shows followed. One painting hung for a year in the Museum of New York. She'd already published a number of short stories by then, one entitled *'Herbie'*; the main character, a midget adored by a lonely, half insane woman for his overwhelming kindness. Kindness from men meant a great deal to Barbara Constance Barry. Vincent Van Gogh impressed her as a kind man in the face of his torment. That brilliant, insane painter became her hero, while she was slowly going mad herself in a violent, alcoholic marriage with limited time to paint and write. The woman was an artist, not a housewife. Van Gogh's insanity justified hers, as if his mental imbalance were the source of his genius. Similarly, she believed her instability was the source of her creativity. I questioned her theory later, after going off the deep end myself in my mid-twenties and still wonder if artists can live well-balanced lives.

~~~

During the father's worst drinking nights, mother huddled her children together in her bed, when his car pulled into the driveway in the wee hours, its headlights casting a bright reflection upon her bedroom's silver asbestos wall.

He was usually drunk.

The nightmare that had become the evening's routine would follow, the man of the house, stumbling over his own vomit, after crashing through the front door like Frankenstein bent on destroying all that had wounded him, the accusatory shouts of, 'bum' and 'pig' that mirrored his twisted impression of his wife, smashed lamp on plaster wall, broken furniture, tuna fish dragged home from a bar in Freeport, foul smelling with bleeding gills, smashed Christmas tree during the holidays, vulgar songs about mother's alleged, sexual diversions, rowdy barroom ditties that described her as a 'whore' and a 'slut,' foul songs, foul language that she, no doubt, had encouraged somewhat with frequent jaunts to New York City to visit her artist friends, thereby making his protests all the more viable to himself. How convenient it had been to use that word, "whore", when he'd returned from a night of whoring himself with barroom battles etched upon his body, split nose, face puffed out like a watermelon from being punched, knife stabs in his back and hand, crashing his car, wrecking it, losing his license, staggering through the house on wobbly legs in a drunken stupor, while his fumbling fingers tried desperately to fit a rubber onto his penis.

A truce would be called at the end of each night, when every member of the family would retreat to separate corners, their bodies cloistered in close quarters, personalities needing privacy, space to think, space to meditate, to stretch, and mother caressing herself as a lonely woman would, when at last the fury of the household gave over to troubled sleep; the man of the house sprawled upon the living room couch, his penis hanging from his shorts. Upon awakening the next morning, after beating his wife bloody with drunken fists the night before, a quiet, repentant expression on his face. In the aftermath of each crisis, reconciliation between husband and wife produced exaggerated, theatrical embraces in front of the children to show they truly loved each other in spite of their indefatigable rage.

Not a pleasant place, called home. Blaring noise described its ambiance, flooding the area with echoes of father's nightly, slurred, drunken fugue. The man hated his marriage but passionately loved mother, although the word 'love' was never mentioned. Husband and wife had become a violent habit without mention of the word 'love'. There had been a sprawling battle then, continuing from morning till night and igniting again, whenever a family member came home. There was no space in that tiny bungalow, only a few tiny rooms and kids and dogs and cats and bodies impinging upon one another's rights, pushing you out of my way before you push me out of the way and all of us pushing each other through childhood, while daddy pushed mommy and mommy cried and they both screamed and the notion of confronting each other without punches and pushes was foreign to us.

Home had become a violent state of mind rather than a physical place, an inheritance bequeathed upon the son from his father, passed down from his father's father, and so on, generation to generation, until it'd become a permanent part of the boy's estate. After three children had been born, there would be no other offspring to continue this lineage. The boy and his two sisters

9

shared its wealth. At that early time, his young life was defined by violence at home, subsequent confusion in school and general neglect. Later, an abnormal appetite for the violent game of football solidified the troubled mold from which he'd been cast.

The boy was skilled at the game.

Memories too of blaring music of Bartok from mother's kitchen radio to drown out the family conspiracy against her. Modern or classical composers' music played from her favorite radio station, reverberating loudly against our bungalow's walls, a symphonic backdrop of Prokofiev, Rachmaninoff or Bach on any given day. Piano or violin concerti were usually accompanied by her shrill whistle, as if she were one of the orchestra's violins, emitting from her pursed lips piercing notes that smothered the boorish sound of her husband's booming voice, as he lurched about the living room, a raging elephant in a zoo, venting his loneliness from being cooped up too long in his cage. Without realizing, the boy's consciousness was being expanded by mother's appreciation for Bella Bartok, Igor Stravinsky and Hindemith constantly blasting through the house.

~~~

Mother's old face expresses shock at the sight of me. She doesn't believe I came, so used to being separated from her son is she. The ninety-four-year-old woman asks why I haven't visited in so many months. There is no answer, aside from my guilt for not having done my duty, for having neglected my mother when her death is imminent. I am guilty, mother's guilty son, offering no gift or flowers to accompany my visit. At least there should be flowers to smell, while we talk. But I bring no flowers. There is no fragrance to brighten our conversation. Instead we deal with each other's smell, the odor of an aging woman and in my case, the smell of an actor's 'hand to mouth' struggle that has miraculously evolved into a legitimate career. We meet for the sake of old times. What else could there be? Love? I could say, "I love you, ma," but "I love you," is a phrase that seems insufficient. I look at mother's wizened face, as her broken voice sends sweet platitudes my way. An old bird she is, croaking away.

"Oh, my, how wonderful you came, my son. How wonderful to see you. And you look so marvelous with your broad shoulders and your fine face. Oh, yes, and you're doing well, I trust? Oh, yes, very good, very good."

She does not listen to my responses. Her ears are blocked with decades of built-up wax. Between us lies an urgency to make something big happen during this short visit, to pack within a few hours what is left to say when life is running out. As I say, she is ninety-four years old and I am sixty-six. The importance of this meeting is palpable, how both of us would like for something meaningful to occur with so little time left. She can barely walk. The most she expects from her remaining days is endless hours of television and naps during the commercials. I sit and smile, the dutiful son, feeling guilty, expecting her death soon after this last meeting together.

I imagine what it must be like to be so old, things that are too intimate to share, the loss of independence, inability to walk easily to the bathroom; asking myself how she bathes herself, how she looks naked with her skin so wrinkled, so shriveled, so loose. Surely she must be horrible to herself, that foreboding aging process that leaves her forgotten, the unfairness of being allowed consciousness enough to value life, while knowing death will arrive soon, the paradox of loving life, when it will soon be taken from her. But mother wants to die. She has said as much. I am here to ease that passage, to affirm that things went well between us. She had a hand in my life. I had a hand in hers. Whatever went wrong during the difficult years gives way to gratitude for all we did in each other's behalf. She was a paradigm of courage when it came to sticking to her personal rules of life, provided wisdom that I still value today; the miracle of creativity, the value of beauty and art in a crass world that worships only money.

Things are somewhat blurred. I've been claiming feelings that are mine one moment and then they're not, after having disappeared without a trace. Feelings aren't the definition of who I

11

really am. Rather they are an afterthought of my condition after action has been taken. I believed it would be a good thing to take action; that is, to visit my aged mother, a good thing to stand before her and express my love to her. Rejuvenating our friendship that once was so strong is my purpose here. There have been times in our past when we laughed together, and our conversations were abundant and rich, demonstrating our mutual interest in theater and painting and writing, but now, as I look into her wizened face, there is little reference to our past, our art, our work together in the theater, and, yes, our love for life. Has she given all this up? Has she allowed herself to lose interest in the things that have given her such vitality? Bewildered by her empty chatter; her words are evasive, avoiding any clear theme that might be meaningful to both of us.

Already the day is passing quickly. Bewildered by mother's empty chatter, my mind is overshadowed by dim memories of our darkened history within the walls of this tiny, suburban bungalow;

~~~

When the boy was eleven or twelve, Barbara Constance Barry introduced him to the local movie house, the 'Arcade'. Tickets were fourteen cents to see great films; *'On the Waterfront'*, *'Streetcar Named Desire'* and *'A Place in the Sun'* with Elizabeth Taylor and Montgomery Clift to name a few. Marlon Brando was bigger than life in the boy's young mind. Brando, Montgomery Clift and later James Dean were fearful, fragile men, atypical of the usual masculine personae of male film stars during the forties and fifties. These new actors seemed accessible to their vulnerability, as opposed to the John Wayne types, flaunting their exaggerated macho image to the public at large. Male sensitivity had suddenly taken its rightful place in the world of film. As a boy, I identified completely.

In that tiny movie house, mother chain smoked non-filter cigarettes, as I watched Marlon Brando vent his passions with Vivien Leigh in *'Streetcar Named Desire'*. The two of them were brilliant, igniting their passions that were seemingly so out of

12

control and yet so artfully performed. Brando's poetic genius mesmerized me as an adolescent, mostly for his vulnerability. His fragility paralleled my own; the depth of his feelings was mine, his pain mine as well. I became Brando, as I watched him perform and fully identified with his struggle within the confines of that tiny movie house screen. In my innocence, his character was a real person, who happened to be in a film.

I was an introverted boy, painfully unsure of myself and very close to my mother. Being macho wasn't in the cards; that is, until years later, when athletics captured my soul. This new, vulnerable image of male movie stars appealed to me. They and I were cut from the same cloth, so to speak; they didn't fit in, out of place, not suitable for public consumption. Marlon Brando and Montgomery Clift seemed more than willing to show their fragility, which was similar to mine as a boy. I identified with that sensitive, male image, so inept to the ways of the world. It never dawned on me that these two brilliant actors had studied the craft of acting, that acting skill could be learned. I had no idea I would become a professional actor someday.

My paralyzing shyness as a boy, excluded me from normal interaction with people, let alone acting before an audience. The thought of it never entered my mind; that is, until a decade later. Meanwhile, my introduction to film I attribute to my mother. Her appreciation influenced me whenever she took me to the Arcade Movie Theater. At that early time, however, Hollywood represented a foreign, inaccessible world of 'stars' and 'fame', so very alien to the small town in which I was raised.

Other times, early in their marriage, mother went to the cinema with my father on Saturday nights. They would dress up for their movie date, mother always looking beautiful and my father so handsome in his suit. During their movie dates, there was never any drinking. Movies became an island of safety for me, since mother and father seemed in love whenever they saw a film. A sense of safety accompanied their movie nights with no drinking and more importantly, no violence. They always came home sober and in good humor and were even what could be called "happy". I stayed with my younger sisters back at the house, but I didn't mind. My

13

parents would be in a good mood when they returned. 'Movie night' for my parents guaranteed harmony in our household.

On Sunday mornings, after my parents' Saturday movie night, mother and I would sit in our tiny kitchen with its green Formica table and the sun blazing through its large, single window. I'd listen to her colorful description of the film she'd seen with my father the night before. Lilacs I'd planted bloomed outside that window in the spring. During the winters, icicles hung from their branches and lots of snow, while mother brought to life the characters she'd seen the night before. Our kitchen became her stage and I her audience, both of us losing track of time, while mother performed each actor's lines. Her skill as a performer was so very obvious, while imitating Betty Davis or Ann Baxter in *'All about Eve'* or Vivien Leigh in *'Streetcar Named Desire'*.

During those Sunday mornings, mother and son were bonded by a world of film fantasy. Her performance over our kitchen table liberated both of us into an imaginary, lush world of Hollywood, enhanced by the message of the film she'd seen the night before. Hours would pass, and the films she described educated me about the evils of racism and anti-Semitism with her description of Robert Ryan playing an anti-Semitic soldier, who killed a man because he was Jewish. This was the first but not the last time I witnessed mother perform. She was a brilliant actress in our kitchen. Years later, I would see on television the same 'black and white' film she'd fully brought to life. Those morning sessions, years before, had fooled me into believing I'd actually seen the film, when in fact, it was mother's vivid performance so firmly fixed in my memory.

~~~

I look out the window, observing the gray clouds that hover above the Hudson River. The sun is momentarily blocked, producing a winter ambiance that embraces the mood between mother and me in her bedroom, where she lies helplessly, while groping for something nice to say. I forgive her. Human activity means little to her at age ninety-four. All she has accomplished in her life has been set aside to make room for death. Death is her preoccupation now rather than life. Random activity for its own sake makes little sense. My visit is all she can handle now. Talk is arbitrary. Serious subjects are avoided for fear of the upheaval they may bring.

In recent years, mother hasn't left the house to take advantage of nature's pastoral scenery. Ninety-four years of living have exhausted spontaneous excursions through the verdant banks of the Hudson. Her bed is more inviting. How useless her life seems, as I witness the old woman before me, who has opted for a sedentary existence. She was such an active woman in her day; horrifying really, to allow oneself such passivity, after surrendering her independence. That's a big one, to allow other people to take the reins of her life. I couldn't do that easily; a daunting possibility really, to be so out of control, while living out each purposeless day. I must remind myself not to end up like mother before me, lying in bed at two in the afternoon, watching television to fill time.

On the other hand, 'doing things' and general 'busyness' may not be all they seem to be. A certain degree of futility is involved in life's sleepwalk, the feeling that one has been here before, and it didn't make much sense then, beyond an endless treading of water without noticing where it spills and little by way of purpose in any of it - aside from the children. They make sense somehow, the love involved in raising them, caring for their welfare. When they grow up, they can figure out what existing on this planet is all about. I haven't much of a clue myself, and yet I've had a decent life and consider myself lucky.

Mother and I stare at the television, as if it might offer a clue as to what to say next. There is nothing to say really and nothing to do. Time passes. We watch a game show called *'Strike It Rich'* that offers a free refrigerator to a couple from Iowa, visiting New York City for the week. According to the husband, they owed themselves a vacation and decided to do something exciting by coming to the big city. In their wanderings, they purchased tickets to the show. Already they've won a washing machine, and if it's possible to answer the next question correctly, they might walk out with a new refrigerator. The fat wife is nervous. The poor woman can barely

15

speak, so taken is she with being on television. Her dutiful husband is gleaming with expectation, eager to get on with it, so he can win his refrigerator. With his washing machine already in the bag, he seems confident. They are Christian, so God is on their side. The wife says as much.

"I hope he wins," mother says, apparently delighted by the man's prospect of going home with a new refrigerator. She has been watching television all day from her bed, the same routine that has filled all of her days from the time she has moved into this little space. That is what a ninety-four year old woman does nowadays, lies in bed and watches television. There is little conversation, while the eager couple struggles to identify the victorious general of the Civil War battle of Antietam, but as soon as the question has been wrongly answered by the disappointed gentleman, the couple forlornly walks off the stage, having won only a washing machine.

There is not much to say, considering the circumstance of competing with the talking box, although I embark upon various subjects, none of which hold mother's interest. My flourishing acting career certainly does not, nor my children, a baby daughter, two young boys and a grown daughter, who give me great joy in my life, but mother never liked children much, relates to them as if they are an imposition upon an artist's busy existence. Her enmity towards children is derived from the restriction she experienced when raising her own brood, three little ones, all of whom impinged upon her career as an artist. Changing dirty diapers simply was not her thing.

Back to the television - the thought of forcibly turning it off occurs to me, but that would be too much of a violation, one which mother wouldn't tolerate. At this very moment, she is laughing and making comments about the humorous talk show host, relating to him as if he were an old friend.

"Why don't you turn the television off, mother?"

I should not have asked the question. It popped out of my mouth without thinking. I have taken this trip to find clarity about what we have meant to each other. Right now this squawking box before us is in the way of that.

16

"Why, son, don't you like the program?"

Mother didn't ask for my visit. I came without warning, hoping she would welcome me, as she certainly did with an open heart. But after the initial salutation was done, it was over, the warmth, the joy of being together for the first time in a year. Back to mother and her television and how to separate the two. I ask her again to turn the machine off, whereupon she again looks at me surprised and repeats herself by asking if I don't like the program she's watching. I try to be gentle, explaining that I would like to spend time together without the television interrupting us, a reasonable request one would think, considering she might be dead tomorrow, or even in a few minutes, although her wizened complexion suggests strength enough to survive a few more months, maybe even years.

~~~

An evening comes to mind. I was thirty years of age and living a 'hand to mouth' existence on the New York stage at the time. Mother paid me a visit at my SoHo loft in New York City. We talked late into the night. Numerous subjects were discussed, including the war zone our family had become during my youth. During the passing hours, my father's roustabout adventures in bars were discussed at length, along with his infidelities. Deep into our conversation, I boldly asked her if she'd had affairs during their marriage. An uncomfortable silence followed, and the question was awkwardly answered that an affair had occurred with a painter, whose name was 'Anton', an alcoholic, similar to my father's drinking. Furthermore, she explained, this affair took place before my mother had a romantic relationship with a woman named Mazi.

I knew her partner well from frequent visits to our house, always adorned in men's suits, men's shoes and sported a 'butch' haircut with a 'part' on the side, similar to a man's hairdo. Mother found an island of security in their relationship, away from the suburban shambles of her marriage. Her women friend provided a sanctuary, a safe space away from home. Mother's partner recognized her worth that was never given credit by her husband.

Mazi supported mother's creativity, her womanhood, and provided a stable anchor in her life for the duration of their twenty-seven year relationship before Mazi finally died.

Mother was always in a good mood when Mazi visited the house. That was enough for me. Their relationship didn't bother me, as long as she was happy. Meanwhile, Barbara Constance Barry's artistic pursuits allowed a breath of fresh air in the midst of my father's punches and raging basso voice that spewed contempt toward all "Jews, Negroes and queers in the world". Mother provided an island of sanity in what was otherwise a mad environment. 'In truth, my father didn't realize that his wife and Mazi were lovers. Essentially, he held an uninformed, primitive view about homosexuality. He was confused by it, and naïve to its source. In his limited perspective, homosexuality was reserved for flamboyantly effeminate males but never women. His few, male drinking buddies in bars were as ignorant as he about the subject. Mother's sexuality was never revealed to him, which might have been unfair, but on the other hand, he surely would have dealt with it in the same manner he dealt with anything he didn't understand and with the only tools he knew – his fists. Mother was afraid of him. We were all afraid of him, and aside from our bonding fishing trips, my father's violence ultimately made him a stranger to all of us.

~~~

Before your frozen face, mother, memories of being suffocated by confusions of gender that came with defending my gay mother's sexuality at age twelve. Your confession to me might have been better left unstated to an innocent teenage boy. Who knows? The question of whether appearances were reality, whether males and females were truly what men and women were meant to be? You contradicted the image of womanhood altogether, dear mother. Womanhood was a role that was imposed upon you at an earlier time of your life before other choices presented themselves. I too have been forced to hold onto old commitments that I no longer wish to obey, but that was my choice in the overview. I left the barn door open, so to speak, and original instincts that defined

18

me as a 'manly male' clearly escaped. As I chased after them with my lasso, those characteristics that remained true and those that were false became the question. In my youth, I was unresolved about this, since my natural masculinity contradicted the fragility that defined the 'real me.' Over time, I discovered far more of my mother inside me than one would ever guess.

In truth, I am not my father, mom. I am my mother. It is your spirit that I carry with me. I too am soft, like you, rather than daddy's hard, male brittleness. I supported who you were, ma, when you lived. There was no choice. You were my mother, after all. Dad represented wonton violence that I abhorred; his raging fists, his brutality that made me aware of my own potential for violence perhaps. I don't know. Even today my physique frightens me for its size and strength. Perhaps I could kill with my bare hands, if the situation were right. I don't like that about myself, preferring my fragility to that drunken brute of my male parent I witnessed so often in my youth.

~~~

But returning to that night in my New York loft, mother admitted she'd had affairs, and her revelation bonded us with the agreement that Mazi had fulfilled personal needs necessary for her to live fully. Her creative spirit would have died had she chosen a more conventional path. We talked for hours into the night, discussing her friendship with Mazi, among other personal subjects. Her visit ended late into the night, and days later, I received a poetically written letter, provocative for its honesty. The letter took the form of a 'no holds barred' confessional that encapsulated her life as an artist, as a mother and a wife. In brutally honest terms, she described the shambles of her marriage, her toxic relationship with my father and her preference for woman companionship.

Mother's letter hit the pit of my stomach like a rock. It suddenly dawned upon me to invite her to perform selected, edited sections of her letter between scenes of an original play I'd been directing with my New York theater company, *'Quena Company'*.

The play was entitled *'Blue Heaven'* and focused upon the universal, psychological complexities within the American family unit. I suggested she wander on stage between scenes, letter in hand, reciting its poetic prose that she'd originally written to me, and then to exit off stage, only to return at chosen intervals to read the remaining parts of her letter.

Barbara Constance Barry began her acting career at age sixty-one. When I was a young boy, she'd introduced me to the beauty of film and specifically to the poetic naturalism of Marlon Brando, James Dean and Montgomery Clift. Twenty years later, I returned the favor by inviting this same woman, my mother, into my theater company. We rehearsed Saturdays through Tuesdays in *'The Annex'*, a space provided by Joseph Papp of New York's *'Public Theater'*. The entire cast enjoyed her contribution to our work. She commuted from the Long Island suburbs, always arriving on time and adding a unique voice of experience to a company of thirty-year-olds. Young and naïve about life in general, this band of actors favored the dark side, a natural inclination of youth, who hadn't the vaguest appreciation for the goodness that had been bestowed upon them from their parents. Mother's role in the play balanced their point of view. She was a parent, after all, and had raised a family, while living a long, creative life. More importantly, she'd been a loving parent to her offspring.

Our working relationship was a healthy one. Mother trusted my direction and was always willing to try something new. We had always been unequivocally honest with each other. Without any sign of resentment, I could ask her to drop the tension in her shoulders, while delivering her letter's prose, so eager was she to perform well on stage. And she did learn quickly, always listening intently to my notes after performances, always seeking discovery that might improve her skill. A 'natural' performer with a wonderfully resonant and articulate voice, her stage presence was exemplary with her white, shining hair and radiant, expressive, blue-green eyes that pleased audiences to no end. Performing strengthened her will to live well into her nineties. At age sixty-one, the last stage of her life, working with my company immediately vitalized her spirits. Theater stimulated her creative juices,

20

rejuvenated her sense of purpose and ultimately liberated her. Her love for audiences was infectious. The prospect of spending four nights each week with her son also appealed to her, as it did me. My father was dead by then, and her three children were grown, otherwise leaving her a lonely woman, living in the Long Island suburbs with little to do with her life.

Barbara Constance Barry knew immediately that the acting profession was right for her. Performing on the New York stage came naturally and suited her adventurous spirit. Fully savoring every moment before audiences who loved her, playing roles became her calling that she'd missed during her youth. When we made theater together, she was always present for me. I too was available in spirit or to visit, to call, to write a letter. Both her director and son, I was obedient to her needs when asked. There was never much to give, aside from meeting for coffee before rehearsals occasionally. What I received in return was her enormous performing talent that'd had its beginnings over our kitchen table years before. She also provided the support that only a mother can bring, while fulfilling the arduous role of directing a company of eighteen, experienced actors.

One performance led to the next at New York's *'Theater for the New City'*, New York's *'La Mama'*, Joseph Papp's *'Public Theater'*, *'Saint Mark's Church on the Bowery'*, Baltimore's *'Theater Project'*, as well as theaters in Philadelphia, St. Louis and New Paltz, New York.

Before long, she'd memorized her letter and was performing it fully on stage, a little old lady with marvelous, expressive blue-green eyes and extended arms and, oh, so radiant a performer. Life itself burst from her body, from her spirit. Audiences were riveted by her presence on stage, a magnet for all to watch. Barbara Constance Barry needed that outpouring of love, needed so very much to be appreciated both as an artist and as a human being. Beautiful to behold on stage, her entrances were a magical addition to our productions. By the time she'd performed for a year, she was well on her way to becoming our company's leading actress. Audiences truly loved her. She became an actress at age sixty-one and continued to be a member of *'Quena*

21

Company' for its six year duration, always with absolute commitment. Theater encapsulated a unique, euphoric experience that she came to depend upon. This has also been the case with her son.

~~~

One morning mother and I met for coffee before a *'Quena Company'* rehearsal. She was very excited.

"Raymond," she exclaimed immediately after we sat down. "I had a visitation last night."

Mother reached for my hand and squeezed it, as if to say the epiphany she'd experienced was not only real but also life-giving.

"A spirit visited me. A presence came into my bedroom. It told me everything I was doing in theater was good, and I was sure it was a sign of the future. The blankets on my bed flew up and suspended above me for a full minute before they came down again. The visitation was joyful, so extraordinary and absolutely joyful."

At that moment, she was enraptured with the spiritual potential of life itself. Theater had become a magical adventure for her. Each moment on stage she cherished with her full mental and physical being, experiencing life at its fullest during that final stage of old age. Creativity by any means possible had always been her passion, whether it be painting, writing or acting. But performing before audiences she loved most, when aging would have otherwise cast her aside from the world.

Sometimes we performed *'Blue Heaven'* on the New York City streets. Once, after a performance from a loading dock in SoHo's lower Manhattan, mother exclaimed euphorically, "Oh, Raymond, acting makes me so much more alive! I feel so alive! Today when I was doing my monologue, I looked up and saw a woman watching from across the street. She was hanging out of her window and listening to my words. We made eye contact, and she smiled at me. I just love this acting business. I just love it."

This is my sentiment as well and the reason why I've stuck to the profession all of my adult life. Acting set my mother free, as it has set me free; freedom to express, freedom to dream and always with standards set by me and not by others. Her belief that all forms of creativity and her children are the most significant parts of her life is mine as well. Yes, acting, painting and writing, not to overlook my marriage and four beautiful children establish the wholeness of my life, as they did for Barbara Constance Barry. Mother's values have stood the test of time, and after six decades, they've garnished the goodness they once promised. By fully living up to her standards, I've endured both the sacrifices and self-examination necessary to escape the mundane, to find my wings and take flight beyond my wildest dreams.

After years of creating theater together, I found Barbara Constance Barry a New York agent, Jerry Kahn. She found her wings in the commercial world of theater, having been cast in some twenty films, including *'Arthur'* with Lisa Minelli and *'Trading Places'* with Eddie Murphy, as well as numerous soap operas and commercials. Two commercials featured her during one Super Bowl halftime. For years, she played David Letterman's mother on his original television show. By then her neighbors were convinced she was a legitimate movie star. A highlight of our relationship was when we played 'mother and son' in Sam Shepherd's *'Buried Child'* with Holly Hunter at the St. Louis Reparatory Company, and later we both performed *'Antigone'* with F. Murray Abraham, directed by the brilliant Joseph Chaikin at Joseph Papp's *'New York Shakespeare Company'*.

At the ripe age of sixty-one to age eighty-eight, performing in plays, films and television rejuvenated mother's interest in life. Performing set her free, providing an opportunity for self-examination and escape from what otherwise would have been dreary isolation and final death in the Long Island suburbs. When mother performed, she was transformed into a paradigm of joy. Nothing else provided that heightened degree of vitality. The challenge of acting expanded her appetite for living.

Barbara Constance Barry never studied painting, writing or acting. She simply engaged herself fully in all three media. She wrote and created art without formal training and without questioning why it should be done, approaching each medium with intelligence and an indomitable will that needed self-expression for the very health of her soul. Willingness to 'try it' was enough, the 'how' of her skill guided by wary instinct alone and demonstrating by example that 'permission to dive into the thick of it' in front of a critical audience was all that was necessary. 'Learning by doing' has also been my way, as it was hers. Blind courage to simply 'do it' enriched her life, as it has enriched mine.

Mother's legacy has been a source of inspiration at every turn, having followed her footsteps, first by learning to appreciate art as a boy and later by actually making it as a grown man. Since she represents the fountainhead of creativity, from which most of my values have been born, she has inadvertently molded the shape of my entire life. I am she in so many ways. We are interlocked in some mysterious fashion, artists both, who live with the understanding that creativity in any form is the most important activity any human being can undertake - not wealth, power or status in society. For mother and me, art has become a way of life, each medium a conduit that allows escape from meaningless activity so visible in the world. Life is a bore without art. The only thing I would add is children, something that mother recognized in her later years, when she could finally embrace us. Before that time, her children were an obstacle to finding her creative voice, which had become her life's mission. The role of motherhood obstructed that mission, until we became old enough to explore our own creative goals.

~~~

A darkness lingered in my soul during my twenties. Mother might have been an influence. Pain was a source of creativity to mother. She glorified artists who were suicidal, as if their depressions were somehow the root of their talents, and without that darkness, their genius would have been absent. According to her, one could not make art without experiencing depression. I absorbed that way of thinking as a boy and carried it into early adulthood. The logic seemed sound at the time with such a long list of artists, who had taken their own lives, starting with the most famous of them all, Vincent Van Gogh, followed by Soutine, Modigliani and later Mark Rothko. The list goes on. I don't remember them all, but I do remember my mother's litany of names, when she was prompted to speak of the link between depression and creativity. They were one and the same to her. There was no separation. An artist had to be unhappy or he wasn't an artist. It was simple, or simplistic, however one chose to interpret her theory. Healthy geniuses were never taken into account. Happy men like Chagall, Matisse, or Picasso weren't given credit for their joyful, creative lives.

And so I grew into adulthood, thinking that depression offered a creative advantage. Depression was a badge of genius to mother, and, of course, advantageous for creativity. Feeling down became normal, and if I weren't feeling down, it would be best to sabotage feelings of well-being.

Eventually I learned the fallacy of that theory.

~~~

"Are you happy, mother?"

I have a nerve asking such a silly question.

"Of course, I'm happy. How could I not be happy?"

The vigor of her delivery fends off any possible challenge. The subject for many women her age could easily be uncomfortable.

"You ask me if I'm happy, son, as if you know what happiness is. Everyone is somewhat 'happy' and also somewhat unhappy, depending upon the direction the wind blows. I don't know if I'm happy. Then again I do know. Happiness is this bed I lie in, or maybe happiness is you visiting me. These give me happiness. Your presence in this room, sitting by my bedside warms my heart. I love my boy, my son. You're growing older, son. Life is passing. Grab onto it with both hands and allow it to take you for a ride. That's what I did, son. I rode on the back of my life and allowed it to take me anywhere it wished. Now I'm resting. I'm waiting for the next stage. Death will come, and I shall ride with that too. I'm looking forward to death, son. I'm tired of this existence. It has nothing more to teach me. I've loved. I've had my children, and I've made art in many forms. There is nothing more to do, after so much passing of time."

"Happy is such a strange word, son. Happy about what? Nothing seems important anymore, except my children. Concern for my children overrides concern for anything else. Art has fallen by the wayside somewhere along the line. I'm not sure when, but it's taken a back seat to my children. You still mean a great deal to me, you three kids, but you're not kids anymore, are you?"

"No, we're not kids anymore, ma."

"I remember each one of you when you were children. You were a sweet child, son. And the girls, they were so very beautiful. I sometimes wish I were a better mother to all of you."

"Don't think that, mom. You did fine."

"I could have done better. So many things were going on then. But I did the best I could, and you all turned out fine, didn't you, son?"

"Yes, ma, we all did fine."

"You've had a good life, son, haven't you?"

"Yes, ma, my life has been very good."

"Makes me proud to think of all you've accomplished."

"I did what I could, ma."

"You imitated me to some extent with your creativity, and I'm proud of that. I'm proud that you saw something worthwhile in my life."

"You should be proud, ma. You were an inspiration to all of us."

"Was I, son? Oh, how wonderful to be an inspiration to my own children."

"Well, you were. Certainly to me. You taught me that art was important. I'll never forget the value of that."

"Oh, son, that's so kind of you to say. You see? Now I'm happy. You asked me if I were happy, and now your words have made me happy. And I'm conscious of that happiness, which makes it all the better. You're good for me, son. I'm so glad you came to visit your old mother."

"I'm glad I came too, ma. And I'm glad you're happy."

Mother perks up for the first time since I arrived, and all I asked was whether she was happy. I never expected such a response. It was as if she had something to prove, that she can be happy if she so chooses, and what's more, she's going to convince me of her happiness. I am convinced. The woman is still in control of her faculties. Her alertness, when stimulated, rises to the challenge. Combativeness is well intact, having been such a large part of her personality years ago. Mother's fight is still in her, which means, of course, that she's quite a bit more aware of what's going on than she reveals. That's encouraging. The old woman's spirit is alive and well.

~~~

I mark the minutes, the delinquent son and his aged mother, aware of the shortness of time, the lack of communication between us, without a simple phone connection that might make weekly calls possible. A mobile phone at the side of her bed would allow that. Mother's hearing loss would make normal conversation difficult, but some words might pass between us by means of a phone. Meanwhile anything can be brought up in this room; little to lose between mother and me at this stage of the game. Conversation resumes again. The television is still a major distraction for mother, dear woman, unable to resist its addictive lure. Her eyes constantly divert back to the screen, while I attempt to sway her focus with idle conversation.

"What have you been doing with your time, mom" I ask during a commercial break.

I know the answer to my question. Don't know why I asked it. Her sedentary condition annoys me somehow. I feel the urge to challenge her.

"Oh, son, you don't want to know what I do," she says.

Mother has always been creative with her time. As I've mentioned, she's been an accomplished painter, a published writer and late in her life embarked on a full acting career in theater and film that thrived until age eighty-eight. Art in all its forms provided the freedom to create at will. One of her paintings on her wall today was exhibited decades ago in the New York City Museum on Fifth Avenue for an entire year, part of a prize she'd won in a downtown art contest.

"You'll find out someday what it means to get old," she warns. It doesn't much matter anymore what I do, and I just don't care the way I did when I was younger. You'll find out what I mean someday."

A smile on her face accompanies her caveat.

I wonder how she cannot care, and why she smiles while admitting it. Having given up certain activities myself recently that I once imagined I would do forever, I choose not to probe the question. Perhaps I am afraid of the answer, and how it applies to me. Mother had that drive at one time, an overpowering will to achieve. Maybe it was her desire to be famous that drove her. In my case, there was certainly a touch of that. The old woman's strength took an exit upon entering her nineties. For some people, the drive to achieve disappears in their sixties or even in their forties, and complacency takes its place. Years pass and then final death. Most people never had that drive to begin with. An ambitious person cannot fully imagine the transition to complacency. Once a person is lulled into a state of inactivity, it is impossible to explain to others. This certainly is the case with mother.

"I'm old too," I say, the statement accompanied by an apologetic chuckle.

"Not as old as your mother," she retorts. The intonation of her voice suggests she has a secret.

28

What I observe before me is a woman who has allowed herself to become irrelevant. For me, mother is not irrelevant. We have this chance to speak from our hearts. My heart is open. My love for her is full. I do love you, my mother. Let us speak. Let us relate to each other as mother and son.

"I love you, mother."

"Oh, and I love you, my son, with all my heart."

"I feel there is a barrier between us that prevents us from communicating."

"What communicate? We are communicating."

"Yes, we are communicating."

"How nice you came, son, to communicate with your mother."

"Yes, ma."

"It's so kind of you to visit."

"Yes, ma, I feel we aren't really talking."

"What was that?"

"I feel we don't really talk."

"Talk?"

"Yes, mother, we're talking, but we aren't talking about anything important."

"Important? Is that what you said?"

"Yes, ma, we aren't discussing real issues. It's all small talk between us."

"Small talk? I'm sorry, son, my hearing has gone to hell. I'm ninety-four years old, you know."

"Yes, I realize that. It's difficult to hear. But it would be nice if we could discuss real issues."

"Real?"

"Yes, mother, issues that really matter between us."

"What real issues?"

"Well, I haven't been visiting you as much as I would like."

"It's so nice you visited me, son."

"Yes, ma, I should have visited you more often, but work has prevented me from doing that. I've wanted to come, but I've been acting in one film or play after another. I've had so many conflicting emotions about this. It's been easier to shut the whole thing out of my mind."

"It would have been nice to see you at Christmas."

"I know that, ma, but it's been so complicated to visit with all the work I've been getting lately. It's not like I can stay overnight with eight shows each week."

"Oh, don't talk about that, son. You're here now. That's what matters.

Mother is partly deaf. She cannot hold a normal conversation and seldom reveals what is really going on. Anything she offers to our conversation is little more than a series of platitudes, expressed with bubbly speech patterns imitating pleasure and hiding any signs of despair. I do not believe her for a second. We have made an agreement not to make waves. She has established that agreement, and I am happy with it. Peace between mother and son is better than conflict. It is too late for conflict. What could possibly come of a battle between us – wounds that have no time to heal? Old wounds are enough without adding more.

"We should discuss a few things before something happens," I say.

The mention of death is not comfortable. I refuse to say it.

"Before I die," she states defiantly. "What do you want to bring up, dear?"

"We should talk."

I'm suddenly at a loss for words when I should be more to the point. This opportunity must not slip by. But my thoughts are muddled. What was it I wanted to say? Something related to love?

I am at a loss for words, faltering. The time is now – not later – but now, but I am wordless, inarticulate and a bit stupid. Why so stupid when it is time to say my final goodbye. Why so inarticulate when I should be clear? I am her oldest child with a right to speak. Her helplessness is partially real and partially a sham. It is true at times she suffers from dementia of sorts.

Flustered for a moment, I become aware of my surroundings, the temperature of the air, the brightness of the sun shining through the window, its warmth when it bathes my face. A healthy mix of sunlight and fresh air washes the room with their balm, softening the energy between mother and son. I am more relaxed than before and do not wish to bring up her imminent death. It is rather a time for meditation between us, time to reflect upon the memories of our laughter together and theater experiences that allowed us appreciate what we've always meant to each other.

It is important to be in my own skin at this moment, to be aware of what I am really thinking, rather than disguising myself with empty words. I notice in detail the room's ambiance. There is an assemblage of wooden sticks in one corner, marking the beginning of an unfinished project, for which someone has brought materials; perhaps the beginning of a bookcase for mother's books. A mattress stands against one wall, slightly ripped. It has seen better days, seems ready to be thrown out. Someone else will do that for her, unless I offer to take it out today.

"Would you like me to take that mattress out to the garbage, mother?"

"That mattress? Oh, yes, it's been there so long that I'd forgotten about it," she says.

"I'd be happy to take it out."

I am in a helpful mood, although I do not move to take out the mattress. Mother does not seem to notice. She is in her own world. Any task that might comfort her would ease the void between us. Any errand completed would show I came on a peace mission. The mattress stays leaning against the wall. I don't make any effort to move it. Paint-spattered rags hang from a screw in the wall. Some workman left them there. An outboard motor runs outside, propelling a small craft along the river's shores. Birds cry out above the shoals of its banks.

My mother died a month later at age ninety-four.

~~~

You seem to hear my thoughts, mom, as you lie in your grave, dead to the world's activity. Some part of me has already died in your absence. My feelings have gone numb. Our entire family has turned off, preferring darkness to light. There is no turning back one's blood ties; they are indelible. Surely mine are, born to a family of mad people, alcoholics, wife-beaters. They are part of me too. They are the dabs of paint that compose this portrait, but the artist's life transforms to surrealism, when I detect the possibility of living a creative life.

I've absorbed my creativity from you, my mother. So very much of you has been passed in parasitic fashion into your son, who has, over the years, nourished himself with a constant diet of your essence. We were fated to bond in the end, as sperm finds egg, swimming to its niche and settling in, or as a baby clings to milky breasts, suckling then, and having been nurtured by mother's milk, growing eventually into a man, who stares at that same dead mother's breast shriveled by passing decades. Something tells me I'm in for numerous duels with imaginary specters bent on punishing me for neglecting you, ma. But on the other hand, your death is the beginning rather than the end.

As I stare, fixated by the memory of your green eyes, I side with women and not so much with men. It's too easy to pass myself off as a 'macho man'. Physically I fill the role, but I am not that. I respond too easily to anything delicate and beautiful, more soft than hard; my proclivity for flowers and pretty things and anything that contradicts the vulgar coarseness of the brute male. I'm adverse to violence, and, yes, I wish to be kind. Just like you, appreciation for beauty attracts me more than some men's bestial ways. No, I am not a brute but rather a sensitized human being, who enjoys the fragrance of honey-suckle and birds in flight. These hold my attention more than physically intimidating other men. I, like you, wish to caress my surroundings, not bash them to pieces with lumbering blows. No, I'm not my father. I am gentle like you, my mother; your fondness for lovely things, your love of art, for good books and your appreciation of fine music. You've instilled in me the notion of harmony with your example. What I naturally embrace, most men ignore; the gentle spray of wind against fresh leaves, washed by spring rain; the soft wave of a grass field, rippled by reflection of sunlight or the innocence of a young child, who looks at life's ugliness in a state of pure wonderment. These are I, as they were you, mother. I'm as receptive to the gentleness of beauty, as you were vulnerable to life's harshness.

How could I not notice how Barbara Constance Barry lived? How could I not be aware of her very high standards when it came to choosing the direction of her life? Survival to her meant survival of the spirit, not of the body. She would have been willing to starve for the sake of expressing what lay so vibrantly beneath the surface. I watched this process for decades, realizing that something was different about my mother. Her passion separated her from most mothers. Her choices seemed erratic and eccentric. There were times she was not present when I wanted her to be. But I grew strong and independent and learned to be self-reliant. With her guidance, work took on a new meaning to me. There were two kinds of work; work for money and the other, more spiritual kind of work that mother did for the very survival of her soul. With her paradigm to follow, my soul became important too, my 'inner self' that knew of a creative world of which most men were unaware. Performing roles in the theater has imprinted upon me a deeper understanding of life, regardless of the difficulties along the way that are part of every person's experience anyway; might as well risk a life that delves into the essence of the soul and by doing that, make something beautiful from nothing.

Those ominous chapters of mother's life, where layers of insecurity forced her to hide from the world, I recognize in myself. As a boy, my fantasies flourished when brutal, domestic reality no longer satisfied. The realm of imagination was pliable to whatever suggestions suited my fancy, not unlike the inspiration of an artist, but instead of canvass and tubes of paint, the medium was the receptivity of my mind to create something beautiful. With regard to my mother, the miracle of our creative partnership is also what I imagined. Mother became a great gift to me in that collaboration. At times, her bewilderment became mine. Her search to make sense of things also became mine. Art in all its forms became our salvation. We searched together in theater, searched to find light above the darkness, knowing always that I could not become one of 'them'. No, I could not live an ordinary life. There had to be some risk involved, freedom to create, freedom to find my own voice. That's what you were about, my mother – always finding a way to speak from your heart, to express the sensations that lay simmering beneath the surface, aching to be released at every step of your life.

The answer to the question of "Who am I?" changes with each breath, with each heartbeat. I am constantly in motion, as mother constantly transformed throughout her life. There is no argument about that alteration. The insecurity of constant transition does not bother me for I have found safety in my observance of you, mother, who like a chameleon, has undergone radical alteration from decade to decade. Change is so very common that even your deterioration from old age to death has not moved me.

Does this mean that I am callous and unfeeling? No, I think not. I am merely sobered to the ways of my family. Mother taught me not to be shocked by right-angled turns in the middle of a straightaway. I have learned my lesson thoroughly, not to be surprised, not to over-sentimentalize and not to be moved by loss of any kind. Mother and I lost each other long ago, when our fierce independence required us to take our own paths. Those winding trails led us to our true selves for sustenance alone, for breath in the middle of this suffocating world. Most of what we discovered along the way is ordinary, but you were not ordinary, mom. The 'others' could never understand you. You never fit in. You were conditioned to ignore anything false that might have lowered you to standards set by others. Pining over mother's death is not in the cards, for you have taught me by example to avoid the trappings of social mores by living the life of an artist-warrior. Your fears never became an excuse to stop believing in yourself. Joyful enthusiasm was always part of your energy, even in death, for having lived so very well and for so very long, a brilliant, creative life.

It is difficult to imagine not existing. To me, thinking involves consciousness and consciousness is life. Consciousness flying out every which way describes the activity of the universe and then death, consciousness in limbo. What happens to all those little souls floating in space? Do they communicate to each other? Will we communicate, mother, now that you've gone? Is my dead father out there trying to speak to me? I feel not. Rather he exists in memory only, sending messages of approval every now and then, supporting my choices when they are sane enough. So much has escaped into thin air; too many thoughts and yet not enough of them.

Heaven is not it, nor hell, nor any pat solution to explain the loss of a mother. There is something simpler going on. Perhaps the incomprehensible nature of things is right and proper; the laws of nature, death, birth, more death, bodies, souls passing on to other plains, this sensation of 'self' when I pay attention to my thoughts. I put my heart and soul into all of it, all the failures and new beginnings. I tried to complete all of it as best I could. God was never in the mix. Maybe that was an error of judgment but probably not. I did it myself with mother's help, the little tasks involved, the workaday involvements that amounted to a life and then what?

Craving a cigarette. Why? Smoking won't solve much. A story lies here, somewhere. I am not completely in the dark. Indeed, there is a kernel of a story here. The idea is forming, some relationship maybe, a linear thought to the finale and possibly a meaningful existence in the end? Wouldn't it be nice to find a beginning? But the beginning was birth, which unfolded into a life, and those dying all around me suggest what this is leading to - those floating souls again in limbo, a kind of purgatory waiting for the next level to happen.

Cork Work, Silence

McCarter Theater, 1963-1964

Memories of a boy descending the stairs to the sound of his mother's screams; blood sprayed upon her nightgown, his sisters wailing like a Greek chorus in the background. The drunken father had punched the mother, breaking her nose, while she slept in her bed. The sight of mother covered with blood remains fixed in my memory today. I've been transformed by that memory, frozen by it for a decade or so, maybe forever. It was impossible to tell father not to drink, not to break furniture, not to punch mother. The boy's rights were ignored in that tiny bungalow that housed a screaming family, desperate for escape.

From that night onward, the boy had no voice. Talk was useless, truth unmentionable. He became withdrawn from the world's violent hypocrisy. He wanted no part of it. Safety in silence became the norm, safety in refusal to take part, silence in the face of his parents' profound unhappiness and his wish to be alone. Days of saying as few words as possible turned into months and then years through adolescence into early manhood. By then, his tongue became dormant. The power of silence became his language. He spoke paragraphs by refusing to speak. The boy's taciturn ways were noticed not for anything he did but rather for what he didn't do; that is, his refusal to speak.

"The boy is so quiet," his family would say.

With so much shouting and noise emanating from their small bungalow, the boy's silence was a relief to all of them. They never forced him to speak, and as years passed, they became familiar with his silence, even learned to appreciate his quietude. Once, one of the boy's sisters asked the father, "Daddy, is my brother annoying like us?" The father replied, "No" and that was that. The man loved the boy deeply. His son's silence was a minor concern. Both parents sensed what was going on in the boy's mind. They were thinking similar thoughts. It was best not to bother him. Each man for himself was their common, unspoken mantra. The boy's brain was churning. They all knew it - impossible to stop the churning. Why bother? Everyone in the family loved the silent boy, whose mind was churning. He loved his mom and dad too and his sisters, but the word 'love' was never mentioned.

Meanwhile the boy's silence was safe. Silence never exposed feelings. Conversation came from others and not from him. Questions were answered with dead, unresponsive vocal inflections. Expressiveness was held to a minimum, leaving a somewhat lifeless persona. Refusing to speak, unless spoken to and then answering with terse, one-word responses was the boy's way of controlling chaos. Saying as few words as possible became his rule of thumb. Full sentences and random conversations were non-existent. Single word expressions became his way, laconic and literal answers to questions asked; the habit of silence when words were expected. When he did respond, only rarely, the boy learned to be brutally honest, his responses always literal and truthful. Truthfulness proved to be a good thing later in his life. Also, silence gave birth to the habit of studying people's behavior, also useful later in his life. Long before he could remember, his basic distrust of humanity, together with an absolute wish to gain its respect, presented a puzzle that someday would be resolved. Until that time, it was necessary to prove his worth to the world.

There had to be a way.

~ ~ ~

At age twenty-three, since I had spent the greater part of my young life in a state of willful silence, my tongue had been rendered somewhat inoperable. Improving my muddy speech became my obsession. The slightest chance of rehabilitation would be difficult at best. The best solution, I surmised, was to place a thermos cork into my mouth and recite passages of Shakespeare to train my wooden tongue to move with a faint glimpse of dexterity. The thermos cork impeded the workings of my tongue and lips, but when the clumsy object was removed, speech became more fluid. In fact, reciting Shakespeare's monologues with a cork in my mouth began my first involvement with the bard's poetry.

The exercise was a sight to behold; mouth stretched wide, tongue laboring to articulate Shakespeare's poetry against the obstacle imposed upon it, resulting in vocal utterances that were barely human. God knows how that cork managed not to dislocate my jaw. Nonetheless, it was only by sheer determination "to learn how to do it," that I dared walk upon the stage, as if a single solution would allow me to speak like the 'others' did. At this early stage of my career, the joy of saying words was new to me. Expressing poetry wasn't a joy really, unless I was prancing about my apartment, spouting the bard's verse in solitude. When people were present, my habit was to clam up. Tightness overwhelmed my voice and body, rendering me to a mere shadow of my true self. Alas, more than a cork in my mouth would be necessary for mastering Shakespeare. The will to communicate would have helped, but that took another ten to twenty years. Unfortunately, I did not have the luxury of time. I was in a hurry. A steady diet of 'cork work' would have to suffice.

After spending a brief stint in the limelight of William Hickey's acting class, all that seemed to nourish me was unequivocal approval from others. I needn't explain. I won't embark upon tangents. My wretched state during my early career in the theater is enough to mention without explaining the reasons for it. Therefore I shall avoid that subject of 'why' at all costs. An analysis of my motivation would surely be a shade indulgent anyway. Never mind. I shall move forward, simply sticking to the facts. Let it be said that the likes of Clark Gable, Montgomery Clift, Marilyn Monroe and Marlon Brando are mythological figures in the American landscape. Naturally, in my naive state of hubris, I assumed I could be one of them.

A personality that was plainly not my own became my trademark. Presenting an 'interesting' presence became my obsession. I developed an unbearable, brooding stance with puckered lips that loosely dangled a cigarette at all times. That rebellious pose included heavy motorcycle boots with tight Levis and walked with an unmitigated swagger. A slightly English lilt in my speech finished the picture. Anything that was different from the 'real me' seemed attractive at the time. A bolstered ego became a habit as well, within social circles where already my infamous reputation had forfeited my welcome. "If only mankind could be blessed with my undiscovered talents, then everyone would love me," was the main theme I professed. As I say, a craving for unlimited approval was the source of my passion and would do anything for it. Of course, I kept that to myself.

At age twenty-three, a few parts came and went along the way, mostly playing soldiers in plays that expressed anti-war sentiments and needed background people to hold guns and wear military uniforms. Bertold Brecht's *"Man is Man"* was one of those plays, starring John Heffernan and Olympia Dukakis, both brilliant actors. The part demanded that I to stand with my gun in hand and appear mean, as any soldier would. The meanness part I did well, being blessed with a face malleable enough to squeeze my cheeks and twist my lips into a furious frown, but often, while daydreaming on stage, my weighty gun, made of hard wood and steel, would drop upon my big toe. A piercing cry would follow the thud of the gun, much to the dismay of my fellow thespians. The limping in the aftermath was the best of it, gimping about the stage with a sore big toe for the remaining two hours of the performance.

Of course, audiences showed concern about a poor lad with a swollen toe, applauding vigorously in my direction at the show's final curtain. It was clear that I was their unsung hero for the night, so brave a thespian to endure the pain of a loaded gun upon a hapless big toe. Once I caught wind of audiences' reaction to my injured toe, I learned to imitate the event skillfully, the heavy weapon dropping close enough to the toe and seemed authentically painful. Being basically a coward, I was always careful not to injure my toe after the original, painful blow. There was a certain cleverness in my scheming mind at the time, originally acquired in the dark corners of my crib, when I'd been beating my rattle for unwonted attention. At last I was receiving the attention I had missed during my fragile infancy. Yes, my acting career was finally marked by some meager measure of success.

Occasionally I even had a few lines. "There's the train," was line in the Brecht play. Thank god the playwright had been dead for a decade. The man probably rolled over in his grave any time I spoke on stage. One line was certainly enough to test my mettle. Two lines would have been the end of it. Perhaps that would have been best. Anyone could say those words as ineffectively as I did, and never did I pick up my cue, which angered the cast, who tired of waiting in silence for me to say, "There's the train," so the play could finally continue. I considered myself a devotee of the 'method' approach without really knowing what that meant. How could I know? I could barely be taught anything, so impervious I was to suggestion of any sort, and so overcome was I with ambition to succeed. Any learning in the face of my thick-headedness was impossible. That 'method' technique I rigidly espoused, was partly at fault here, which, in my misguided understanding, meant 'feeling it' before I spoke. The simple task of story-telling was roundly defeated by my approach and not atypical of my futile attempt at making things more complicated than they should have been. In truth, I didn't have a clue. Everything was too important for me then, the art of acting, the craft of it and so-called 'honesty,' a term I'd heard somewhere in acting class. Any trace of sensitivity to events on stage was beyond me.

Every night I earnestly refused to deliver the line on cue, until it was clear that I actually heard the train. I was so very responsible to the idea of the so-called 'reality'. Everything had to be real, but nothing was. I never did hear the train, of course, but I convinced myself that I did. And every performance, the line took longer to say and sounded more wooden than the night before. The length of silence before I said, "There's the train," sometimes lasted as much as a half a minute in a vacuum of nothingness. The cast was annoyed beyond measure, I'm sure, even though they never showed their enmity, except once when a portly performer directed a derogative comment about "empty space on stage" pointedly at me. I stared off innocently into space, pretending to be deaf, wearing my mean expression to protect myself.

~~~

God knows how I managed it, but in the year 1963, at age twenty-three I landed a job doing regional theater in Princeton, New Jersey at *McCarter Theater*. Two small roles were offered in Shakespeare's *'Julius Caesar'* that mercifully required only a few scenes on stage. The larger role; that is, the one that had words to say, was the role of 'Titinius'. My acting talent surely wasn't the reason they hired me. Perhaps my full head of hair had something to do with it or my physique that slightly resembled a cross between a ballet dancer and a weight-lifter. Or possibly my modest triumph could be attributed to the affected speech patterns that I'd incorporated into my audition. Performing the *'Henry the Fifth'* prologue for our director and properly butchering it with a sufficient number of rolled 'rrrs' barely left the impression that I might have been 'classically' trained, whatever that meant.

For whatever reason they offered me the roles.

Every night I made my first entrance as a Roman plebian, dressed in a leopard skin designed by a costume designer, who no doubt had a fetish for taut male thighs. The 'Roman plebian' had no lines, thank goodness. My oversized muscles were neatly exposed and were, I might add, the crux of what I had to offer on stage. The entire package gave the impression I was a leftover Cro-Magnon wandering through the streets of Rome. I had been pegged as "the body" of the company that the designer could exhibit in whatever outfit might suit his aesthetic taste. Leopard skin pleased him most, and since it was my first professional job, being passed off as a physical specimen was the least of my worries. I was sincerely determined to learn the craft of acting, not to overlook my refusal to pursue a normal profession.

Nonetheless, the show must go on. In my state of youthful earnestness, my 'plebian' character swaggered across the boards nightly, dressed in his leopard skin outfit. One fateful might, during Mark Anthony's "Friends, Romans, countrymen, lend me your ears" speech, while running across the stage at Mark Anthony's beckoning, I tripped over a flat and fell forcefully onto my face, thereby demonstrating the futile hours I'd spent in ballet class. The concussion of my weight on the wooden stage partially tore my false beard helplessly off. Without realizing something was amiss, after my clumsy pratfall, I quickly gained my bearing and presented an earnestly attentive pose, dutifully listening to Mark Anthony's speech with a pathetic-looking piece of false beard, hanging by a few strands from my chin. The sight of that appendage, together with my fixed, earnest expression, as if I believed my own impression of myself, was too much for cast and audience to bear. Everyone, except me, were convulsed with laughter, including the cast that was trying its best to hide its reaction for the sake of a paying audience.

Indeed, I took myself very seriously after my stumble, unaware that a few pathetic strands of beard were dangling from my aforementioned chin, which together with my leopard skin outfit must have been a sight to behold. As I say, both cast and audience were double over with convulsions throughout Mark

Anthony's speech, much to the dismay of the sixty-five year old actor, playing twenty-year-old Mark Anthony, who was furious for weeks afterward for ruining his alleged "brilliant performance." In his defense, I was his understudy. Thank the goodness of the Gods he never took sick. Had I played *'Mark Anthony'* in his absence, it surely would have been the end.

But not to dwell too long on a minor incident, I mustn't neglect my portrayal of *'Titinius'*, who appeared in the fifth act and whose single monologue eulogized Cassius' death. This character was regaled in a glorious costume of a Roman general, complete with cardboard sword and tunic, not to overlook his ornately plumed helmet made of the highest quality plastic. Roman sandals completed the image. Indeed, ensconced in that glorious outfit, I embodied the figure of a gallant warrior, confident enough to confront any military challenge. Unfortunately, acting skill was required to please a paying audience.

A fine actor named Gwillum Evens played Cassius. Unlike myself, he was both extremely talented and bald. He served the bard well, this man. Comparing myself to others had already become one of my many character flaws. In my naïve way of thinking, Mr. Evens would not have a chance at movie stardom without hair, I reasoned. I imagined such glory then. A thick mien of brown hair on my head assured that I was destined for Hollywood, while Gwillem did not stand a chance for such fame and glory with his bald pate. My logic was a meager attempt to compensate for the man's formidable acting skill that dwarfed my own. While changing from my 'plebian' leopard skin into *Titinius'* Roman tunic, Gwillem Evens and Lawrence Luckenbill, who played Brutus, brilliantly performed the well-known 'tent scene'. Their performances were truly compelling, thereby shaking my confidence. My full head of hair did little to assuage my doubt. Vanity seldom did much in a pinch.

Before making my entrance every night, after my interpretation of the leopard-skinned plebian had been satisfactorily purged, I climbed the stairs to the fifth floor of a stone tower adjacent to the main stage and passionately performed *Titinius'* suicide speech to a blank brick wall with a colorful array of vocal effects that included intermittent inflections of fake crying.

The bareness of my legs allowed freedom of motion from my lower half. Adorned with a lofty plumed helmet ornately placed squarely upon my knobby dome, I presented a fine figure of a Roman general engaged in the perilous fortunes of war. While the play continued downstairs, I paced in the belfry of that tower, reciting improvised military commands with my cardboard sword in hand, gallantly swinging at imaginary enemies lurking in the shadows. My figure demonstrated a regal pose and a rare sureness of purpose, as I raved and ranted to that wall, while waiting for my entrance down below. The strutting was the best of it, along with the deliberate swing of my sword through the thick shadows of that tower's belfry. My gait was strong in my scuffed leather sandals, a size too small for my ungainly feet that pounded heavily the rough floorboards five stories above the stage. This was no ordinary general but rather a noble patriot at heart, who was wont to committing mayhem for the sake of Rome's destiny. His ferocity was real, as he plundered with abandonment, slashing his trusty cardboard sword at imaginary foes, bravely defending Rome's fortune with the onslaught of his deadly blade.

To be sure, I was my own man in that lonely tower, spontaneous, brave and rambunctious, not to mention pronounced leadership in my carriage. It seemed logical at the time to slice my cardboard sword at the blackness of my surroundings, if only to save Rome. At last, I was a free man, playing the role of a noble general, eulogizing Cassius, my deceased friend. Undaunted in my quest for a Roman victory, I refused to relent, until the battle would be won. I dueled with scabbard and sword against the tower's main supporting post, beating it interminably, the sound echoing throughout the lower floors of the tower. Continuous slashing brought me to a state of absolute frenzy, while down below Shakespeare's play droned onward toward the moment of my entrance.

Sufficiently convinced that loudness was the proper ingredient for a thespian's preparation, every night in that tower I shouted *Titinius'* monologue five times with what I thought to be

44

full emotion. In truth, I was merely loud. How I came to the number five, I have no idea. I've always been a bit of a pedant. Forget the joy of creativity. My approach was so very rigid, dutifully memorizing, drilling Shakespeare's words and suffocating the freedom required for any trace of spontaneity.

My diligent work ethic failed to be a labor of love, but rather labor for the sake of itself. Thank God the playwright was dead, although Shakespeare probably suffered posthumous humiliation from the inadequacy of my new-born thespian skills. He would surely have removed me with the proverbial 'hook' had he witnessed the strain of my efforts. The notion of 'effort' always came first, thereby limiting any possibility of discovery on stage. Plugging away at Shakespeare's verse became more the point than the performance itself. Why 'effort' alone meant so very much to me was incomprehensible at the time, aside from the fact that it served as an earnest substitute for creativity, about which I hadn't a clue. Hard labor alone has too often fooled me into believing it would bring about a satisfactory result, overlooking entirely that 'spontaneous enjoyment' might have been a more fruitful approach. At any rate, "See how hard I am working," became the whole of my performance and left little to brag about. Youth and naïveté did not discern the difference. Nonetheless, the audience would have loved my earnestness in that tower above, yelling Shakespeare's words to my heart's content at a blank brick wall. My leopard skin, of course, had been replaced by that aforementioned Roman tunic, well suited for *Titinius'* military stature. I was quite full of myself really, strutting about in that tower with my cardboard sword, flowing tunic and bared, hairy, knock-kneed legs.

Imaginary Spartan warriors lurked in the shadows for the duration of my histrionics. My preparation seemed to go on for hours, although, in that limitless expanse of time, it could have been weeks or even months. These marathon battles that I always won were followed by a strutting victory walk, chest out, knees highly penetrating the space, as I marched beneath the tower's peak, waving to an imagined plebian population below, no doubt enthralled at the sight of their general. No question that I was a general. Any lesser rank would not have matched the glorious stance I presented in the wake of victorious celebration. Crowds of common folk were also participating in the festivities, although they could not be seen. All of this was purely the product of my vivid imagination. Their absence by no means daunted my aspirations for lofty heights of victorious celebration. My cardboard sword had performed its deadly purpose for the state of Rome, after all. Its population, as I saw it, was indebted to me and demonstrated their joy enthusiastically. That scenario was all I needed to invent the rest, which I did by means of a lofty speech to the imagined crowds of Roman men and women, all of whom adored their general.

"Romans do not fear the outcome of war!" I announced vociferously. "Yes, noble Cassius is dead, but I have driven away our Spartan enemies form the north and the Huns from the east! We are saved once again! My armies are united in battle and we are victorious! Celebrate as you have never celebrated before, for I am your beloved leader now, and I shall protect you forever from harm!"

I was indeed loved by the commoners in that dark tower.

A loud roar came from the crowd as I performed. At least, I imagined so. If any actors in the cast were to witness my preparation in that tower during those outbursts, the proper authorities would be summoned immediately, and I, no doubt, would have been escorted to the nearest mental institution. Notwithstanding, immense pleasure I found in embodying the character of *Titinius*, festooned in his plastic helmet and brandishing his cardboard sword, as if his very soul depended upon victory against an imagined barbaric enemy. Walls were thick enough to block the volume of my histrionics. At least I thought as much. One never knows. Such was the depth of my naïveté at the tender age of twenty-three.

Nonetheless, after one month of performing the play, *Titinius'* lengthy monologue eulogizing Cassius had already reached what I considered a high degree of rhetorical skill; that is, when I performed alone in that tower. Aside from a few futile attempts and false starts, I delivered the Roman general's words with confidence that far surpassed my leopard-skin adorned plebeian's mutterings only moments before. Only one monologue was required. The audience could not have endured more. Neither could the blank, brick wall that was beginning to show signs of cracking from my nightly purge.

~~~

This was my warm up, I reasoned, for what would follow on stage. After this private ritual, the strategy was to descend to the stage and imitate each sound and gesture exactly as I had performed them to that blank wall. Indeed, I was an optimistic, young fellow then. My private performances, isolated in the stone tower were always skilled demonstrations of my talent; that is, at least to myself. Once in front of an audience, however, it was my habit to crumble under pressure of being judged. Rigidity overtook my body and mind, and the question of whether I was 'a good actor' or 'a bad actor' plagued me whenever I performed. This was my first professional job, and I had much to learn.

After finding Cassius, his beloved general, deceased, *Titinius* commits suicide by plunging a cardboard sword into his breast. I stabbed myself nightly with that flimsy prop and died convincingly, I would say. Unfortunately, the aforementioned monologue had to be delivered first, and that I plainly mangled in an over-wrought fashion with raging gesticulations and passionately false vocal tones, all of which compensated for my fear of not doing enough to please my audience.

My solitary performance in that tower expressed freedom I never attained on stage. The audience made the difference. Before a crowd of expectant onlookers, an overwhelming tension gripped me, obliterating the freedom I'd attained in that lonely tower. Along with audience came a subliminal belief that I hadn't the right to perform at my best, similar, perhaps, to not having the right to express myself in the house where I'd been raised, where as a child I'd been rendered speechless, while witnessing brutal violence. That early condition of helplessness was surely repeating itself during early adulthood. This realization never came to full consciousness, however; that is, until years later. Nonetheless, before an audience, an indescribable tension held me in its grip, indomitable, abstract terror that left my brave Roman general compromised by self-doubt. Tension impeded my delivery, as well as fear of being myself, a persona that was cloudy at best.

In truth, I had no idea who I was under pressure of audience. No matter how simple were the requirements of the part, my tendency was to raise the decibel level of Shakespeare's words to convince both myself and the audience of the sincerity of my grief. The prospect of simply communicating was foreign to me. No, to be normal was never enough. I was compelled to impress the invisible 'them' with a variety of phony accents, exaggerated posturing and cascades of voluminous vocal effects in order to achieve something more. "More what?" was the question? I hadn't the vaguest notion of what 'more' meant. Everything I presented on stage was geared toward proving 'more' to the world. 'More' was all I would accept of myself. It never dawned on me it would have been enough to quietly communicate, as one might talk to a friend.

Placing a worried expression on my face convinced the sea of faces in front of me that I meant every word, or so I thought. I could barely comprehend the meaning of Shakespeare's verse, much less realize the character's intention. My concern had more to do with the impression I was giving, rather than any experience I might have had on stage. Any gimmick to win an audience's favor was amply implemented to impress them. Trembling my lower lip, as if about to cry was one of my favorites. Looking back on it, trembling lips and raised volume were never useful, but I didn't know better at the time. During those early days, 'loudness' combined with an array of sincere grimaces, ranging from 'happy' to 'sad' with seldom a nuance between, were synonymous with 'feeling it.' The entire performance became an elaborate study of physical tension and all of its ramifications. My interpretation of 'Titinius' had become little more than a poor imitation. Turning my back to the audience might've disguised my struggle, but the director would've fired my ass had I done so. He knew he'd made a terrible mistake hiring me, not for my talent, but rather, I suspect, for my bushy head of hair. As weeks passed, performances became increasingly strident. To be blunt, I was not very convincing in the role.

My gallant attempts on stage were, alas, ill received and outright repugnant to my director, an anal fellow he, whose area of expertise was the so-called 'classics', whatever that means. In his defense, my ineptitude was slowly driving the man out of his mind. Some nights the poor fellow would approach me after the last curtain, shaking his head and standing before me tongue-tied, as if my performance were beyond the pale. This good man's sincere wish was to nudge me towards adequacy on stage, at least within the range of the audience's forgiveness, while not allowing himself to injure my spirit in any way. No, he refused to be bluntly critical and in fact, was a rather kind fellow, although I'm sure the purpose for which he'd hired me for the role remained a daunting question.

"Couldn't you connect a bit more with the character?" he might say with a bewildered expression on his face, after which he would walk away bowing his head, as if words to explain were useless. Aware that something was awry, I was helpless to correct the flaws of my dreadful performance. In truth, I was fulfilling my meager capabilities during the incubation of my career.

Exactly what made an artist was still a mystery to me. A full head of hair was only part of it, I suspected. But I was not sure. 'Hair' might have been all of it for all I knew. The question left me in the dark, aside from my suspicion that artistry was something mysteriously projected from the likes of Lawrence Luckenbill and Gwillem Evens. They were plainly gifted artists in my view. I had not the vaguest hint of what blessing had been bestowed upon them that allowed their skill to shine night after night, although I did notice that they enjoyed themselves fully as they worked. Could this possibly be the ingredient that enhanced success on stage? Perhaps so, but enjoyment was an unattainable concept for a young man of twenty-three years, obsessed with results to the point of blindness.

~~~

One fateful night, Gwillem Evens, who was, as I say, playing Cassius, lay dead on the floor. As I delivered 'Titinius' monologue, my oversized foot mistakenly stepped upon his finger with the full weight of my body. The journeyman actor grimaced in pain, but if I removed my large foot from his finger, I would surely forget my lines. I stood stupefied before Cassius' body like a wooden stick, unable to speak, vaguely aware of what Cassius' death meant to me; my lover, my friend, my general. At that moment, I wished I could stab myself with a real knife, but the cardboard number would have to do. Who ever heard of a man committing suicide with a cardboard sword?

Needless to say, I became increasingly paralyzed in that unrehearsed situation. After all, I hadn't practiced stepping upon Gwillem's finger during my warm up in the tower. How could I possibly handle such an unexpected event on stage, particularly at that point of my life when everything had to be planned beforehand? The guilty foot remained steadfastly planted on the poor fellow's finger. Predictably I went blank. Poignant silence throughout the theater hung in the balance, the audience aware that something was awry. That silence crushed me. My memory failed me, and I fell to the floor, as if an invisible spear aimed from the wings had found its mark in my flank. George Reinhold, another talented member of our company, carried me off stage, and I escaped to the theater's lonely basement, where Titinius' shame could be negotiated in privacy.

At the risk of boasting, I suspect *Titinius'* exit convinced the audience that a wounded Roman soldier was being carried off stage, perhaps to one of their famous Roman baths where he might heal his wounds. At very least the audience's sympathy accompanied his exit. Of that I am sure. Five decades have passed since that evening. In my subsequent assessment of the situation, I have surmised that forgetting my lines was the single most interesting event of the evening, much more so than four and one-half hours of Shakespeare's play, which in spite of its wonderfully rich characters, is a bit lengthy and much too predictable. At very least, forgetting my lines, while my large foot crushed Gwillem Evens' finger, added a note of spontaneity to the evening, for which the audience might have been most grateful.

Today, I wish that to be the case.

The show must go on. Indeed, my so-called career was progressing in its bumbling fashion. Up to that point, five disciplines had been learned through various forms of misunderstanding. They were lessons well learned, nonetheless. They are, in the order I acquired them: the ability to stand in one spot for an interminably long time, like a very well-trained German Shepherd; the dubious skill of taking inordinately long pauses, until my feelings coincided with the words I was about to say; thirdly, tripping on stage and entertaining both cast and audience with false hair dangling from my chin; fourthly, my ability to convince an audience that I was mortally wounded, when in fact I had merely forgotten my lines. Another skill I developed to perfection was the ability to appear disinterested, when I really did care so very much.

~~~

Young students of the theater took naturalism so very seriously during the sixties. Being 'real' meant everything to young actors then. Brilliant, naturalistic performances by Marlon Brando, Montgomery Clift and Marilyn Monroe had enthralled most inexperienced thespians like myself at that early time of our careers. But the so-called 'Method' approach also bore with it hazards too dangerous for a young actor's obsession with so-called 'truth'. Actors at the birth of their careers, required of themselves to create 'reality' on stage, to 'feel' before they took action, overlooking that human beings are 'feeling' every moment of every day.

If I could have for once relaxed that desperate 'holding on' mode I could have, I'm sure, dived for pearls unimaginably sacred, but, alas, at age twenty-three, I was not given to impromptu acceptance of things beautiful that came from chance. No, the child in me hovered for protection from all that was outside my control. There was the untamed beast in me to consider, and therefore my performance of *'Titinius'* had to be planned beforehand in detail, while, a plethora of demons gnawed at me for their freedom.

But a young actor's obsession with 'being real' can be dangerous; a twenty-three year old playing a character, who commits suicide, doesn't have to kill himself to fill a role. I didn't know that then. After my first few weeks of having difficulty with the role, a haunting image of stabbing myself with a real knife on stage to reenact Titinius' suicide had plagued me for months. I didn't have the vaguest notion of what I was doing at that innocent time. Such are the dangers of naturalism, especially when a young man's sincere wish to be 'real' comes to play. And, oh, how sincere, how earnest I was, hoping to be a great actor, hoping to be 'real'. That's what the Actor's Studio's Method training had imbued upon me, my sincerity so extreme, so willing to do anything to fulfill the role of 'Titinius', while endlessly floundering, like a gaping fish out of water, gasping for breath, wide-eyed and desperate for a cold ocean to swim.

I rose to my feet and staggered downstairs to the basement of the McCarter Theater bound to do damage to myself for my horrible blunder on stage: forgetting my lines before a full audience, no less! Oh, my goodness! The show had been ruined, and in my young mind, I had failed miserably. What had I done to myself? What did my colleagues think? Why had I been so out of control? Forgetting my lines? How could I forgive myself? Why had I behaved like an idiot on a weekend night, when the house was full?

At that innocent time of my life, everything was overly serious to a young man, who gave the appearance of refusing to care, when I did care so very much. Dear God, how much I did care. I was going to see this acting thing through if it killed me – not because I enjoyed my work, no, certainly not, given the rigorous regimen I'd imposed upon myself. Work, work, work was the whole of my approach. Enjoyment never entered my mind. Creative imagination was a lost cause. No, I was determined to be an artist without fully comprehending what that meant. Artistry on stage had something to do with Lawrence Luckenbill's and Gwillem Evens' approach, but how they came to that level of expertise remained a daunting mystery.

Enjoyment had something to do with it. The question was "How?"

Surrounded by the cement walls of McCarter Theater's basement, I stood for an interminable length of time. The first urge that came upon me was to breathe, also perhaps for the first time in my life. Freedom came next - that faint voice within my brain that had been pounding on my skull since birth, if only to be freed, raised the decibel level of its shouts. That was a good thing for in my shameful state, I could finally hear its cries.

"Feel something for goodness sake, feel anything!"

That faint voice had been calling incessantly into my deaf ears with no response, until I listened to my heart, and subsequently, stuck my hand into a bonfire, not to burn but rather to feel something, to feel anything. Even raging impulses that threatened to devour me were worth pursuing for their sensation alone. Without stubborn logic to rescue me, animal intuition was all that was left.

An unshakeable anxiety governed me with a terrible constriction along the sides of my head. Playing the role of 'Titinius' had gotten me into a fine mess. It had been a memorable performance to be sure. The audience had surely been entranced by my dumbness on stage, but after the play ended that night, the tightening along the sides of my skull, as if a large hand were gripping my head, suggested what was in store for me. Anxiety gripped me with its nasty talons the following day and on to the next. The more I attempted to rid myself of fear of forgetting lines, the more fully it engulfed me. Perspective scenarios of forgetting lines in future productions haunted me. I wrestled with severe anxiety for the remaining two days of the run, while I played the role of 'normality' to my colleagues with a pleasant smile plastered upon my face and an abundance of vacuous small talk.

Outside, the splendor of spring burgeoned forth with full rays of sunshine and a brilliant array of yellow flowers. It was the beginning of April, and daffodils were blooming. Coldness of winter was preferable, since it offered something to struggle against, which might have allowed me to forget my blunder on stage, but alas, the spring weather was invitingly warm. Birds and plants were waking. I should have felt joy, after three months of performing *'Julius Caesar'*. But a foreboding anxiety marked my condition, based upon inexorable doom about remembering lines in future productions. Tension within my head, a 'vice-grip of anxiety' was squeezing the life out of logical thought. I couldn't in a word, 'think straight', and no matter how hard I banged that damned head with the ball of my palm, my brain refused to function properly, as if a helmet on my cranium was five sizes too tight. An internal tugging held me at bay in the aftermath of my failed performance of *'Titinius'*. I was not able to handle gracefully my mind's compilations that most people seemed to balance so well.

Perhaps I was mad.

Shame of failure became my daily condition. I was a kid, not a fully mature man, who knew nothing about my craft nor about myself. Somehow I'd become my own worst enemy. The bar had been set much too high for any real success. Only failure was possible with the bar so very high. Actor my ass - I couldn't act out of a paper bag and what an inauspicious beginning for someone who wanted so much from himself, some abstract notion of 'greatness', whatever that might have been.

My fellow actors hardly knew me, except in the context of my earnest portrayal of *'Titinius'*. They perceived me as a 'would-be actor' with the body of an athlete but lacking any real talent. They also realized a lot more was going on inside my mind than what met the eye. The oncoming spring, so visible outside my window, was juxtaposed against deep depression; a curious mix of nature's lush beauty burgeoning outside, while I was so very ashamed within an abyss of self-imposed failure. I longed to smell spring air. Any actor who would forget his lines during a performance of Shakespeare's *'Julius Caesar'* could not be trusted.

Indeed, I could not trust myself.

My melancholy deepened. Waves of anxiety grew. Fear became part of every thought and every act. I pretended to the cast that everything was perfectly fine, when in fact I was in trouble. Obsessive thoughts of forgetting lines and what a fool I'd made of myself on that fateful night recycled themselves continuously. The more I struggled with the fear of forgetting, the more vehemently my terror obsessed. Afraid of fear itself, a continuous onslaught crippled any possibility of finding peace of mind and well-deserved punishment for my inadequacy on stage. An empty, meaningless dream of becoming a 'star' had become nothing more than a self-serving fantasy.

Finally it was time to go home. I would be on my own for the first time since this mess happened. If only to repair myself, to heal myself, steps had to be taken. Some ineffable, inner strength had collapsed, and it was all I could do to function from day to day. My life had spiraled out of control. Or was it the beginning of my life? I did not know which; a young, inexperienced actor tortured by his profession - the horrific memory of my last performance incessantly plaguing my mind. I even hated the word, 'performing,' as if I were a dancing bear, willing to do anything for a meal.

Simply said, I had to regain confidence, but to do that it would be necessary someday, not then, to face the music by putting myself in front of an audience again to recover from somewhat of a 'breakdown.' Funny word that; to 'break down', to crumble to pieces. That is precisely what I had done. Barely able to function, I was still plagued with the notion of being an actor. Returning to the stage to take my licks was necessary for recovery. It was risky business, and I wasn't ready yet. Pressure to be the best, as unrealistic as it was, still tormented me. Recovery would require a more forgiving approach to my work, not to mention courage I didn't possess. Fear confronted me at every turn, blind trepidation that knew no boundaries. But I simply would not admit to failure. What else but to try? I'd been trying all of my life. Yet I was a coward and by no means a warrior.

Playing 'Normal'

McCarter Theater, 1964

In the aftermath of McCarter Theater's travails, I pretended that I was, for all intents and purposes, completely normal and perfectly fine. Upon returning to New York City to get on with my life, I plastered a pleasant smile upon my face, trying my best to be a just 'normal guy'. A vague memory of joy informed me about how it could've been, if things had gone well. Imitating that memory of 'well-being' completed my disguise. I had been conditioned to be quiet and self-contained in my youth. Now that quietude, combined with a slightly upturned smile could fool most people, although the sadness in my eyes gave away my despair; that is, if one were astute enough to observe.

Playing 'normal' was my most difficult role to date, but I was finally learning the craft of acting. Role playing came easy during those dark days. I played at being a 'normal guy', a functioning human being, using the tool of pleasant, 'small talk' with anyone willing to listen, always accompanied by lots of smiles and intermittent chuckles along the way. Oh, yes, I was having a grand time of it, convincing everyone that I was a 'normal, happy-go-lucky guy'. Humoring my fellow actors was the best of it. My skill was honed to perfection with numerous jokes and a plastered expression of 'happiness' upon my face.

That was the beginning of my becoming a skilled actor, using all the tricks to imitate a genuinely 'happy person' without planning beforehand what I would say. I began to trust my skill at improvising, convincing anyone willing to listen. In truth, personal demons had brought me to my knees and were still dancing through my head, but I became quite skilled at performing a pleasant, somewhat jovial character with his acquired, charming countenance, all of which disguised the obsessiveness of my fear of 'forgetting lines' in future productions.

~~~

After returning to New York City and immediately before I arrived at my East Ninth Street apartment, I bumped into an old, high school classmate of all people. A few moments before, I had stepped off the train from Princeton, New Jersey, and she came into my view suddenly, like an apparition from the past, standing before me with her arms extended, as if we were old friends, which might have been the case had we spent more time together in high school. My memory of her as a cheerleader with large breasts that stuck out like pineapples and whose thighs were brown as maple syrup was most appealing. But sex was definitely not a priority for me.

Again, 'playing normal' was my role upon meeting her, conversing as if little of note had occurred in my life and convincing her that my career as an actor was unfolding on course.

"I just did a season at McCarter Theater," I exclaimed cheerfully. "The season went really well. I played some great roles. Life is good, no, more than good. In fact, life is great," I boasted, trying my best to be convincing, half believing what I was saying was true. Of course, I was aware of the lie I was perpetrating, but 'playing normal' was my role now, and my acting in her behalf seemed more skilled than any performance I'd ever done on stage.

"You look great," she exclaimed exuberantly with a big smile plastered upon her face.

"Thanks," I said a bit shyly. "You look terrific too," I answered with an even bigger, flirtatious smile.

We were fully aware what was in our minds, those years in high school, during which we'd been attracted to each other but too shy to do anything about it. That said, I took her to my Ninth Street apartment on the Lower East Side, and we did it for old times' sake, half enjoying it too. That helped me forget myself for a few hours. But afterwards the same obsession about 'forgetting lines' recycled itself. I was plainly in trouble. The city distracted me to some degree, but life did not work anymore. Something had to be done.

~~~

Failure marked the beginning of my career and a true test of my mettle. I knew nothing for the first time in my twenty-three years of life. No longer was I the center of the universe, a useful lesson to be sure. Plainly I was worth nothing to myself. Furthermore, I knew nothing and was becoming aware of what was really involved to become an actor. No logical formula was applicable. The original plan had failed; that is, the struggle, worry and insurmountable effort to become in the eyes of strangers the greatest performer in the world. I had no idea why I wished to please people, especially strangers, but I did, and that ambition for public approval had been a part of me for much of my young life.

58

But now 'fame' was irrelevant. Living through each day was enough to handle. My ego had evaporated. Fear of the unknown haunted me. Struggling to maintain equilibrium in a world of despair took priority. Most of all, my peers mustn't discover what I was experiencing. And, above all, I would not succumb to pity. I would be strong. I would pretend to be normal.

"You have to pay your dues," is a statement I'd heard often in the theater but never fully realized its meaning, until the spring of nineteen-sixty-four. I was beginning a new chapter from the rubble I'd experienced in my first acting job at McCarter Theater. A humbled person had been born, a new person, who realized that a successful acting career takes more than sheer will. Other ingredients are required, 'trust in oneself' for one that allows an actor to do his work openly from the heart and not so much from the logical mind. Sometimes logic is intuitive without planning beforehand. On stage, I'd been operating from a preconceived notion of what 'should be' at the sacrifice of discovery, not to overlook an inhuman work ethic, drilling Shakespeare's words incessantly before each performance, without ever quite arriving at a level of freedom on stage. Constant worry was also part of the mix. What was wrong? Why wasn't I doing well? Wasn't I as talented as the rest of the cast? My mind refused to free itself. In my overwrought condition, tension and all of its ramifications was all I offered to any audience.

But as nature has learned to compensate for such dark incursions upon the soul, I began to feel myself through the complexity of each day. After my blundering attempt at Shakespeare, 'intuition' was the part of me that functioned best, and for the first time I realized how intelligent my feelings were compared to my logical mind that was so slow, so methodical and in some respects rather dumb. How could I trust logic after all? Logic had brought me to my knees in the first place.

My mother once suggested I attempt another profession, after seeing my dreadful performance of *Titinius* in Shakespeare's *'Julius Caesar'*. Of course, I sensed her concern. In her opinion, my talents were limited and even more alarming, I was on a suicide mission bound to destroy myself by pursuing a goal that was surely out of reach. But how does one know a goal is out of reach, until one has tried it to its end? And what does "out of reach" mean? Impossible or very difficult? Out of reach now and possible with passing time? Is a person required to avoid anything difficult, simply because it is difficult? I think not. Most people pursue what is convenient, but willingness to pursue what seems out of reach might very well separate a joyful life from a vacuous one.

I'd paid a heavy price. Now it was time to do something about it.

~~~

Acting was placed on hold for a while, perhaps forever. Meanwhile, in the face of failure, I learned to fake normality, while I gave up acting and moved out of New York City to Newburgh, New York. At Oakland Academy, I took a job teaching English and of all things coaching football to teenage boys, who wore white, plastic helmets to protect their heads from the routine collisions that came with the game. Faking 'normal' was always part of the job, using the tools of agreeability and fully aware that most people generally survive in what Thoreau refers to as a state of "quiet desperation", which accurately describes my condition at that formative time of my life.

Coaching came naturally, having played the game for a dozen years or so. Working with boys was a palliative really. Their enthusiasm allowed me to forget my failure at McCarter Theater and enlightened me to some degree. On the football field, I was quite brilliant at motivating the boys to play at their very best, having mastered very well the phenomenon of trying one's hardest, even when missing the mark *(as in my first attempt at acting)*. Oh, yes, 'effort' was certainly my field of expertise during that time. Indeed, I knew about so-called 'effort', perhaps too much so. 'Trying too hard' to achieve meaningless public approval had been my undoing by age twenty-three, but a good day's work was still necessary for any kind of success. One must try one's best to succeed. Balance was the main lesson I was forced to learn; to what degree should a man push himself? And in what direction? That requires wisdom, which I sorely lacked.

'Normality' too was a subject I willfully explored, to behave the way 'real people' behaved, thereby disguising my general disappointment. Most people fulfill the role of 'normal folk', while plodding aimlessly through their dull existences, and I was no different than they, while guiding the boys through studies of poetry, grammar and composition. Thank goodness for my interest in the puzzle of words - sentence structure, grammar and general mechanics involved in expressing ideas. Poetry taught as much to me as it did to my students. For the most part I modeled myself after those young men, who were functioning from a 'feeling' plain as well, particularly when they blocked and tackled, while wearing their helmets on the football field. They were just boys, you see, trying earnestly to pull it together, as I was trying. But my helmet was on backwards, you see.

Theater still was where my soul lay. Acting was my heart, while I lay shivering early mornings in a state of wonder, in a state of absolute chaos of mind. My brittleness had been successfully softened by the poignant memory of my absolute failure as an actor. Perhaps that memory was necessary to melt what had previously frozen my soul into a solid block of ice.

During that period, carving huge wooden logs into sculpture provided self-expression; also painting on canvass in the small room provided by the private school that had hired me. Painting and sculpting provided a creative outlet, if only to heal myself. My painting and sculpting began earnestly in my spare time and continues to this day. Meanwhile, I had a professional job, a teaching job no less. What could be more respectable? Teachers are a paradigm for youth, a model of good citizenship, allowing me to fake 'being normal' for the time being.

Whole series of events are missing, but dogged recollections continued to press at me; green, green fields, even cows and purple lilacs outside my kitchen window when I was a boy; peonies too and later a memory of a long train ride, during which I dutifully memorized words from a biology book on my way to New York City from Providence, Rhode Island, where I was a student at Brown University. I was traveling home for the holidays, and how I longed to put that biology book down to flirt with a girl standing in the aisle above my seat, but did nothing about my urge. Memorizing my biology book guaranteed my future, after all. We rode silently for five hours, and I, forgetting my lines at McCarter Theater in the aftermath of too little flirting between hours of work. Could that have really happened? And what if I had refused to memorize my biology book to insure my academic future? Would I have fallen in love on that train from Providence to New York? And what of that? And if so, then what? Was I numbed from too much memorizing?

~~~

Already I had become a suitably insignificant man, not an important one, compared to those dressed in suits. At some mysterious point, I seemed on my last legs and no more than a tangential part of mankind's herd. I had turned away from that herd, had taken myself completely out of the loop, so to speak. Something fundamental had died inside. It was time for the final flight, the flight of all flights, escape from the largest obstacle of all, namely the world at large with all of its entanglements. My impulse was to run away. But where, after all, does one run? Some anonymous space might have provided suitable seclusion. An East Tenth Street storefront for forty-eight dollars a month in the Lower East Side of Manhattan would suit my needs, yes, at least while I sorted things out. I bolted from the field and took my ball, tore myself away from all forms of activity and barricaded that storefront door to think things out, until a proper plan could be formed.

Walnut Logs, Storefront

1964-1967

Originally published in 'Florida Review', volume #39, 2015

    I had a way about me then, often sitting idly to fill the time in that rented Tenth Street storefront with the low murmur of cars beyond its bay window. Thank God I was capable of thought. Some mechanism within that dome of mine functioned well enough to think. I certainly had leisure time to think. It was not as if I had to work. There was little requirement on that front; three nights a week washing dishes for rent and a fresh tube of toothpaste every now and then. My needs were simple – a mattress on the floor to sleep upon, a small sink for washing, toilet in back that I used whenever the urge came upon me. Food was available often enough without planning in this rich country of ours. 'Thought' was the commodity valued and not food. 'Thinking' was the activity held in such high esteem, not the filling of my stomach. The cutting of logs was part of the daily routine, large ones that weighed half a ton.

Carving wood was a religious ritual. That storefront studio was an altar upon which I said my prayers every day. Woodchips covered its floor. Chopping one ton walnut logs for the life of me, my back was to the wall. I wasn't timid about chopping those huge chunks of wood that symbolized the largeness of my ache. Or was it my heart? Something was larger in me, some bigness that needed to be expressed; my desire to impress perhaps. That was big, my need to cry out for people to notice me. Yes, that was big. There was no reservation when it came to throwing my soul out in front of people. I wasn't shy about that, not at all shy about that. If it came to large chunks of wood or small chunks of wood, I would choose large. My heart was in it, chopping away at those huge hunks of walnut. Their hugeness balanced the smallness of my self-image, the humble impression of me that could never be guessed by appearances. Everything I represented appeared big, my sculpture, my shoulders and thickened hands, not to overlook the intensity of my persona that pierced through space, as I stared confusedly at the busy world outside. 'Big' was everything to me. Size was the standard, and weight, much heavy weight. Those were my criteria of worth.

Freedom itself was what I thrived for in that storefront. Although its space offered little aside from the darkness of solitude, I felt free within its walled confinement without judgment from others. Let live; let be free are the operative phrases here. It was all about my freedom, all of it. A certain random waving of arms was necessary to proceed through each day, merely to exercise my ability to choose and be done with it. I had become quite skillful at giving the impression that there was indeed a reason for those random movements when I swirled the air about me, and given the proper facial expression that accompanied said movement, I could convince most any man of my genuine contribution to the general "mish mash" of things, thereby ensuring myself a place in the world of some respectability, regardless of certain facts that suggested otherwise.

'Respect' was plainly not due me by ordinary standards, aside from my own to myself, but that was a given. Without self-respect I would have been in a sorry state indeed. Of course, there would be a need eventually to proceed in some direction or another, some humble activity that would lead me out of the condition that fixed me in its grip. Was I not destined, after all, to be a success? That is, if I were patient with myself, if I held myself in check, while what was left of me dangled helplessly from a hook with fine toothed fish nipping at my heels and subsequent dissolution of my parts. But, of course, my newfound freedom was my success, separate from the world, living in a Lower East Side storefront by my own choice and answering to no one. Alas, it is easier said than done, this freedom business.

Where had I disappeared to during that time? Where did I go? Some private place, deep within and so difficult to return once having arrived, and then back to the chilling reality that I just had to make something of myself, but there was so little upon which I could lay my trust. What could possibly offset the windshield wipers, oscillating before my eyes? I was awake, but I seemed not at home. When I knocked on my head with my folded fist there was no answer. No part of me was willing to respond. Everything had come to a halt one day *(lucky event)*, when I was wise enough to recognize the pleasure of solitude. I became a friend only to myself, as my bones were dragged from front to rear of that tiny storefront, chair to bench, chisel to paint brush. I needn't mention the burning cigarette taste in my lungs, sharp and acid. My attention span found barely enough focus to chop my logs, while passersby busily darted on nearby New York City streets. Was it nine thirty? Was it five thirty? Was there no top or bottom? My eyeballs twitched. With droplets of cold faucet water I sprayed my forehead, while somewhere in the dark cavern of my brain a little man waved to me with a smirk on his face, hounding me for my attention. So much time had already passed, an unexpected event, since it crept by unnoticed, one fallen hair at a time, leaving barking, random commands from invisible, superior officers urging me to carve those blocks of wood.

In my numbed state, I dutifully chopped and chiseled month after month. Two years passed rather quickly, I would say - an enormous body of work produced as well; that is, by ordinary standards. All the while, the halo enveloping my head had been tarnished like spoiled silverware that needed polishing. There was no shine.

Glancing outside my studio occasionally at people passing by, they seemed so very busy, walking with such purpose, hustling about like ants. It was not in the cards that I could be one of them, scurrying along the street. I was an unpaid log-cutter by trade and that was solitary activity suited only for those who could handle mallet and chisel, an endeavor that was not for the faint of heart, carving logs into shapes that suited my sensibility. At night I carried on with part-time jobs, waiting on tables, longshoreman, busboy, plumber, dishwasher, bouncer at a bar to name a few; anything that required the most rudimentary training and simultaneously paid the rent. Depression was part of the experience, a deep one that lasted too long and took me on a ride I shall never forget. I am not one to complain. It was all a learning experience. I would take whatever goodness came of my situation and forget the rest.

The even tone of trucks' engines passing outside my storefront and the sound of mallet upon chisel were the only consistent measure of forward ascent. Few understood a grown man burrowing holes into the bark surface of logs. I certainly was not interested in their opinion, hard enough on myself as I was. Self-criticism abounded at every turn, no matter what my thoughts. Every log I carved represented another passage of time, but little changed internally. I was anxious about something invisible and saw fear when I looked into a mirror; the deepened lines on my face, the flushed complexion, ears that stuck out too far; everything put together awkwardly with little consideration for the person

66

inside. Carving huge logs was a secondary result to what really was going on. I hadn't the energy to pay attention to a career. Oh, yes, there were gallery shows occasionally and a few pieces sold for a pittance of their worth, but doing well never entered my mind. That meant thinking of the future, which I never did. Everything good in my life was a side-effect.

Part time jobs taught important lessons about people and me. I washed dishes in a Mexican restaurant with an open kitchen, wearing rubber gloves and making seven bucks an hour. One night a familiar voice called in back of me. I turned around and found an old school chum, a fellow student from Brown University, puzzled at the image of me washing dishes. Not that he said anything. He merely looked at me pitifully, as if I'd fallen to the depths of despair. I did not explain myself, as I removed my rubber glove to shake his hand. Dressed in a power suit with a power tie, the good fellow looked like a million dollars, obviously making big money on the stock market. An economics major, having studied the subtleties of finance at Brown, my old friend was doing very well. Contrarily, I had been a philosophy major, an alleged 'thinker', well versed in the writings of Aristotle and Plato, and earned a living by washing dishes, which provided ample time for deep thought. Our stations in life had taken radically different directions, a fact clearly registered in his bewildered expression, a cross between wonderment and shock, although his dismay at my lowly station in life remained unspoken. On the contrary, the fellow offered a warm, albeit uncomfortable handshake with lots of, "How ya doing? You look great!" His highly visible disbelief was awkwardly ignored with lively small talk mixed with undercurrents of my alleged plight, a man lost without a future, an anomaly for a Brown graduate, a dishwasher, no less, at the age of twenty-six.

I played along as if nothing were unusual. Washing dishes was dignified work. Like childbirth, it cannot be explained, unless an artist lives it. Dishwashing provided enough income to pay my storefront rent and ample time for chopping walnut logs. Nothing could be simpler. I was a log cutter by trade, and that's all there was to it. A sculptor of walnut logs survives in whatever way possible.

Washing dishes was a means to an end. Alas, from the look of my friend's expression, it was indeed 'the end'.

~~~

One day a woman pleasantly smiled at me when we passed each other on East Tenth Street. We had noticed each other in the neighborhood a few times, and she'd often nodded approvingly as she passed. I always nodded back and smiled, but furthering our acquaintance never entered my mind. Weeks later, a note taped onto my door invited me to an experimental theater workshop that met once a week. The word "experimental" immediately appealed to me, implying that skill wasn't required. Various failed attempts at reading my bumbled poetry within the confines of my lonely storefront confirmed I still knew nothing about acting per se, not to mention the travesty of my failed attempts at Shakespeare five years before. According to the woman's note, whose name was Lee, the group needed men, and, since I looked like one, they might welcome me; that is, if I didn't take up too much space.

As I say, I was busy sculpting walnut logs at the time, but the solitary stand I had taken was weighing heavily on me. Plainly spoken, I was lonely. Relationships were few. I could not handle them. Something had snapped, making the notion of sharing a life impossible, when partners buried me with affection. My feelings were tender beneath the hardness; that veneer so impenetrable, so rigid, so cemented into the fabric of my life and so very frightened of people. Brittleness would be the term used, hard and brittle and so liable for breaking, so easily smashed into unrecognizable pieces, out of control in a state of rigid control. It was not possible, I thought, to change.

Contact with people had been held to a minimum with the exception of a beautiful German woman, who had walked by chance into my studio and seemed to show mercy for my humble circumstance. She was a welcomed visitor and shared the mattress I laid upon in that storefront floor more than once. Love was surely part of it and enough to bond us for an interlude, if only for her bravery, until firmer commitments could be made by her; a dear person she. Most partners were passing fancies I loved briefly and then who knows where they went? Some married and that was the end of it. Others just moved away. One moved down south and opened a dress shop. She was a sensitive girl but a bit cruel. Maybe we're all a bit cruel when things aren't going well.

Be that as it may, regardless of the hours needed to bore holes into aforementioned logs, I took a night off and showed up at the workshop, seeking human company to help bear the burden of another lonely week with my walnut logs.

~~~

The group as a whole seemed a benign bunch, all of whom, without exception, were aspiring actors, while I was unable to present an occupational definition that might deem satisfactory in their eyes. Categories that described any suitable profession escaped me. 'Porter' was my title at the time, or, better described, a combined dishwasher/janitor, who cleaned the dirty crockery, took the garbage out and washed the floors when the bar closed. Plainly I was not an actor as my colleagues were, who had studied the craft, and in some cases, actually earned their livings by doing theater or television or whatever actors did for pay. I was a voyeur in that setting of professionals, who, at their young ages were searching for the "truth". Oh, yes, that "truth" word was mentioned repeatedly. The group seemed earnestly seeking it out, while I sought little more than friendly company for a few hours to forget the tediousness of carving walnut logs.

I wished very much to hide within the group, feeling, as I did, not to be part of humanity's plan, which worked so well for those allied with the system. Taking my exit from that workshop was a constant subtext, back to the storefront with its mattress on the floor and tiny wash basin. God knows what kept me from retreating to that dark hole. Vanity, I suppose. The prospect of sleeping in a real bed had not crept into my consciousness yet. The actors, on the other hand, all had beds. I was sure of it from their general scrubbed look, not to mention a subtle fragrance in the air, a saccharine aroma that suggested access not only to regular baths but also to a fresh supply of cologne every day. In my way of looking at things, that luxury alone was something worth the hours spent with those good people. Their smell brought me back to civilization, if only to draw into my lungs the odor of their abundance. I had been cleaning unmentionable orifices with the assistance of my little storefront sink, so I passed muster mingling among them, I suspect. At least nothing unsavory was mentioned. Thank God for running water and other small pleasures and so very grateful for my good fortune at the time.

Our leader *(Lee was her name)* was a lovely human being, who, I sensed, favored my presence in that spacious, white hall, not to make too much of it. It was by no means an occasion for bolstering egos. No, there was adventure to be had on those workshop nights. But getting back to the group and our leader Lee, a kind woman she, and so very alert to the needs of the group. Actors tend to be a mean bunch, sort of ravenous, considering their overwhelming need to gain favor from strangers. At the time, I certainly needed attention as well, or I would not have been there. As I say, my need to mingle with humanity served to balance the lonely days.

The one night each week I spent in that workshop was little more than a social event for me, a time to hold hands and talk, not to overlook the touchy, feely exercises that were the best. I did not speak much but that didn't matter. Politeness and obedience got me by in a pinch. When it came to doing the exercises suggested by Lee, these could be executed by anyone really, guaranteeing that my lack of skill would not be discovered. I was a charlatan, could not act to save myself, but I could easily move with the others and make odd guttural sounds that resembled the utterances one might hear in some faraway jungle, various "uggs" and "oohs" and "ahhs" that anyone with the barest of training could execute with a minimum of talent.

As far as movement was concerned, I did what the others did. Within the walls of that vaulted, airy space, I was indeed a skilled follower. Yes, imitating behavior led by others was my proclivity in those magical surroundings, down any path that met Lee's fancy; sometimes extending our arms like human airplanes and gliding through space, until we gently collided against a wall and crumpled to the ground. I followed their repertoire when they insouciantly leaped or pranced like horses, as if they were little children. Something liberating about the exercise calmed me. There was always a suggestion of the beast within our behavior, whether in the realm of the sounds we made or our movements. A child again, I played freely with the other children and was not particularly interested in the meaning of it all. Perhaps this was the childhood I'd missed. I never quite comprehended their message with the bizarre behavior they demonstrated, but that did not bother me. Really it didn't. The girls were pretty, and no one asked what I was doing there. Information about me was never proffered either, which secured my position among them. For what little they knew, I was an actor. Nothing could be farther from the truth.

Meanwhile, the work seemed designed for some higher purpose that our leader Lee had in mind. The other actors seemed to be aware of that purpose. The vocal gymnastics, otherwise known as grunting, was not communication in the true sense of the word. We had been reduced to the level of primordial beings devoid of social grace of any kind, let alone communicating. If we had been on the street we surely would have been arrested and the proverbial key thrown away, but thoughts of imprisonment did not bother me then. I was not a criminal, having lacked the courage to harm anyone, or to steal anything. There was nothing I wanted and therefore nothing to steal and no one I wished to injure in any way; that is, aside from myself at random moments. Generally speaking, I was a benevolent fellow but lacked the resources necessary to do anyone much good.

~~~

Story-telling was usually the last part of each workshop. With our colleagues serving as audience, the actors recreated personal experiences of their lives. Upon being given a chance to perform, their formidable skills flourished. Highly imaginative verbal accounts of hair-raising events were often embellished with vocal sounds to heighten dramatic moments. Those accompanying sounds were somewhat artificial and definitely avant-garde, I would say, but their skill was extraordinary, their grace exemplary, as they passionately related secret memories of their pasts. Some even cried. No, I could never do that.

Meanwhile, no skill was involved on my account. No one asked me for anything by way of thespian craft. It was a victory merely to breathe in a world so complex, let alone act on stage where people would be watching my every move. No, I was not meant to be watched. Thinking clearly in front of a group was beyond the capability of my overwrought condition; a tenuous cross between high ambition with one foot in the loony bin, so racked I was with self-doubt and fear of forgetting my lines. It could have been fear of anything really. 'Lines' were merely a convenient tool with which to prevent myself from accomplishing God knows what. Fame or fortune were somewhere in the mix, but they did not comprise the entire picture. But getting back to forgetting lines, I could just as easily have forgotten to wear my pants due to some phobia about buttoning my fly.

For me, telling a story was impossible, although I must admit there were numerous lurid tales I could have related to a very close friend, but definitely not to a group of strangers. Audiences frightened me. I've always been afraid of being a total laughing stock in the public eye. Still I admit that a story based upon a personal event, even though embellished, cannot be challenged for its accuracy. My story would be my story, improvised by its owner for public view. What could be simpler? There would be no words to memorize and no threat of forgetting lines. My life could not be forgotten after all, and better if it were, considering the numerous travesties I had brought upon myself; my storefront living quarters for one, among others in a series of mishaps that through sheer perseverance had summed up to a questionable whole without the slightest notion of where it was all heading.

To fill a void of my life was the reason I was there, not telling secrets that would raise hairs on backs. As I say, I was a voyeur and not so much a participant in that workshop; that is, aside from the few noises I'd offered to the group during ensemble exercises, merely to accommodate and nothing more. Voyeurism suited me just fine too, to sit back and listen to my comrades reveal their darkest secrets, and always with the hope that they would become better actors. I carved walnut logs in my storefront to fill my time and washed dishes for a living. That was enough for me. Acting was not my ambition, and yet, I must admit, my retreat from the limelight was a performance unto itself, well aware, as I was, of my colleagues watching me closely, while I lingered in the shadows of the back row.

Besides, I was too dumb to speak to an audience. There was nothing of merit I might have revealed. Not that I wasn't interested. I was, but that interest was overridden by the amount of effort it would take to move my rump from the back of the room if asked to join. Of course, fear was a factor too. The actors' willingness to put themselves through a maze of personal tribulation for Lee's approval was both impressive and frightening for a layman such as me. It took a certain degree of courage I didn't have. As one can well imagine, my limited logic did not fully grasp the purpose of exposing secrets. No, those were my secrets, reserved only for me. I would have jumped through hoops for our teacher, but the threat of performing a personal story boggled my mind and ruined my digestion. Every Friday night, I was a mess, after an hour of sitting helplessly in the rear, separate from the rest.

As weeks passed, I listened to elaborate accounts of their private lives and all was hunky-dory, but one evening I attempted to ease myself out of the workshop before the inevitable might happen. I sensed my time was approaching. But it was too late. When I moved toward the door, Lee stopped me in my tracks and asked me to tell a story like the others had done.

Predictably, I was mortified by the prospect. The long walk to the front of the room seemed a lifetime, my body trailing the chemical odor of a frightened animal, punctuated by a very long and awkward silence. I faced their expectant faces. What story to tell? Something from my childhood, possibly an anecdote, having to do with sucking my mother's breast at a tender age? No, that wouldn't do. There might be something in the area of politics. Vietnam was raging at the time, but I was unconnected to the brutality of that war, except for Mai Lai. That horrific massacre affected me deeply. On the other hand, such subjects were risky. I have been known to come to tears at awkward moments and would not risk such vulnerability in front of that group of professionals. Imagine a grown man. No, my bricklayer father would never approve. It would be better to relate something nice, but nothing seemed particularly nice. My general state of disappointment could be a suitable subject, dealt as penance for my sins and derived from the wrath of, let us say, some long forgotten Assyrian God. My original perfect state at birth never went beyond the first moment. Yes, that first moment of life was the best of it, after which I was forced to duck and writhe from the deluge of compromises that followed. "We are not who we wished to be in the beginning" could be the theme. No, I didn't wish to be anything; that is, beyond a sculptor of logs. They'd know I was lying.

Lee asked everyone to be quiet. This was to be my first story, she explained. Some of the real actors, while sincerely working on their craft, had skillfully related three or four stories by then, as opposed to myself, who had sat on my bum with a pleasant countenance to be sure. I was there, after all, to spend time with people and then go back to carving my walnut logs and part time job. And yet I wished to excel. That was a definite flaw in my character, wishing to win a contest that was not clearly defined, having to do with applause perhaps, or being the most imaginative in the group. My thoughts were running away with me. I wanted so very much to beat everyone else at story-telling - an odd pursuit if there ever was one and surely aimed for disaster.

'Greatness' was irrelevant in that setting. Living through the story would be enough. Forget greatness. My entire being embraced a fresh condition of alertness. Poignant stage fright forced heightened perception. I was open to impressions, unguarded, insurmountably vulnerable. Innocence came with helplessness that I did my best to hide from those 'real actors'. I looked in wonderment at my audience, as a child does, when he hasn't learned to comprehend the logic behind events. Cause and effect no longer made sense. I connected intuitively. Struggle to maintain equilibrium in a haunting world of performing took priority. Most of all, people must not discover what I was experiencing. I would be strong. I would boldly tell my story. I reminded myself not to try

74

too much to please my numerous judges. Henceforth, I began to speak with a new sense of purpose.

My mouth had trouble forming the words at first, starting with the pronoun, *"I. . ."* and then, *"I'm nervous."* confessing my condition as if it were past tense. That part of my story was true. I continued.

"It was always my way not to talk, let alone tell stories to a group."

At that point I paused again, feeling the fool in front of them and quite unsure of myself, but there seemed no alternative but to get on with it. I was trapped like a proverbial rat. My audience seemed riveted to something on stage. It could not possibly be me, although their eyes were staring in my direction. I opened my mouth again and words escaped.

"There was mention of divorce. The father threatened divorce. The mother agreed and searched for another place to live in that small town with its cool shade-trees blocking out the hot summer sun, like a thick, green-leafed roof. The mother walked with three young children in tow through the neat, lawn lined streets bordered by friendly white houses. The boy knew the purpose of their wanderings. He was the oldest at age nine, a child refusing to speak, since speaking would mean revealing the truth, and the truth was dangerous for a young boy's survival. He followed his mother through that small village and listened to her ask landlords how much they charged for apartments. It never occurred to the boy to put a stop to any of it, given his reluctance to express rage. Sons are often silent in the presence of their parents. What was a child to say when his mother and father were separating after years of hell? The boy chose to speak by not speaking. That was his opinion – to say nothing in the wake of his parents' noise, silence in outrage toward all of it, and most of all, the wish to be alone."

Faces before me seemed oversized, having never observed them all at once nor as intently. One actor was completely bald. I studied his shiny pate for the very first time. 'Peter' his name, a friendly fellow and workshop partner, but now transformed into my hanging judge, as was the blond, pretty woman, 'Jane', sitting next

75

to him with her quizzical, wide-eyed stare and another fellow in back, the one with a deep, stentorian voice and dark hair, just plain 'Jim' his name. At that moment, the fellow witnessed a frightened little boy trapped in a man's body, unleashing his personal history to strangers. My voice barely audible, I opened my mouth and articulated words from a body that was separate from me, describing the most remarkable image of an unkempt, somewhat scruffy looking boy.

"More naïve than stubborn, the boy denied his parents' pending divorce, refused to give up his home or his father. Both were part of his roots, and he was unwilling to separate from either of them, certainly not from his dad. The boy looked up to his dad and loved him deeply. He loved his dad, didn't want another one."

Another pause ensued. I sneaked a glimpse to see if they were still there. They were and waiting for more.

"From a nine-year-old's perspective, the boy analyzed the nature of permanence, learned to appreciate anything with roots, admired the lushness of trees and flowers and bushes and grass. He noticed how they dug into the ground to stay alive and observed how they insisted upon growing, and unlike his parents, how they stayed in one place and refused to move. He decided to plant living things, went into the nearby woods to dig up wild tiger lilies that grew by the thousands, padding the ground with their orange brilliance. The boy studied the sturdy, thick trunks of trees, the towering mass of their girths and the tenacity of shrubbery that held onto the earth like tentacles with their roots sucking into it, studied with his young eyes the green, green fields, where cows grazed on sod layers of grass, a thick woven rug, stitched by a Master Craftsman."

Someone mumbled something inaudible under his breath, a word of encouragement, something like, "Yeah", an expression of support. God knows how I appeared to them - a failed actor or simply an overwrought, writhing fool? Or was I simply one of them, doing my best to express myself? There had to be something brilliant inside, I reasoned, if only I could locate its whereabouts. Stage fright was the worst of it. Terror gripped my body to such a degree that barely was I able to whisper the words. The audience inched forward if only to hear. My clumsy delivery did nothing to enhance the message of my vapid prose. Again I paused for breath. Some of the real actors interjected a few more, kindly intended, "Yeahs" to show they were genuinely interested. Oh, yes, I admit a few were drifting off, but only a few. I could not please everyone, I reasoned. Besides, I was encouraged by their few utterances of support. Or was it pity? Hard to tell and wasn't able to dwell upon the question since the moment had passed. Again, I spoke softly, my rhythm hastening, if only to finish, partially out of breath.

"The boy replanted tiger lilies and tiny birch trees in the yard of their little, white bungalow, digging, planting, making permanent what was falling apart at home, hoping they would grow in their new environs and also that his parents would see the permanence those plants represented. In different locations throughout the backyard, the little boy nourished with his watering pot the hearty roots he'd planted and raised into full grown, brilliant lilacs, tiger lilies, daffodils, birch trees and a few peonies thrown into the mix."

For minutes I carried on like this. My tongue seemed too large for my mouth as I spoke, causing my delivery to stumble at times, but in spite of this, words found their own momentum, my tongue operating in full gear by then. God, help me. Oh, God, please help me.

"Those flowers guaranteed roots for the boy, roots that would penetrate deep into the earth, roots that would suck nourishment out of the soil and sink down deep, and the sun shining high above with light rain showers occasionally, a nice situation for growing. And those flowers did grow years afterward and they still grow in that same yard today. The young boy planted shrubbery too, taken from a nursery nearby, but they died, as his parents' marriage was dying."

"In the face of his parent's pending divorce, the roots of what he planted sank deep. In time, two tiny birch trees in the front yard grew taller than the house. One still thrives today. Lilac bushes still flourish outside the mother's kitchen window, as do

peonies and daffodils and more Tiger Lilies. The mother and father did not separate quite then, threatened to, but didn't carry it out; that is, until later. 'Habit' was the glue that bonded his parents' marriage, as well as fear of the unknown, afraid, as they were, to dig up their own roots from the soil of their common, dysfunctional marriage that had blossomed into an addiction. Each year those flowers bloomed into a blanket of orange, white and purple that surround the same bungalow, defiant in their permanence."

Was that my voice? Surely that was not me, those words, describing a boy's softness, his affectionate tendencies, and the sensitivity of feelings. Why did I dare reveal such a personal memory? What on Earth had I dared to expose about myself? Couldn't I have presented a more manly stance? My voice had cracked more than once. The truth is I almost, not quite, shed a tear in front of them. God, the absolute shame of such a prospect and before a room of strangers. Exposing my vulnerability had always been out of the question, an absolute nightmare. Imagine I - a grown man! What would my bricklayer father say? What had I become? A slobbering fool? No, no, the 'strong, silent one' had always been my way. But, oh my, I'd revealed my soul before that workshop audience!

But my words continued and arrived of their own accord. I could not be blamed. Furthermore they described the truth; that is, my proclivity toward anything fluffy, soft or flowery. All of it was true and in violation of the masculine pose I'd feigned for weeks. On that informal stage, I imposed upon my captive audience the dulled fruits of my labors, much to the dismay of all who were forced to watch such a spectacle. But, no, some seemed supportive, yes, if only a few. My story, for all of its pitfalls that nearly brought me to the brink, was at very least the truth. Honesty surely has its merits. The story was not nice and it was not planned and it wasn't even the best story told. What I described was not a story at all, but rather a paroxysm, the subject of which had bound me within is grip for years to the point where sleeping on a mattress on a storefront floor seemed my natural fate. All beds had been taken by professionals, who had studied their craft. I was no doctor of medicine. There was no expertise available that might untie my knotted head. For years, only sleep had soothed my mind and at times food to fill the belly, but I was a prisoner of feelings relentlessly assigned to my keep.

Feeling the fool, my impulse was to flee but did not, preferring awkwardly to say, "Thank you" and returned to the back row, hoping to evaporate or to die. Lee complimented me, while I sat mortified at having touched so raw a nerve. I'd almost come to tears for goodness sake, a grown man and in the presence of strangers. I would never, ever forgive myself for that. After all, there was a time and a place but not in front of professional actors, who were skilled at controlling their emotions, who had studied their craft, as if they were dabs of paint rendered upon a canvass, as opposed to myself who had recklessly splattered colors with no more than a palette knife and without concern for structure or purpose. There had been no purpose to my choice of words. My emotions had given birth to them, and they had gushed forth from my mouth, like a broken fire hydrant into the gutter of a New York City street.

And yet, regardless of my doubt, a seed had been planted. During the telling of my story, another person had been reborn from the ashes of what had been me, soft and not hard, doubtful and not sure, helplessly open to feelings and not brittle, confused and yet still wishing so very much to express myself as an artist. On the one hand, telling my story had been mortifying, but on the other, it had released an unbridled, raw and vulnerable presentation before an audience, which, even if not fully recognized while in the throes of improvisation, must have been a spark and perhaps a glimpse of what acting could someday be; that is, if I were willing to open myself up again and return to the stage.

I'd experienced absolute surrender before Lee's group, a condition that, until I told my story, I'd been avoiding. The gift of 'weakness' was discovered while telling my story, plain weakness, a gift that exposes the actor's soul, from which a fountainhead of emotional truth can be explored. But an actor must assimilate to the pressure of audience gradually, until he masters that condition of extreme sensitivity and is able to speak clearly from that place. Years of risk, years of placing one's hand into the fire are sometimes required before an actor's balance, while in a state of absolute vulnerability, is found; to function on stage while weak, fragile and absolutely vulnerable. I'd only done it once, but that was enough to see the light.

My story was told intuitively and not so much from logic. Absolute terror had been part of the experience, but the challenge to bring it forth at all costs had carried me to the end. My natural instinct had always been guarded. Telling that story about a boy planting flowers for their symbolic permanence, if nothing else forced upon me a fragility that served the event I described. Furthermore, it had brought me before an audience again, after two years of solitary chopping of logs.

~~~

The following day, Lee Worley left another note on my storefront door inviting me to work on an original production of 'The Serpent' and become a member of the 'Open Theater'. Unbeknownst to me, Joseph Chaikin, the company's director, had been sitting in the audience the night before, during my 'Lilac and Daffodil' story, and the impression I'd left upon him generated his interest in my joining his company. I'd been unaware of his presence in Lee's workshop and in fact, had never laid eyes on the man, so it would've been impossible to recognize him. But his New York production of 'America Hurrah', which I'd seen, had confirmed that his directing skills were exemplary. His performances with the famed 'Living Theater' directed by Judith and Julian Beck had also been heralded by the New York press. The 'Open Theater' was about to tour through Europe and the Near East. I was inexperienced to be sure, but the troupe needed men, so Mr. Chaikin asked Lee Worley to invite me to join.

What I really wanted was to act, but I was cautious after my initial failure at McCarter Theater. Performing wasn't a natural fit for me, having injured my spirit so deeply during my first attempt. My compulsion to perform was reignited without fully trusting it was the right thing to do; yes, foolish man, so very willing to follow one's dream, so willing to 'dive into the fire again'. I would show up at the rehearsals of *'The Serpent'* as a committed member of the cast outwardly, but secretly I was cautious. Acting had been a precarious choice to date, but the prospect of working again in a controlled environment, under the guidance of Joseph Chaikin, had ignited that old, familiar and addictive adrenalin rush that brought me home to my roots.

My excitement about joining the company was somewhat confused further by my commitment to carving logs into sculpture. Sculpture and painting appealed to me, and I had a talent for them that was derived from my gene pool, I suppose; a lot of artists in my family, a sculptor grandfather, an artist mother and one sister was a painter as well. Carving logs came easily, by intuition alone, and I didn't want to give it up. Perhaps I could do both. Also the *'Open Theater'* would provide a weekly paycheck, a factor that couldn't be overlooked. I could finally quit my dishwashing job and still pay the bills.

~~~

A Paycheck at Last, 'Open Theater'

1967-1974

I won a small victory when Joseph Chaikin invited me to join the *'Open Theater'* to collaborate in the creation of *'The Serpent'* that would eventually tour through the United States, Europe and the Near East. Like a baseball player, who'd been hit on the head by a fastball, it was imperative to place myself in the batter's box once again. Five years had passed since the travails of McCarter Theater, when life had gone off the rails, a difficult period that represents today the uncertain reality of youth.

The *'Open Theater'* was known as an avant-garde theatre company, under the guidance of Joseph Chaikin, whose unique vision fully engaged audiences both politically and aesthetically. The man was truly a genius. It was a time for change during the sixties, when every conventional form was being questioned from marriage, to racism, to government, to war. Theater was also experiencing growing pains, and privately I was going through a major transformation as well - sculptor or actor or possibly both? I was in the process of discovery, a process that has lasted for a lifetime. Continuous touring through Europe, America and the Near East stimulated both creative and political awareness. Vietnam had altered society's collective consciousness, as well as the assassinations of great leaders like Robert and John Kennedy, Martin Luther King and Malcolm X. As a well-known, political, avant-garde company, *'The Open Theater'* rode on that wave, or perhaps I did, as if it were going to last forever.

When I began working with the company, my contribution was a limited one, since my shyness rarely offered a full sentence during normal conversation with company members. At first, I added little to the work; that is, aside from my size and ability to move with a modicum of grace. By that time, unwillingness to communicate had become a firmly embedded habit from boyhood and such contrivance really, posing as the strong, silent type, allegedly thinking 'deep thoughts' seldom expressed to others. What complicated matters was my oversized, muscled body and somewhat brutish countenance that completed the picture. God, what a sight to behold. A mute, overly muscled male with limited intellectual capacity was the image I projected, indeed a somewhat curious figure to anyone bothering to notice.

Being a physical specimen certainly didn't help matters. "Anyone with that body couldn't possibly have a brain," was the general consensus within the company. A few knew differently, but others did not. It was difficult to perceive what was going on inside a man too shy to speak. Engaging in conversation would have so easily added fluidity to relationships. Alas, I offered what was possible at that early stage of my life.

In truth, my brooding stance, although blatantly an affectation, did attract attention from other cast members; not the sort I desired, however. At very least, I was 'different' from that talkative bunch. Everything about me was methodical, my speech patterns, even my movements that were forced to accommodate the thickness of my thighs, below which hung a pair of feet barely large enough to support my hovering weight. To make matters worse, walking on my heels created a banging sound whenever I crossed the rehearsal hall. Our director, Joseph Chaikin, cleverly found stationary positions in the background for interminable periods of time, while the real actors fulfilled most of our workshop's action. Having little training, absolute stillness was the function I served best.

On the other hand, personal thoughts connected to the theme of our work raced through my mind at a frantic pace. Often I was too shy to express them. Much of my time was spent hiding. I needed rest above all. I certainly wasn't of a mind to 'beat' anyone. Just 'getting by' was enough, feeling whatever I felt along the way. I had my sculpture and painting back at my storefront to bolster my spirits. That was enough for me. My life had taken a turn toward the bare essentials; living in a storefront, isolated and sleeping on a mattress on the floor, out of touch with the practical world. When we weren't rehearsing, I carved wood and painted pictures to satisfy my soul, even had a few exhibitions and sold some work.

Whenever Joseph Chaikin was present, sinking into the background became my habit. The man was a masterful actor and director. He was also well read and erudite, capable of conversing about many subjects both political and philosophic. The man's availability to words allowed him license to expound knowledgeably on any subject, while I listened intently in the background, hoping to garnish a few gems from his wisdom. What I noticed most was his modesty. He wasn't aggressive when he directed, often speaking as if he were unsure of the answer, always leaving the door open for the actors to explore the question at hand. He seldom spoke as if he were sure of how a scene should be executed. The answer always was left for the actors to solve without his defining the solution beforehand. He asked pertinent questions about the theme we were exploring, questions interesting enough to stimulate our imaginations. In return, our minds were constantly searching for useful material. Knowing intuitively what would pique our imaginations, he chose the right questions that would inevitably result in finished, somewhat brilliant productions. At the risk of repeating myself, the man was truly a genius.

Plainly the company did not need me, and my silent presence among those chatty artists didn't match, but that didn't register enough to refuse traipsing along with the group. I was collecting a salary, after all, and the prospect of washing dishes in a Mexican restaurant seemed a repugnant alternative. My needs were simple; a full head of hair and a paycheck, enough to pay the rent, and occasionally a hamburger with an onion on top filled my weekly requirements.

Meanwhile, as far as I was concerned, my silent pose could continue for the rest of my life and that would be just fine. It didn't occur to me that my mute stance was robbing me creatively. Any play requires the use of words, but from lack of use, my tongue still lacked the dexterity required. Joseph Chaikin was under the impression that I'd had a stutter at some earlier period of my life. Little did he know that 'willful stubbornness' was the source of my deliberately slow and excruciatingly labored speech. On one rare occasion, after the company had left for the day, he called me aside and gave me a few pointers to enhance the subtleties of my performance abilities, which, as I say, amounted to little more than standing in one spot, looking as if I cared. The appearance of caring was easy for me, for I did care so very much. Still do in fact.

Once he asked, "Ray, is it possible to speak a little faster?"

We both smiled then; his was a kind, forgiving smile. We genuinely liked each other. At least I sensed as much. Fact was that I had few lines in 'The Serpent', but Joe was trying to help me become the person I really was. Anyway, his remark was amusing to both of us. Generally, he tolerated my taciturn composure, as well as my slowness. More importantly, I never questioned his aesthetic judgment, whereas the company's main actors challenged him continuously. Their resistance was a Godsend with his attention constantly diverted towards them, leaving me for long stretches of time safe from his perusal. The director was even thankful for my silent presence *(at least I believe this to be the case)*, mostly for staying out of his hair and respectfully nodding my head whenever he passed. Joseph Chaikin was a kind man and certainly aware I was doing my very best. Once he told me my fly was open, a revelation for which I was indeed thankful. I was not on stage at the time, so it didn't bother him much. He even smiled, not the mocking kind that I received from other members of the company; more of a joke between us, as if we were old friends, which we were by then. Seven months of continuous workshop rehearsals had passed between us by then, and I was serving his vision more skillfully every week, a factor in our relationship that bonded us for years afterwards during our work together.

In my fragile state, working with Joseph Chaikin was a Godsend. He was an extraordinarily gentle man with unusual intelligence, especially when creating our original plays. After the company's critical success of *'America Hurrah'*, our aforementioned production was *'The Serpent'* based upon episodes from the Bible; Adam and Eve's bite into the 'forbidden apple' in the Garden of Eden; the *'Cain and Able'* scene, otherwise known as the first murder; also the first copulation to name a few. These scenes were integrated together with scenes of pungently sad moments of modern history, the assassinations of great leaders like Robert and John Kennedy, Malcom X and Martin Luther King.

While creating *'The Serpent'* by means of actors' improvisation with the assistance of two writers, Jean Claude Van Italie and a young Sam Shephard, actors were not required to portray the arc of a full character from beginning, middle to end. Our work was "episodic", which meant 'pieces of a whole', consisting of a series of iconic vignettes derived both from the Bible and from modern history without a plot to tie them together.

In his mild tone, Joe would explain what we were attempting to accomplish for the day, and the actors fulfilled his vision by improvising upon a specific theme. Complementing the actor's improvised monologues were Jean Claude Van Italie's or

Sam Shephard's written speeches, often derived from the company's improvisations. The collaboration of scenes and monologues from both writers and actors became the scripts of our finished plays. The daily work was based upon exercises taken from Viola Spolin's book, *'Theater Games'*, consisting of 'conductors', 'worlds', 'sound and movement' and 'story-telling', all useful for establishing the *'Garden of Eden'*, from which the *'Serpent'* character was created, consisting of five men mounted upon the stronger ones' shoulders and all of us delivering lines in chorus. I could handle that with relative ease, since we were an ensemble, and I wouldn't be particularly noticed on the bottom tier of bodies with Peter Maloney on my back, while we flailed our arms, wagged our tongues in serpent fashion and delivered our lines in chorus, tempting Adam to bite into the apple, which he always did ravenously.

~~~

The very first murder between *'Cain and Able'* from the Bible was the highlight of my contribution to *'The Serpent'*. Joseph Chaikin cast me in the major role of Cain. I don't know why exactly. I was very quiet during those days compared to other members of the company, which, as I say, encouraged me to take a modest position within the group. Becoming one of the main actors wasn't part of my thinking, although the leading role of *'Cain'* became memorable in the public eye. Chaikin directed the *'Cain and Able'* scene with artist's eye for simplicity. Nothing was done in excess. Athletic, big and capable of moving well, I offered a degree of masculinity on stage, although, as I've said, verbal dexterity was still sorely lacking. The scene required physical action without words, which was a blessing, considering my neurosis about remembering lines.

The *'Cain and Able'* scene portrayed the 'original murder', the very first murder in history, as recorded in the Bible. The two brothers were the offspring of *Adam* and *Eve*, the first man and woman created by God, so death was universally unknown to the human experience. Ralph Lee played *Able*. In the beginning of the scene, my blows did mortal damage to my brother in the background of which the entire company exhaled rhythmic sounds of breath that accompanied the physical action on stage. Aside from that chorus of audible breath, the scene was done in silence. At age twenty-eight, I was able to lift Ralph high above my head and kill him with convincing, pantomimed blows night after night, after which, the character *Cain*, not knowing what 'death' was, attempted to bring *Able* back to life, naïve to the fact that his blows had actually killed his brother.

When *Cain's* blows exhausted themselves, *Able* was dead, but according to the Bible, this was the first death in human history. Murdering *Able* was the more predictable 'first beat' of the scene, but what followed *Able's* death added a dimension of emotional depth. As I say, this was the first death in the history of man. *Cain* was dealing with unchartered territory, the 'original murder', without *Cain* knowing what death was. The futile task followed of restoring his brother back to life by hugging him, by caressing him, by shaking him and physically expressing his love for his brother's unresponsive body. But *Able's* limp condition would not transform back to life. This was a puzzle to *Cain,* who hadn't realized his violent blows would result in injury and ultimate death. *Able's* permanent loss of life presented an incomprehensible mystery to Cain. His confused facial expression searched for answers. Why wasn't his brother moving? Why wasn't he breathing? Why was his body so limp?

'The Serpent' achieved great success in New York and later in Europe. When we opened in New York City, the *'Cain and Able'* scene was highlighted in a spectacular, New York Times, rave review, written by Walter Kerr with dramatic headlines and a photograph of Ralph Lee and myself on the front page of the theater section. Inadvertently, in my stumbling fashion, I'd become part of an artistically innovative, brilliant theater experience, miraculously celebrated by the illustrious New York Times. I was still unsure of myself on stage, but I was being celebrated for my work, an outcome derived from pure chance to be sure, similar to Lee Worley's invitation to join her workshop by leaving a note on my storefront studio door, also by chance.

Luck was beginning to come my way. My availability to the work at that uncertain time of my life was also by chance. Mr. Chaikin's invitation to his workshop had revitalized my latent desire to perform on stage. Also Joseph Chaikin's approach to the work allowed me permission to grow at my own pace. His gentle way enticed me back into the theater, also a stroke of fortuitous luck. I never would've returned to acting if it weren't for Joseph Chaikin's unassuming guidance and the nurturing environment he established for our work. Truth be said, I owe the man my professional life in the theater.

~~~

Romance came after the *'Open Theater'* returned from Europe. That scared me a bit, moving off a fixed spot to share a life with a beautiful, German woman. *'Regine'* was her name and a kind, lovely lady she is. Sharing with anyone would have been most difficult. My heart was not in it for the longest time; always 'close to the vest,' so to speak. Although I'd moved away from a mattress on the floor to a makeshift bed made of plywood and steel pipe by my own hands, there was little I dared to share with another human being, aside from my handmade, plywood bed and wasn't about to give that up without a struggle. Sleep was the most pleasurable part of my life, after all. In that regard, sharing my bed was no small matter. It had taken some twenty dollars for materials to build, not to mention the expense of foam that served as a mattress during those years. I could never give up that bed with its little television sitting on a nearby ledge. That bed represented a small measure of stability, perhaps for both of us.

My new lover and I shared that bed. I was cautious at first, but ultimately I became familiar with the arrangement, two of us lying on that foam rubber mattress, mounted on a rough piece of plywood. Four pipes served as legs. This was a bridal bed to beat all bridal beds. We slept. We made love. Oh, yes, minor scuffles arose between me and my German friend. I was mostly to blame, if blame were necessary. Who knows if blame ever solves conflict between two people at odds? I loved her deeply; no question about that. We lived our lives in luxury paid for by my income from the avant-garde theater group that required me to stand sedately in one spot, followed by my portrayal of the first murder, which by that time I'd learned to execute with maximum efficiently. At long last, I had job security. Familiarity with my role in *'The Serpent'* negated the need for preparation before each performance. Nervousness was out of the question. I showed up every night and performed dutifully, similar to a night watchman guarding the First National Bank and never missed a performance.

~~~

When the *'Open Theater'* created our second play, *'Terminal'*, by then telling stories directly to the company was an integral part of the rehearsal process. The main company had collaborated with Joe for years by then. Their advanced skill at telling stories was palpable, and again, in spite of the attention I was receiving for my performance in *'The Serpent'* I was still somewhat of a voyeur. During the last two hours of our workshops, some actors would relate a personal event in his or her life that would parallel the theme of the play we were constructing. For the most part, I would listen to the others relate their personal accounts based upon those themes. Joseph Chaikin never forced me to deliver improvised monologues before the group. Each actor volunteered when he or she was ready to do so. This allowed me to assimilate gradually, to sit patiently and watch the others work, until I found inspiration to relate a personal monologue before my more experienced colleagues. Sometimes I observed for weeks before I finally told a story. When inspiration arrived, *(only when comfortable and not beforehand)*, my offering to the group was rooted in the deepest, most personal place of my soul. Joe's patience and his refusal to pressure me resulted in the most personal work I'd ever done. I'd already grown to trust and respect the man unequivocally, which gave me permission to explore honestly life experiences that were relevant to the theme we were exploring. In the case of *'Terminal'*, the subject was death.

So much confusion had been part of my history that anything I did or said, while relating a story, was emotionally full. Waves of feelings permeated all of my work. My very first story was a passionate description of what eventually evolved into a character called the *'Executed Man'* in our second play, *'Terminal'*. The *'Executed Man'* was a prisoner of his mind, as I had been, when I first created the character. My first improvisation was expressed in a state of heightened anxiety and described the emotional imprisonment of *'The Executed Man's'* daily life *(or was it mine)*. What surprised me was my willingness to say it like it was, the freedom to articulate words without thinking beforehand and perhaps for the first time in my life. Verbiage gushed out of me without judgment. My soul's essence, keenly attuned to a state of continuous, moment to moment anxiety was the improvised subject matter of my story. Heightened vulnerability at that time of my life prompted me to reveal repressed, forbidden subjects that had been previously hidden. Perhaps for the first time, words became my tools to express freely without a plan, without contrivance of any kind and most importantly without censorship. Joseph Chaikin was taken with the *'Executed Man's'* speech; it's rawness, its blatant honesty and integrated it into our play, *'Terminal'*.

Performing monologues in 'story form' was awkward at first, clumsy at best. Emotion came easily to me. I was a raw nerve during this period. It was impossible not to feel. This was a good thing. Summoning enormous depth of emotion came easily. My vulnerability during improvised stories allowed me to create characters that contributed solidly to our plays. The original inhibited person, who had been me, was transformed into an expressive, yes, even an 'articulate' performer under the umbrella of Joseph Chaikin's nurturing direction. Rigidity fell by the wayside, and confronting openly what lay ahead became the norm. Self-doubt gave birth to softness and malleability, openness to suggestion and easily swayed by stimuli around me. Less muscle was required in performance and vocally softer tones easily expressed a vulnerable state of mind, rather than hiding it with loudness. Aggressiveness had left me for good. Stillness became more prevalent in my work and in my life. Another person had been born from the ashes of what had been me; soft and not hard, doubtful and not sure, open and not shut down, somewhat confused and yet now willing to expose the secret part of me that I had heretofore hidden from public view.

In fact, all my stories in those workshops were emotionally full. At the mercy of my fragility at that time, passion permeated everything I said or did. My state of mind was born from heightened, moment to moment vulnerability of daily life. Contrivance was unnecessary. I was so very thin-skinned those days. Planning beforehand wouldn't have brought the same results. When prompted to offer an improvisation, I simply stood before the company and said whatever came to mind. The words fell in line with feelings racking my brain that I needed so desperately to express. Improvised words had a will of their own, and the insurmountable rawness of my emotions spewed forth, like lava vomiting from a mountain top.

Would anyone consciously plan such a condition? I doubt it. Such an uncomfortable burden to carry, but on the other hand, so very useful creatively. The delicacy of my mind during that period was a fortuitous stroke of luck that filled any character's emotional availability. A mind at peace with itself wouldn't have been accessible to such a deep sense of personal truth. Also, if it weren't for Joseph Chaikin's approach of telling stories to explore subjects for our plays, I would have been less useful to his vision. Mr. Chaikin's process of building plays by means of 'story-telling' provided a conduit to express each actor's personal, inner life, which in my case, was highly sensitized during that youthful period. Joseph Chaikin's process exposed the company's deepest consciousness based upon the themes for each piece we made.

At the risk of braggadocio, I seemed quite skilled at telling stories, although I seldom gave myself credit. Executing them in front of the group in my fragile state, required little by way of effort. Permission had been granted by Joe to reveal the truth, and our personal connection to ourselves did the rest. For me, any effort 'to feel' was unnecessary. Emotions lay at my fingertips and permeated my entire being, available anytime under any circumstance. In my sensitized condition, along with heightened awareness derived from that condition, poetic description of political injustice and a reservoir of emotion were available at the drop of a hat. And I was finally able to speak spontaneously! I was actually motivated to communicate with words fluidly! God, what a miracle to finally express myself freely after so many years of silence!

Gradually the *'Open Theater'* liberated me from the inhibition I'd imposed upon myself all my life. That nurturing experience allowed me to grow as an actor without pressure to achieve. But touting my value as a performer never entered my mind. The event at McCarter Theater had put me in my place, had permanently left its mark. Arrogance was out of the question. I'd been humbled by failure at age twenty-three, and that lesson encouraged me to take a back seat, unless called upon by Joe. The resulting stories often became permanent characters in our plays; *'The Executed Man'* in *'Terminal'*; the *'Boy in the Box'* in *'Mutation Show'*; the *'Transvestite Travel Agent'* in *'Nightwalk';* *'Cain'* in *'The Serpent'*.

The origins of all of these characters were derived from personal improvisations based upon the theme we were exploring at the time. These themes were always introduced by Joseph Chaikin, whose vision knew intuitively what was worth exploring, always gentle, always nurturing and always astutely aware of how to structure our original material. The man was truly a genius. More importantly he was very kind.

As time passed, I learned to perform monologues in our plays directly to audiences, a task I feared at first. By placing my hand in the fire night after night and acquiring a willingness to articulate words to an audience, I gradually healed my phobia about forgetting lines – scary business when you've been traumatized the way I'd been. More importantly I began to speak as a normal actor would, conscious of rhythm with willful purpose of communicating to an audience. The pleasure of spontaneity began to affirm itself. Verbal dexterity was no longer lacking.

Truth meant everything to Joseph Chaikin. His work represented a search for the truth. The man embodied the truth. His thoughts were profound, his demeanor humble, never arrogant, never obnoxiously full of himself in spite of his accomplishments.

Everyone in the company admired him, his mind, his unassuming way, his submissive personality that never fell into the trap of 'hubris'. We were his flock to his shepherd. I wanted his approval, so I always gave him the best I had to offer, simply to please him. This required communicating openly, using words as a tool to affect an audience. For his approval alone, I dug deeply into my innermost soul and revealed secrets that I never would have otherwise. That was one of Joe's great talents, his uncanny ability to summon my most creative self, my best self, the part of me that was so very private and so very much in line with the truth. His profound influence upon me offered confidence enough to speak openly to an audience about subjects that mattered to me.

I loved Joseph Chaikin, and I loved our work together. I loved telling stories during our process of making plays. So much was going on in my mind during those early years, insecurities, outright fear and reticence about self-worth and becoming a so-called 'real actor'. I wanted what so-called 'real actors' had, and I was learning to trust myself within the *'Open Theater'* environment that, above all, was safe and provided serious exploration of personal subjects that, after years of improvising with the company, transformed me into a skilled actor. I was starting over again, slowly discovering who I was; that is, the healthy part of me. Also, my modest income allowed me to live comfortably.

I was part of an important company that was gaining fame for its work and most importantly performing two hundred times each year. My *'Open Theater'* involvement lasted from 1967, until the company broke up in 1973. Travel was frequent to exotic locations like Denmark, Zurich, Paris, London at the Roundhouse Theater, Copenhagen, every city in Italy, Berlin, Frankfort, Munich, Iran at the Shiraz Festival, *(when the Shah was in power)*, Algeria and most cities in both America and Canada. We also did performances in numerous prisons. The *'Open Theater's'* work was brilliant, thanks to the talented company of actors and the genius of Joseph Chaikin, whose vision surpassed expectations. Some of the plays we created are in publication today – *'America Hurrah'*, *'The Serpent'*, *'Terminal'* to name a few. Later Joseph Chaikin directed

94

'The Winter Project', of which I was also a member. My skill developed fully through the work.

Drawing and painting continued. When I wasn't acting, I worked in my loft studio, large paintings and more manageable drawings that I carried in a plastic tube when I traveled through Europe and the Near East during our tours. When traveling, I worked in my hotel room during the day and performed our plays at night. The drawings were large, two feet by three feet and could be rolled up into a plastic tube when we traveled. I needed to draw. Acting wasn't dependable, an art form that disappears into thin air as soon as it is executed. Acting exists in memory only after each night of performance. The performance itself is cathartic and tactile but lasts only during the moment it is happening, after which it disappears. Drawings and paintings are permanent, tangible evidence of any artist's existence. I paint today, fifty years later. I'm challenged by painting and enjoy working alone in my studio.

The safety of the *'Open Theater'* work environment allowed me to take a back seat, when I had nothing to offer to the group. No one pressured me to contribute to the workshop. I contributed to the process only when I was inspired to do so and not before. Days would pass, sometimes weeks of offering nothing to the work, until some event would prompt me to do an improvisation in front of the company. Joe's permission to tell a story only when inspired served me well. An actor is always more creative when he's not forced. The work, although in my case often rooted in a state of anxiety, was often inspired, after long periods of waiting and watching the other actors improvise their life experiences. Out of that void came my personal truth that had time for incubation without pressure to perform before I was ready and mostly without requirement from our director, who, in his wisdom, was patient enough to wait for an eventual payoff. Joe knew intuitively what was inside me and was willing to wait for my soul to reveal itself.

I would not be an actor today if it weren't for Joseph Chaikin's *'Open Theater'*.

Meanwhile, inexorable stubbornness remained firm. As I say, I wished with all my heart to be an actor. After spending a brief stint in the limelight of Lee's workshop, followed by a dozen *'Open Theater'* tours, what seemed to nourish me was unequivocal approval from strangers. I needn't explain. I won't embark upon tangents. My wretched state during the bungled birth of an unlikely acting career is enough to mention without explaining the reasons for it. Therefore, I shall avoid the question of 'why' at all costs. An analysis of my motivation would surely be a shade indulgent anyway. Never mind. I shall move forward, simply sticking to the facts. Let it be said that a magnetic force pulled me toward the invisible 'them'. Audiences attracted me, their applause representing visible public approval that I could hear more clearly than the sound of mallet and chisel chopping wooden logs. Perhaps public approval became more important than art. But, no, I'll always bear the weight of an artist's soul. Performing became more attractive than carving sculpture that was so very lonely compared to the adrenaline burst that one feels in front of an audience. That drug seduced me from chopping wood into living forms. I was a whore at heart and turned away from sculpture for the sake of love generated from audiences.

It was a fickle love really, an unrequited love, an addiction to public approval that has become a blessed albatross upon my back; "blessed" only because the theater has provided, in its odd fashion, the desired privacy that was so much a part of my existence in that Tenth Street, storefront studio. Audiences took my solitude from me, but, no, not really. Something in me insisted upon privacy; my struggle to be my own man – to be different by avoiding the commercial, by avoiding the tawdry.

I almost managed it, but not quite.

Today I don't wonder about my decision. Whether it would have been better to choose another profession is a useless question. Sculpting and painting would have held my interest, I'm sure, but always in the back of my mind I would have wondered, "What if . . ?" I have made sense of my choice, having stuck to it through hell and high water. "Fear is never a reason for doing or not doing something," I say to my children today. Fear is derived from caring too much. If I didn't care about acting, I wouldn't have been afraid of it, but apathy would have left me unconnected to the core of my being. With the limitation of 'not caring', my life would have been otherwise vacuous.

~~~

How different it was later, compared to then, when I traipsed the streets of New York City, looking to find my place within the world of theater. There were ethical values that I absorbed during my daily travels on subways. I remember the warm sun in spring, after long, gray winters and walking miles from block to block, visiting friends, having a beer in the neighborhood bar. New York City provided a community of artists, who sensed the truth about what was happening in the world. I was part of that aware population. There was no family, as I have now. I led a loner's life with an estranged wife and a lovely daughter, Oona, who lived with me half of every week. Later, a girlfriend, a beautiful black woman, was part of the mix. I loved her dearly too. During that period, I attempted to catch up to myself. I'd lost ground during the earlier years, but confidence was slowly being restored. Audiences' recognition of my worth still mattered to me.

~~~

Years later in 1974, before a performance of Buchner's *'Voychek'* performed at Joseph Papp's *'New York Public Theater'* and directed by Leo Shapiro. I sat in the dressing room next to Jake Dengel, a fellow cast member, extremely gifted and sadly deceased. In the production, I played the *'Drum Major'* and the *'Grandmother'* to Joseph Chaikin's *'Voychek'*.

A moment before we went on stage, I whispered, "I just got laid."

Realizing it was true, Jake doubled over with the giggles. Soon afterwards, we made our entrances and had a ball on stage, discovering fresh and delightful moments in our mutual state of relaxed enjoyment. Our laughter in the dressing room had set the stage for openness in our performances. The work became fun.

When an artist accomplishes a sense of 'play' within his creative process, a high level of ease and intelligence is derived on stage. Enjoying the work is a key factor and a far cry from grim determination to force results. Forcing is never fun. Forcing involves arduous, muscular labor that is not particularly creative. Playfulness on stage involves an uncanny awareness of the absurdity of life that can be assuaged by means of humor. Humor offers buoyancy to the creative process, whether it be painting, writing or acting. My storefront days were a metaphor for grim determination to survive as an artist. Not so anymore. Today, performing is what I do, and what I do is not particularly important to the universe as a whole. I enjoy it simply for what it is - playtime for building castles in the sand.

Another lesson learned: Humor among actors breeds freedom and trust.

"Simply do the work with dignity and enjoy the income, as well as the result," is my motto today. But 'play' is not enough to bring depth of emotion in films like Oliver Stone's *'Born on the Fourth of July'*, Tim Robbins' *'Dead Man Walking'* or Neil Burger's *'Interview with the Assassin'*. Performing those films wasn't what one would call 'playful.'

In two of them, I played bereaved fathers whose sons had either been murdered or paralyzed by war in Vietnam. The third film, *'Interview with the Assassin'* featured the alleged 'second gunman' assassin of President John F. Kennedy, played by me. What situations could render characters more emotionally distraught? Making 'play' of the work alone would not have brought a satisfactory result. A deep, personal exploration and technique were also required. I cared deeply about the subjects of all three films. I suspect the depth of the work speaks for itself.

~~~

After eight years with the *'Open Theater'*, my acting career seemed somewhat on its way. With a dozen plays to my credit, Joseph Papp, the well-known producer and founder of New York's Public Theater, grew a fondness for a young, talented actor with a modicum of skill. He hired me often enough to make a living, and I always performed for him to the best of my ability. Joe Papp liked my work ethic. Shyness was always part of the mix, but he forgave me for that, realizing it never stopped me from serving his needs. I'd experienced all sorts of mishaps by then, 'forgetting my lines' type events that occasionally had left me distraught, after which I'd pick myself up and continue the struggle. A core of toughness enabled me to keep myself balanced. My work in the theater had been hampered by an underlying trepidation of failing or plainly being a 'bad' actor, which admittedly I was at times. "So what?" became my usual response and on to the next. I'd learned to overcome inadequacies by returning to the stage to straighten it out in front of audiences, similar to pushing a proverbial boulder up a mountain top.

At times too, performances were actually pleasing both to me and to audiences. I am hesitant to admit this. The important thing was not how good or bad performances were but rather the entire package that came from that naïve, existential choice made as a young man to become a working actor. Today I take full responsibility for everything positive and negative that came with that choice. Embracing all the side-effects that accompanied that decision was part of the journey. The rawness of my talent was irrelevant compared to earning a living. Menial jobs to make a few bucks were a given. I was an actor, and that's what New York actors did. We found a way to make a buck. Whatever that original choice included, lack of income, part time jobs, learning the craft, failing and succeeding, all of it had to be embraced, until glimpses of 'nirvana' arrived during moments of clarity.

Chopping holes in logs was a constant subtext, back to that storefront with a mattress on its floor, conveniently equipped with its tiny wash basin. God knows what kept me from retreating to that dark hole. Vanity, I suppose, along with a sincere wish to learn how to act, the challenge of it. Perhaps it doesn't matter. For better or for worse, I continued moving forward into the fray.

Fragments of a Miguel Pinero Interview with

Raphael Sa'adah

(Full Interview has been lost)

BARRY: "Once Miguel Pinero brought me below Houston Street to Ludlow Street full of dealers hawking drugs, guys, calling, "Hey, bro, you looking? You looking?"

SA'ADAH: "That sounds like Eldridge Street. . ."

BARRY: "Maybe it was. I forget. It was in that . . . It used to be a Jewish area turned Puerto Rican. The street had been transformed into a maze of drug dealers. I walked ten feet in back of Pinero, amazed at the scene that I didn't know existed. All of a sudden he pulled me into a storefront that was totally pitch black inside with deep-pitched male voices calling, "Hey, man, hey, I got some good stuff. Hey, bro, what do ya want? Hey, man!" As I said, it was completely dark inside, and he told me to stand in a corner, that he'd be back in a minute. I swear to God I didn't see one face, just heard those voices and the sound of bodies milling around in that pitch black room."

"Mikey Pinero said to me, "What do you want, man?" I explained I wasn't doing drugs, but he scored a little coke for me anyway, and we returned to my loft in SOHO, where he mixed up the coke and heroin and speedballs; he mainlines, and that was the only time I'd ever seen a guy shoot up. Next thing, he got a rush after he shot up. He's shaking his head, and hyper from the coke, and we went out to the street, where he suddenly took his shirt off, and he's talking to everybody

100

passing us and tripping a mile a minute. Pinero was talking so fast that I could barely understand what he was saying. With me following him, he went into a grocery store, but the owner kicked him out of the place immediately."

"This was the guy's life! This was the way he lived! There was something fascinating about how far on the edge Mike Pinero was every day of his life."

"I'm giving you little pictures that hit my mind, you know?"

"Another time Mike said, "Hey, man, I'm going up to Papp's office. Come with me.""

"So we walked to Joseph Papp's office on the fourth floor of the *'Public Theater'*, and Mikey announced to the secretary, "I want to see Joe Papp," and immediately, without permission, he walked past the secretary, opened the office door and boldly entered Joe's office in the middle of a board meeting. I heard Pinero's voice before he closed the door, "Hey, Joe, how'ya doin', man?" Pinero barged into that office and borrowed a hundred bucks from Joe Papp, which Papp pulled out of his pocket and gave to him, while introducing him to his board of directors, as "Miguel Pinero, the celebrated, Pulitzer Prize nominated author of *'Short Eyes'*". They had a short conversation, while I waited outside. I wouldn't have been able to pull something like that off anyway, walking into Papp's office like that, and, you know, he was in there with all these suits, and he walked out with his hundred bucks, and Papp gained a little bit out of it too, 'rubbing elbows with the streets' sort of thing, which I'm sure impressed the board of directors. Mike had the balls to pull things off like that in a spontaneous, natural way without any repercussions, whereas I'd be thinking too much. Mike didn't think beforehand. He spontaneously took action and directly went after whatever he wanted, usually having to do with getting high or producing his plays."

BARRY: "While directing the *'Puerto Rican Playwrights' Workshop'* in Manhattan's Lower East Side, I was the only person who wasn't Spanish or black, so I was a bit of an outsider. But I did have a wide theater background that was useful to the company. Miguel Algarin invited me to direct, but at times there was confusion between us, because I directed the plays, while he was the 'head honcho' who'd founded the company. Miguel Algarin was running the group, but without a theater background like mine, a kind of 'push-pull' dynamic happened between us about who was actually running things. Mikey Pinero was part of that tension too. Pinero was so much from the heart and so directly connected to the writing. He wasn't interested in running Miguel Algarin's *Nuyorican Poets' Café'*. He wasn't interested in becoming famous either. He lived for the moment and wasn't driven by ambition. Anyway, in the end, we managed to create our plays."

"One time I directed a reading of Pinero's play, *'Irving Horowitz is a Homosexual'* at the *'Public Theater'* for Joseph Papp. To inform Mikey about when to show up for the reading, I ran uptown to the Chelsea Hotel on Twenty-Third Street, where he was living at the time. This was probably 1978 or so. The door to his room was opened, so I entered and found him in bed with some young boy with dope paraphernalia all over the floor. I asked him if he could make it on the date for the reading."

"Mikey, Mikey, is it okay if we do the reading on October seventeenth?"

"Pinero opened one eye and said with a bleary drawl, "Yeeeahh, man, yeeaah, yeeaah," and fell back to sleep. I got my answer and left. When the day arrived, we did the reading under a lot of pressure, because Papp and his wife were there.

Mikey, of course, didn't show up, and Papp's wife called me into the office afterwards. She was angry and stated her case.

"We don't have this kind of time, and Mike asked for this reading, blah, blah, blah, blah . . ."

"They'd watched the reading of Mike's play. What more did she want? On the basis of the reading, Mike could win a grant, see? That was the hidden politics of the situation from Pinero's point of view. Miguel Pinero was awarded his grant, but *'The Public Theater'* didn't produce his play. Papp claimed the writing wasn't about anything more than a homosexual coming out of the closet and needed work."

"Here's another one. He was working on *'Miami Vice'* as a consultant and a part time actor. I believe he did a couple of episodes, playing a legitimate gangster. He was making a hundred fifty grand a season and was required to be in Miami for shooting about six months of the year. I believe he did it for two years, but behind the scenes, his relationship with Michael Mann was really based on drugs, which probably nobody knows. They got high together, and that's probably why he was hired to do the job in the first place. Michael Mann was into drugs as much as Pinero was, but Mann covered it up. Now if you print that . . . What you gotta do is an anonymous deal, because I don't want to . . ."

SA'ADAH: "Gotcha."

BARRY: "One day Mikey says to me he wants to study with me. I taught acting classes at the time. We're at a bar near Miguel Algarin's apartment on East Fourth Street. Miguel has sold that apartment since then. So he says to me, "I'm not getting any pleasure out of acting anymore," and I explained, "Mike, you can't get pleasure out of acting if you're high all the time. Your preoccupation with 'feeling high' will fool you every time you act. You think good acting is about

103

getting this 'fresh feeling', but that's about how you feel, not about intentions, so you'll take an arbitrary cross on stage, or you'll say an improvised line or you'll start shouting all of a sudden or whatever it is that an actor does to 'feel fresh', but meanwhile the intentions within the scene are sacrificed."

"We talked about it at length, and finally I said, "The only way you can really enjoy your work again is to get away from drugs."

"I can't," he said.

And I said, "I know."

Then he explained sadly, "I've tried, and I just cannot do it."

"It was one of the more honest discussions I've ever had with Miguel Pinero, where he wasn't totally stoned out of his mind and able to speak the truth."

"Mike was feeling desperate at the time. What we usually witnessed was the showy part of his personality. Taking drugs is an avoidance of a kind. If you feel bad, you just get high. I seldom saw Mike Pinero depressed. He was constantly sidetracking the issue. And because he was constantly under the influence of drugs, people only saw the more surface part of his personality. In fact, it affected his plays. Not his poetry. Many of his plays are unfinished, not an 'in depth' study. He wrote them very fast, and they were accurate in terms of subject matter, but in terms of depth, the only play that really hit the money was *'Short Eyes'*."

'Short Eyes' was explored at length under the tutelage of Marvin Camillio, starting when Mikey was serving time in Sing-Sing Penitentiary. He was sober in prison, and there was plenty of time to develop the play with Marvin's input and patience. That's the reason *'Short Eyes'* is a fully realized play, whereas *'The Sun Always Shines on the Cool'* and

'Irving Horowitz is a Homosexual' are merely sketches. They're wonderful sketches, rough diamonds, but ultimately they lack depth."

"Marvin Camillio was a brilliant craftsman. When he worked on *'Short Eyes'*, he spent years refining it first when Pinero was in prison and later during the *'Public Theater'* production and later at *'Lincoln Center'*. He developed the work with tenderness and care, until it was finished, and the result was a wonderful production with actors, who had worked on the play for years both in and out of prison. He had wonderful actors in the production, people like Bimbo Rivas, who's now dead. Tito Goya . . . all those guys. Anyway, as I mentioned, most of Pinero's plays were unfinished, since they didn't go through the same process that *'Short Eyes'* had, again thanks to Marvin Camillio's endless patience."

"Miguel Pinero's poetry was fully explored. Any poem is a brief encounter with an idea; it is a short description of thoughts and poignant moments in life. In writing a poem, Miguel Pinero didn't necessarily need a beginning, middle and an ending. He simply described his immediate impressions of the world with wonderful poetry. He was so very sensitive to what was happening around him, so on the edge and so alive to the moment. With poetry, he was able to complete an idea in a relatively short period of time, which suited his limited concentrative powers. But Mike Pinero needed endless time to write his plays and the contribution of a committed, disciplined director, a man like Marvin Camillio, whose collaboration was necessary to bring Pinero's plays to a satisfying whole."

"Unfortunately after Miguel Pinero's *'Short Eyes'* became so famous, a rift arose between the two men. Marvin was jealous of all the publicity Mike was getting, the result of the successful Lincoln Center production that went to Mikey's head. Also Marvin wasn't given full credit for his creative input, and the cast began to dream about becoming film actors in Hollywood. As a matter of fact, some of those guys did go out to Hollywood. Marvin's company, *'The Family'* began to disintegrate, and Pinero's publicity began to undermine things; 'who was getting the most attention' type of stuff. The unity of the company was threatened, and Marvin Camillo pointed the finger at Miguel Pinero as the culprit. Mikey was taking full credit for the production of *'Short Eyes'*, but Marvin Camillio had contributed structure and numerous ideas written into the script. He had reshaped the play into a finely tuned gem and had accomplished what Miguel Pinero wasn't trained to do; that is, to make a finished, in depth production. So they began not speaking to each other, and . . . *(break)*. . . And a rift between Marvin Camillio and Mike Pinero was born. Their friendship gradually dissolved."

"There's a part of me that's proud to have collaborated with both Miguel Pinero and Miguel Algarin, the founder of the *'Nuyorican Poets' Café'*, where I worked for years as a director. If I had taken the normal route, Yale Drama School . . . I went there for a year and dropped out, didn't have the tuition money. If I had finished, I wouldn't have acted with Joseph Chaikin's *'Open Theater'* nor would I have directed the *'Puerto Rican Playwrights' Workshop'*, and I never would've been influenced by those Puerto Rican writers like Miguel Algarin and Miguel Pinero. I'm privileged for having collaborated with them. The Puerto Rican barrio is a world that very few white people are aware of, but I was permitted to collaborate with them within the bowels of their community."

"Meanwhile, somewhere down the line, after *'Short Eyes'* closed with great success at the *'Public Theater'* and at *'Lincoln Center'*, Mike Pinero began doing heavy drugs again and returned to his life on the streets."

106

"When he'd been released from Sing-Sing Penitentiary, he was relatively clean, and he looked wonderful. His skin looked great. He had an Afro. He dressed clean and was a strong, healthy man with the success of his play running to sold out audiences. This was a different Mike Pinero, who had control of his life. But after his play closed, he hung out with male prostitutes in Times Square and returned to his drugs. New York, Puerto Rican lifestyle is well described, by the way, in a book called *'La Vida: the Life of the Puerto Rican in New York'* by Oscar Lewis. Apparently, these young boys don't have fathers and live in poverty, ending up prostituting themselves to homosexuals for a few bucks at a very young age, twelve or thirteen, up in Times Square. They become bisexual at a very tender age, around puberty. And then they get busted. They're in prison where they get raped, and by the time they're twenty years old, they're sexuality is all over the place. That was the case with Miguel Pinero."

SA'ADAH: "Did he ever come straight out and tell you about his hustling, when he was a kid?"

BARRY: "No. No matter how I attempted to offset this, I was liked and respected, but I was always the 'outsider'. I was a white man, and I was also conservative compared to those guys. I didn't pack a gun, and I was a graduate of Brown University. But after seeing my work with the *'Open Theater'*, Miguel Algarin invited me into their world by asking me to direct the *'Puerto Rican Playwrights' Workshop'*. When I worked with Miguel Algarin, a very strong bonding took place. With Pinero, the same thing happened. I loved both of them. I wouldn't be a writer today, if it weren't for their influence."

"Eventually I bonded with all the members of the company. Sometimes a 'chance event' outside of our work would establish unequivocal trust between me and one of the actors.

One time, I saw Lucky Cienfuegos up on Fifty-Seventh Street, stopped by a cop. I don't know what was wrong. Maybe a light on his car was out of order or something. I owed him a hundred bucks, and I had it in my pocket, so I crossed the street, while he was being interrogated by this policeman. He was standing next to his car, and I said, "Lucky, I got the money I owe you," and I gave him a hundred dollar bill. And with that, the cop, for some reason, maybe because I was white or something, finished his interrogation and left. But after the cop left, Lucky gave me a ride downtown, and he admitted he had drugs on him, and he was so thankful that I'd come up on the scene at that moment and had gotten him off the hook, and, believe me, I don't know how I did that. I interrupted the flow of the cop's interrogation or something. It wasn't because I knew what I was doing. I didn't even know Lucky had drugs in his car. I wasn't doing drugs at that time. Drugs weren't on my mind at all."

"The event bonded Lucky Cienfuegos and me, you know? He trusted me after that. First of all, I paid back my debt. These guys were street people with a code of ethics that was primal, very simple. They understood certain codes of honor. If you paid back a debt, they noticed it. If you were unafraid of a policeman and you just walked straight into the fray, like I had done with the cop . . . There were certain things. I don't know what it was . . . Also, I brought my mother to the 'Nuyorican Poets' Café' to perform in my plays, and I think they dug that. She was sixty-one years old at the time, and she played a lead role in a number of my plays."

"At any rate, what happened eventually was Miguel Pinero formed a company called the 'Young Family', which was composed of Puerto Rican male prostitutes from Times Square, boys between the ages of eleven to about sixteen. And my favorite of these kids was a guy named Hector . . .

(break). . . He was a charming young kid, a male prostitute, who did his business with homosexuals. He wanted to escape that life and started to write plays, like Mike Pinero, but with a tape recorder. A lot of those kids couldn't read. Those kids in Mikey's company were all male prostitutes from broken families, sleeping in Joseph Papp's rehearsal space called *'The Annex'*. They put together a play, the name of which escapes me, *'Carnival'* or something?"

SA'ADAH: "Sideshow."

BARRY: "That's it! They put together *'Sideshow'*. Pinero directed and named the company *'The Young Family'*. Naturally it was short lived, because Pinero couldn't really hold it together for a long enough time to make it last, but it was a wonderful idea, because Pinero had these young kids working together toward a mutual goal! But unfortunately, Miguel Pinero's lifestyle influenced the kids. And people like Bimbo Rivas, who was very community minded, began to resent Miguel's influence on youth in the barrio. Also the name *'Young Family'* became an issue to Marvin Camillio. He went through litigation to sue Mike Pinero for the name of the company. He felt *'The Young Family'* title was a rip off from his own company, *'The Family'*."

"Marvin's litigation against Pinero caused conflict within the Puerto Rican community. Miguel Algarin was in on it to too. Suddenly Marvin Camillio became the bad guy in the Lower East Side, whereas Baraka in Newark sided with Marvin Camillio. Baraka was a powerful figure at that time, and the two factions were at odds with each other, constantly bad mouthing each other. One thing I notice about the Third World, when somebody gains a little success, there's so little to go around for blacks and Puerto Ricans that they resent anyone who pulls himself up by the bootstraps!"

SA'ADAH: "Believe me, it's not just in theater. It's in almost any aspect of life."

BARRY: "I hear you. If a black man becomes middle class with a house and a car, the community resents it. It's like . . . I don't know. It's jealousy. And jealousy was certainly a source of conflict between Camillio and Pinero."

"Coupled with this, Mikey molested a kid, and the kid was upset and told or something. I don't know what exactly happened, but Pinero left the Lower East Side for maybe a year and a half or so. A contingency of Puerto Rican men resented him for molesting the kid and vowed to kill him. Anyway, all of these dynamics began to chip away at Miguel Pinero's godly reputation in the barrio, to the point where he was forced to run for his life."

"The next time I saw him was about a year and a half later. I was working as a bouncer at the Broome Street Bar in SOHO on Friday and Saturday nights from ten o'clock to two in the morning. One of the bartenders, Wilfredo Hernandez had worked with the *'Puerto Rican Playwrights' Workshop'* in both *'Apartment 6-D'* and *'Olu Clemente'*, both of which I had directed. By the way, you can verify this with Miguel Algarin. He has a tape of *'Apartment 6-D'*. In the introduction of the tape, he gives me credit for "techniques". But I directed the play! . . . *(laughs)* . . . And you can tell him I said so! Actually that was a low point in our relationship, a lot of politics going on. But the next time I saw Mikey was in the Broome Street Bar. I was working the door, and who walked in but Miguel Pinero with a cane and the most exaggerated limp I've ever seen in my life . . ." *(break)* ". . . Whether he could return to the neighborhood and not be shot was the question in his mind. By returning in such a fragile condition, people were given the impression that Pinero was on his way out anyway, so it didn't make sense to kill him."

110

SA'ADAH: "Wow, he's coming back on the humble."

BARRY: "Exactly. He was like a chameleon. Compare the bravura of the man walking into Joseph Papp's office, saying, "Hey, Joe, you got a hundred bucks? I need a hundred bucks, man!" And he's saying this in front of board members. You compare that to his walking into the Broome Street Bar with a cane and limping and barely able to talk and . . . he's just faking it. This guy had a 'get-over' a mile long. And the long and the short of that episode was that he was given entrée back into the community."

"Bimbo Rivas I knew fairly well. I did a play at La Mama with Bimbo. Bimbo was never a part of the *'Puerto Rican Playwrights' Workshop'* at Papp's joint, but I worked with him with a company called the *'Talking Band'* at *'La Mama'* in a play called *'Hot Lunch Apostles'*. He's a man with great integrity. He opened a school that had been shut down on the corner of Avenue B and Tenth Street."

SA'ADAH: "Charas."

BARRY: "Exactly. I lived on the corner on Tenth Street, right on the park there. At any rate, Bimbo was very community minded and he opened this school that had been abandoned; no heat in the building, and he performed all kinds of theater there . . . *(break)* . . . A lot of resentment was building up towards Pinero, mostly because he was so famous, and yet he never really contributed anything to the Puerto Rican community. His influence on young people became an issue. One man in particular started doing drugs because of Miguel Pinero's influence, Wilfredo Hernandez, the bartender I mentioned before. He died of an overdose in Los Angeles. He'd worked with the *'Puerto Rican Playwrights' Workshop'*, so I knew him like a brother. Physically he was one of the most beautiful human beings I've ever seen in my life and spiritually he reminded me of a young boy ready to

111

take on the world. When I saw him the last time, he'd lost fifty pounds and was a junkie. He'd started shooting drugs after emulating Miguel Pinero. I know that for a fact. Pinero's drug influence happened more than once too. This is the only example I know, but . . . people in the community saw what he was doing and resented it."

"The last time I saw Miguel Pinero, I'd moved to Hollywood. I had to get out of New York City because the rents were going up, and the scene in the Lower East Side had gone its route. The theater scene was at a stalemate, and I was treading my wheels. A great role came my way too, the second lead in *The Year of the Dragon'*, directed by the 'Oscar-winning' Michael Cimino and written by 'Oscar-winning' Oliver Stone. After finishing that film, I moved to Los Angeles and pursued a film and television career. And I'm glad I did. I'd done twenty-three years on the New York City stage by then and had performed in some forty plays Off Broadway and Broadway, and it was time to do more film, which I did."

"I moved into an apartment at Park La Brea . . . *(break)* . . . I was totally clean and felt good about myself, partly because of my work in *'Year of the Dragon'* and I was sort of a different person on a certain level. I was making decent money, acting in films and television . . . and living a different life."

"Pinero had a relationship out here in Los Angeles. *'Short Eyes'* had been produced by Bill Bushnell at the *'Los Angeles Theater Center'*, and they did very well with it. They also produced my play, *'Once in Doubt'* that won a *'Los Angeles Drama Critics Circle Award'*, three *'Dramalogue Awards'* and a *'Maddy Award'* for playwriting. He was also in Los Angeles trying to do some business with Bill Bushnell about another of his plays, *'The Sun Always Shines on the Cool'*, which is probably his second best play. I'm not really sure of that, but . . . probably his second best developed play, because they actually did it earlier at the *'Theater for the New City'* in New York. Mikey had a good director working on that production. I'm not sure what his name is, but he did some creative work on the play, which made Pinero's writing better . . . As I say, I forget the man's name."

"Bill Bushnell loved to ride on the coattails of people like Mike Pinero. And that seemed to be one of the dynamics that happened with white people at the *'Nuyorican Poets Café'*. You'd be around these criminal figures, who were also poets, and as a white man, I was the token white guy, who admired guys like Mike Pinero and Miguel Algarin, but at some point, I realized I was seeking some kind of identity within the Puerto Rican community, which was a bit of a lie. Maybe I wasn't special enough to myself in the white community. I don't know, and I don't care. I loved the work we did together. With the knowledge gained from my vast experience as both an actor and director, I bonded with the Spanish barrio, as well as with prison inmates . . . I worked in prisons for five years; Sing-Sing and Grasslands County Jail doing theater workshops with a company of ex-offenders. The company was called *'Street Theater'*. We owned a large truck with a backside that opened into a stage. The cast consisted of very talented black men who'd served their time and had been released from prison."

"There is some idealism that goes into that kind of work, and some of it is very real; not that I wasn't learning anything. Those men taught me all right. Today I write plays because of their influence. Working with them felt good too, the 'giving part of the experience'. I knew something about theater that many ghetto people didn't, mostly what I had picked up from Joseph Chaikin and the *'Open Theater'*, which taught me both how to create and how to direct original plays. The Third World community is starved for good

113

directors. Marvin Camillio was a great loss when he died of AIDS. The man was a great, great loss. There are so few artists with his vision and patience for a creative work process among people educated only by the streets."

"Another time and this was so bizarre. I attended Mikey's marriage in a SOHO loft. I don't know anything about his wife . . . *(break)* . . ."

SA'ADAH: "It's amazing. Nobody know anything about this woman."

BARRY: "Yeah, I didn't know her. But I was at the wedding, and the wedding consisted of the ceremony and a party afterwards. Everybody knew Pinero's wedding was ridiculous, everybody. Miguel Algarin approached me and said, "I don't know what he's doing, but he's doing it.""

SA'ADAH: "After Pinero died, did you go to the memorial services in New York?"

BARRY: "No, I was out here in Los Angeles, but I saw it on tape. The white guy I tried to describe to you showed me a tape of it."

SA'ADAH: "Was that Jack Brown?"

BARRY: "Yes, that's him. Jack Brown was on the outs with Miguel Algarin. There's a . . . I don't know what that's all about . . . (break) . . . There are all these memories. Everybody's dead in that company of twelve actors. Although there's a woman named Maria Landau, who is probably alive."

SA'ADAH: "Yes, I just talked to Maria last week."

BARRY: "She's still alive? She's a very intelligent woman, very educated. She's got a degree in biology or something, and she knows about the history of *The Puerto Rican*

Playwrights' Workshop', since she was a member of the cast."

"When I worked those workshops, I'd show up at *'The Annex'* where we worked, and the conga drums would be playing, amidst the smell of marijuana that usually inundated Joseph Papp's rehearsal space, called *'The Annex'*. The space was always loud with much dancing and music, and whenever I showed up for our rehearsals, they'd yell, "Hey, bro! Hey here's Ray!""

"I could never say, "Okay, everybody, line up!" That would never work . . . *(break)* . . . The material for our original plays always came from them. We'd begin the workshops with their music and dancing. There's a Viola Spolin exercise called 'storytelling' that allowed them to uncover material for our plays. Each member of the company became quite skilled at relating personal stories told from a private place and related to the theme we were exploring. A skilled director can shape personal stories by introducing rhythm to them or by encouraging the company to add vocal sound to accompany the words of the storyteller, not necessarily loud but rather a soft, vocal accompaniment to the storyteller's words. Actors can also be encouraged to use their bodies to express a story, which adds physicality to their performance. In order to connect their private, personal monologues into a solid play, I wrote scenes that formed a bridge from monologue to monologue, always with the intent of embellishing the actors' original stories. Those workshops stimulated me to write for the first time in my life, so in truth, the company educated me. Guys with eighth grade educations read brilliant poetry that they themselves had written, but I had a philosophy degree from Brown University and had never written anything. I said to myself, "What is wrong with me?" So I began writing myself under their influence."

"That's how significant these people were to me; Miguel Pinero and Miguel Algarin especially. I've written a dozen plays by now and published a book of five plays coming out this year. *'Chicago Plays'* is my publisher. They're connected with *'Act One Bookstore'* in Chicago. I've also published about ten short stories and essays in various literary reviews and a single play called *'Once in Doubt'*. They educated me. I was a white man educated in an Ivy League school, who knew nothin' about nothin' from a writing point of view. Suddenly I became a man of letters, like Miguel Algarin and Miguel Pinero and Lucky Cienfuegos and all these gangsters from the hood, who unlike me, knew the power of the written word and who originally began writing in prison. It was a profound event for me personally to know them all. They changed me to a better man, a writer."

"Miguel Algarin introduced me to Pablo Neruda too. I had never heard of the man. A Nobel Prize laureate, and I hadn't even heard of him! I remember Miguel Algarin visited my loft in SOHO in the early seventies and insisted that we read Pablo Neruda's poems out loud, and they became part of the play, *'Apartment 6-D'*. We selected some poems and . . . that was the first time I saw the value of writing . . . *(break)* . . ."

"Mike Pinero was the essence of an artist in my opinion, although his subject matter mostly dealt with being a drug addict in a Third World community, which is a viable thing to write. He wrote about it from the bowels of his experience. That's what Miguel Pinero knew of life. I remember him one time walking into the *'Nuyorican Poets' Café'* stoned out of his gourd on heroin, approaching the microphone and reciting a poem that had to do with a back lot on East Third Street, where a lot of people had been killed. He recited the poem by memory. It was wonderfully done. The words were so powerful. When he finished the poem, he placed the microphone back on its stand and walked out of the café with the entire audience cheering him, as he took his exit. That's the type of thing he would do. He'd just make a visitation, read a poem and leave abruptly. Probably he'd be back there again at two o'clock in the morning, just wandering around, usually scoring and copping, whatever."

"I think I've run the gamut."

Work for a Buck, Part Time Jobs

1968-1973, Pier #28 on the Hudson River.

Originally Published by 'The Storyteller Anthology', 2020

Martin Luther King's Assassination, Existential Choice,
Free Will, Stubbornness

Part time jobs were frequent during my twenties; less so in my thirties. Those gigs taught me more about the world than the study of acting itself. They taught me what might have been, if I hadn't toughened myself in a field I loved, how trapped I would have been, if I hadn't educated myself at Brown University, how frustrating it would have been without theater to educate me further, without opening my eyes to the ways of the world and to its working populace, providing awareness of political injustice and informing me of the universal human dilemma the struggle of life brings; questions of survival, how to make a buck, how to make ends meet and how little it all means; that is, if a man doesn't provide a means for himself of personal expression to make sense of his existence.

There isn't a time in my life when living out one's dream didn't take priority over practicality. To execute what is wisely practical, to do 'what is best' has always taken a back seat to pursuing my dreams. My goal of 'becoming an actor' was firmly fixed by age twenty during my third year at Brown University. My ambition to rise above the so-called 'bewildered herd' involved risk that was never an obstacle to that pursuit. Somewhere, deep inside, lay the confidence that I was capable of accomplishing anything I wished; no doubt lay within my mind. 'Deservedness' was the ingredient missing; that is, the subconscious sense that success was well-deserved.

Between acting jobs, from 1968 thru 1973, I worked on the docks at Pier Twenty-eight on Laight Street on the Hudson River in New York City. Here, huge black men, dressed in layers of clothing for warmth, unloaded the freight from boxcars brought in on barges. After the 'Civil Rights Act' had been passed, the Longshoreman's Union had been forced to integrate, but all black union members were placed on one pier, Pier #28. This maintained a policy of continued segregation, while obeying the law. On weekends, when an excess of incoming freight necessitated more longshoremen, white hippies, Vietnam veterans and out-of-work actors and artists with temporary union cards were hired to increase the labor force. I was one of those men.

~~~

I am twenty-eight years old, strong as a bull with long brown hair down to my shoulders. There is much about the world and about me I do not understand. The assassinations of John Kennedy, Malcom X and Robert Kennedy have left me with a remnant of outrage. I'm grateful they were once part of the political mix. Basically, I'm sympathetic to civil rights and voting rights for all men equally, but I'm not actively involved in much more than my survival.

It is early evening. I'm going to work. My wife is used to my laboring for the entire night on the piers. Two pair of pants, two shirts, a sweater, a heavy coat and cumbersome work boots is my outfit for the freezing night ahead. I do not use a longshoreman's hook. The blacks use hooks, but gloved hands are enough to grab heavy boxes of fruit from South America and throw them onto rollers all night. Teams of men unload Hudson River barges and stack boxes on a huge platform, where they're loaded on trucks and sold to markets the next morning.

This night is unusual; riots raging throughout the country. Martin Luther King has been murdered. It doesn't occur to me that Pier Twenty-Eight, where black longshoremen work, might be a dangerous place on the night of Martin Luther King's assassination. But his death won't interfere with earning a paycheck. Work is an automatic requirement. Acting is my life, but I need the money, fifty bucks in one night, money for rent and food that allows my wife and me to live. After I earn the money needed to live, I'll pursue an acting career and not the reverse. 'The long and short of it' is that my art is supported by mule-work at the docks. The job is a not-so-subtle 'sellout' for money in exchange for my time. Working at Pier Twenty-eight on the night of Martin Luther King's assassination might someday be translated into art, but tonight I don't think of it as anything more than a job that I need to live.

My wife seems quiet. I don't know why. Quietude doesn't necessarily mean something is wrong. Quiet could mean she has nothing to say.

I kiss her goodbye, but she decides to walk with me down Grand Street. We walk together holding hands. Something seems strangely tense between us. My wish to communicate cannot find suitable words. Words are uncomfortable. Things do not feel right between us. Our union is not going well. Infidelity has been part of our history. We're young and unaware of how much damage that would do. Now we're stuck with each other, in love, yes, but confused and angry too. I can't be bothered tonight. Work comes

120

first. A conversation will have to wait until another time. I love my wife, but work has always come first before love, before relationships of any kind, except for my children. Work has always been too important, as if it were a penance that must be paid before one gains self-worth. Meantime, my wife and I are having serious troubles, more serious than we realize. We have difficulty communicating in a kind, rational manner. Our tendency leans towards silence. Riots are raging throughout the country, but that isn't the source of our silence. It's the first marriage for both of us. We're simply unable to speak, perhaps too stubborn to speak. Finally we part ways. She heads back, and I am on my way to work.

~~~

When I join the 'shape up', which is nothing more than a group of longshoremen, waiting to be picked for a night's work, I'm the only white man. Other whites stayed home for fear of reprisal in the wake of Martin Luther's assassination only hours before. As I say, riots are already a scourge throughout the country. None of the black men speak to me. Nor do I speak to them. I've come for work and not for small talk. There is nothing to say. Martin Luther King has been assassinated. "I am sorry," seems inadequate. My shame for what has happened is private, along with a helpless feeling that little can be done. Aside from the general somber mood of the men, there is the matter-of-fact efficiency from the 'shape-up' boss, who goes about the business of picking men for work. I am picked and assigned to the specific barge of freight cars that will keep me busy through the night, until sunrise.

River barges loaded with six train cars filled with boxes of fruit are moored at bulkheads along the shore of the Hudson River. Melting ice floats by in the darkness, making an eerie sound as frozen blocks collide in the water's current. I go to my assigned barge, walk into one of its freight cars and begin throwing the boxes of fruit onto rollers that send the boxes down to a landing, where they are caught by black men who stack them on the pier.

That is what I'll do all night, lifting boxes of fruit and sending them down rollers to men receiving them on the landing.

121

Back bent, muscles straining, warm from working, my time is money, a trade off of my soul to behave like a pack horse for ten hours. More significant is the rage of these black men and America's racist brutality that has taken their leader. The weight of Martin Luther King's senseless murder by a white assassin's bullet has fully registered throughout the loading platform's heavy atmosphere. I don't feel hostility from them. I don't feel threatened. Instinct tells me they won't harm me in retaliation for their leader's death. The weight of the evening and the strain of the work is the whole of it, not to overlook palpable despair indelibly etched upon those black faces.

On a normal evening, work would take on a lighter mood of joking and laughing through the night with enormous energy exuding from their baritone voices, similar to an African tribe, celebrating a change of seasons with their cascading voices resounding from the pier's rafters. A ritualistic dance of the docks describes its usual ambiance with arms, legs, backs, hooks swinging, chains clanking, loading and unloading, muscles aching, backs bursting, and through all of it, the cacophony of their big, strong, Negro voices, vocalizing various opinions about the world's harsh ways. On an ordinary night, the bustle of huge, laboring black men express the subtle rhythms of a modern jazz concerto, embellished by the clamor of clanging chains, whirring boxes on rollers, grinding go-cart motors and bosses' loud, guttural, masculine voices shouting orders during the unloading process; black men jibing and cajoling each other unmercifully, as they haul freight, their work an afterthought to their camaraderie.

But not so on this night. A pregnant, ominous silence dominates the mood tonight. Only the sounds of freight cars and chains that hold the boxes in place can be heard and motors of pull-carts stacked high with boxes, carrying the freight to waiting trucks. Barges buttress against piers, as they drift to bulkheads from downriver, providing percussion to the night's somber mood. Beneath the overwhelming shadow of Martin Luther King's brutal assassination, some men are quietly crying as they work, masking their emotions as best they can. As they unload the freight, few words are spoken out of respect for Martin Luther King's memory,

"That's what happens to a black man," under their breaths; "Some white cracker, son-of-a-bitch, shot him," loud enough to be heard. They move vigorously to maintain warmth, covered by layers of heavy clothing to protect from the cold, beefing up their already thick bodies to enormous proportions. They are huge, solidly built men. Some are drinking hard liquor from pint bottles as they work. Half drunk, they manage to load boxes onto the right stack.

Martin Luther King represents their manhood. He gave the black race in America a voice that was heard around the world. His intellect and uncanny ability to speak poetically, politically and universally for the black race offered hope for fairness in an ugly, racist society. But Martin Luther King has been eliminated by an ignorant white killer's bullet. Martin Luther King might not have changed the plight of these men. Had he lived, they most likely would still be working for a meager sum at Pier Twenty-eight for the remainder of their lives. But Martin Luther King offered a visionary symbol of hope that life for black men would someday transform to a level of fairness, when racism in America would end.

Meanwhile I'm a young actor simply making a buck, straining to maintain their pace. Earning a living any way possible is a habit I cannot break, a habit so deeply embedded that staying home on this night of Martin Luther King's assassination wasn't possible. My presence among them might offer a modicum of hope. One white man among a throng of bereaved black men sends a message of equality. My back aches, as their backs ache. Our bodies are close enough to bump shoulders, as we work together under the weight of a political crisis that has befallen the entire nation. I do the same work that a black man does. The work is real. The work is hard. The work hurts. Perhaps that makes me a real person. I certainly need the money. Lack of income from my profession has placed me in this setting – the quiet dignity of bereaved men deprived of their inspirational leader. When I glimpse at their faces, their expressions imply that nothing will change. Each man, white and black, shares a common goal, to unload the damned boxcars and have done with it.

This white man is willing to stand side by side with them in solidarity against ugly racism in America. I'm here, unafraid, a witness to their grief, privileged to be in their presence at this profoundly sad moment in history. They are aware of me laboring among them. We are beasts of burden, hauling and lifting to earn a simple buck, the utter exhaustion of the work, the strain of bent, muscular backs. They tolerate me. We are equal for the night. Exhaustion unifies us, working together in silence, respecting each other for our willingness to perform a back-breaking job for survival. Subjecting myself to their grief has made me a better man, laboring side by side with these forlorn figures through the night, a lone white man in a black man's world.

In silence, they permit my presence in their moment of deepest grief, the intimacy of that, the vulnerability of their sadness, the personal nature of their fragility in full view - some crying, others drunk from the contents of stashed pint bottles. Martin Luther King's death suggests that racism will always rear its ugly head. But some whites are different. Some represent hope. I am different, although merely a voyeur, visiting for a period of time to make a little money, until the next theater gig comes along. The guilt of being white is poignant. The sadness of Martin Luther King's death is intensified by the mood of these men for whom he fought and died. Working beside them is an honor. This night has given me palpable insight into a black man's world. My empathy is full, as is my sorrow for the plight of all black men in America, striving to survive in a harsh, racist world.

If I weren't an actor, I wouldn't be privy to their pain. Pursuing an acting career has placed me on this pier at this historic moment. When the job ends, I shall have furthered my dream of being a professional actor. But these same men will be stuck on this pier for as long as their bodies can bear the strain of backbreaking work. Maybe black men will always be the ones to unload freight from barges in America. The 'mule work' of loading and unloading will be their destiny perhaps forever. Those saddened expressions, on the night of Martin Luther King's death, signify a life of deprivation, lack of education, hopelessness and an understanding that Pier Twenty-eight on the Hudson River is the last stop before death. Whenever a black leader dares to speak out on behalf of their entrapment, he will be shot dead. That is how white men insure racism in America. When the leader is dead, the rest will take care of itself.

I too offer the strength of my back, unloading heavy wooden boxes to pay the rent. That is what actors do when they are out of work. That is what I do. I have worked with dignity for years at numerous part time jobs. Those jobs have raised my awareness of what most people do for money. The sadness on this pier adds richness to a life well spent for having performed the same labor as they, particularly on this night of all nights. Someday I hope to earn a living in theater, but this night of Martin Luther King's death will remain locked in my memory forever. My decision to become an actor has embraced all that has accompanied that original choice; lack of money, discouragement, hour upon hour of manual labor to earn a quick buck next to these men on the night of Martin Luther King's assassination. All of it is an unexpected side effect of that original choice to earn a life in the theater, both a gift to me and a privilege to be witness to the world of Negro despair in the face of racist ignorance.

At midnight, during my lunch half-hour, I call my wife, but no answer. I don't have much time, so I don't call again. Wondering where she is, I wish to make contact, tell her I love her, nothing more. It will not save my marriage, if she answers the phone. The night certainly would have been easier had she been at home. When tension lies in the air, it is easier to say nice things over the phone. It's late when I call, and she should have answered. She did not. Those black men probably have marital problems as well, with so little money to raise a family. Calling home is not usual for them. Neither is it for me.

My wife and I parted ways one week later; my first marriage of two - a dear woman she. We were too young for wisdom in a complicated world. Today, thirty years later we are close friends.

~~~

That job on Pier Twenty-eight offered the gift of an unforgettable memory. If I had not been an actor, I would not have been privy to that momentous night. There were other jobs too. I was a social worker on Manhattan's One Hundredth Street, where threat of gang violence and extreme poverty of black families entrapped their children within one, city block.

Part time jobs seemed always to involve black people. I do not know why, but I learned to admire and identify with the culture; something about their beauty attracts me. Once I directed theater workshops in Grasslands County jail in White Plains, New York, working again with black men convicted for one thing or another. Those men are dead now, killed below the age of forty. Prison is a pungent memory, working with black men interested in theatre. Their formidable talent knew intuitively how to pretend.

Within the confines of prison, I directed the men to act out events of their lives by means of improvised story-telling. Some characters they invented were brilliantly funny, a hypocrite preacher or a theater director stoned on heroin. One of them, John Davis, was a six foot six, jet black man who had a hilarious sense of humor. The man was superbly talented but addicted to heroin. His father was a well-known drug dealer, who worked with Nicky Barnes, the notorious Harlem drug entrepreneur. John was raised in that illicit environment. He's probably dead today, as so many of those men are dead below the age of forty.

~~~

Alone in my Los Angeles storefront, I am writing down random thoughts, nothing much of interest. The men working on the building across the street meet my eye. They seem an uninspired bunch, laboring for survival. Their work is physically difficult but impersonal, lifting sheet rock, digging holes, putting on flooring, nailing boards, sawing wood, general duties of a laborer, a dulled existence that I once lived and am no longer forced to do. Long ago I made that decision, nothing mindless for me, nothing that requires sacrificing my thoughts, my understanding. It took years of that kind of work to establish myself as an actor, freedom to create, freedom to be me. As a young man, I wanted to be an actor, and now that I'm older I've fulfilled that dream, having little to do with income, although that was part of it too, to make a decent living, so I wouldn't have to be a dishwasher or a longshoreman or a bouncer in a bar. Success had to do with 'sticking to it', until the profession worked for me. At this time in my life, I look back at the small victories and personal satisfactions, where I came from and where I've arrived, the past struggle, compared to the present equilibrium of my life. It was worth it, wasn't it? Doesn't matter.

It had to be done.

Write Your Own Damned Plays

1980-2018

With the exception of eight years with Joseph Chaikin's *'Open Theater'* and various Joe Papp productions at New York's *'Public Theater'*, directors did not always offer characters that inspired me. My athletic appearance too often limited possibility for roles that matched my inner self. In many casting directors' eyes, I was in too good physical shape to play artists or a poets. The hardness of my facial lineaments and hair grown down to my shoulders during the sixties 'hippie' period didn't help much either. There were some exceptions; *'Rory'*, a vociferous anarchist, in Michael Weller's play *'Fishing'* was a role I savored. Joseph Papp produced the play at New York's *'Public Theater'*. The character of *'Rory'* suited my sensibilities, and I certainly looked the part with my lengthy head of hair. Dennis Reardon's *'The Leaf People'* at Broadway's *'Booth Theater'* was another favored leading role, not to overlook the characters I performed with *'The Open Theater'*.

But too often my roles didn't match my appetite to dig further into my subconscious. Simply said, these roles weren't challenging enough, and the hardness of my appearance limited possibilities. Expanding the characters I was playing became a requirement. Henceforth, I wrote plays with leading roles that titillated my imagination. Pleasure for acting itself was fully realized when I began to write characters for myself to perform in New York's Off-Off Broadway theaters, *'La Mama'* and *'Theatre for the New City'*. Later I found venues in Portland, Oregon, Colorado Springs, Chicago, Dublin, Ireland and the Edinburgh Festival in Scotland; also numerous Los Angeles theaters, *'The Cast'*, *'Los Angeles Theater Center'* and *'The Odyssey'*. I wrote personal monologues performed directly to audiences and toughened myself by playing leading roles that required being on stage for long periods of time. As decades passed, my original plays enabled me to become a truly seasoned and toughened veteran on the boards, and, yes, I even enjoyed myself. Acting became pleasurable. I became a true professional, earning money enough to support both myself and my four children, feeding them, clothing them, educating them fully.

When I was a young man about to choose a career, I was under the impression that I did not have literary talent. Believing that writing requires one to be an 'intellectual', I didn't realize that writing must come from the heart and not only from intellect. Passion is involved for good writing. I've always been passionate. Only after the words are written from an emotional connection to the subject can 'intellect' provide the architecture necessary for shaping the work into a finished form.

Sculpting and painting had been a major part of my life for two decades by then; that is, when I wasn't acting. An artist's awareness I fully embraced from that dark period in my Lower East Side storefront during my mid to late twenties when I'd been painting and burrowing sculpture from one ton, black walnut logs. As I have mentioned, I continue to draw and paint today. The soul of an artist was planted solidly during that period. Subsequently, realizing the limitations that casting people had imposed upon me, I began to write characters for myself in plays that suited my so-called 'real self'' and performed those plays throughout the United States and parts of Europe. Complicated, leading roles that I wrote portrayed more accurately my inner life and have provided a personal voice for some thirty years now. My plays have filled a gap that more commercial theater, films and television too often ignored.

Doing long monologues directly to the audience frightened me during the early years of my career. Too often a cloud of fear held me hostage to that old demon of possibly forgetting lines. But I remedied my fear by giving myself sizeable speeches at the top of each play I wrote. Facing audiences directly became second nature after hundreds of performances. Also, I conditioned myself to being on stage for the entire length of the play by playing leading roles. My writing has provided continuous exposure to audiences and has toughened me as a performer by performing large, complicated roles before full audiences. Essentially I put my hand in the fire and left it there, until I no longer felt the burn.

~~~

My first and arguably my most successful play, 'Once in Doubt', was written in a New York City loft on a Saint Patrick's Day, 1980. I'd never written a play, and a slight hangover tinged my frame of mind. Achieving greatness as a writer was never part of my thinking. I wasn't a writer by definition, but in my state of mind, I desperately needed to write. At first, I faced a blank slate. Ideas pressed against my brain, as my hand held the pen. The main character, 'Harry', an artist, a painter, is involved in a toxic relationship with 'Flo', his live-in lover. During that writing session, ideas flowed upon the white page of my writing book and at times in meter, no less! An invisible muse enraptured me, as words developed into sentences and sentences into monologues. Characters evolved immediately. Their voices needed to be expressed. My compulsion to write became the main character, 'Harry's' obsession to create a final collage onto the fourth wall before death. His painting is composed of objects in his studio, mixed with sprayed blood from his wrist. Blood is imagined and therefore unseen by the audience. I held the pen, but the characters I imagined wrote the script during the day and night.

Failed relationships seemed my destiny at the time. Not long before I'd ended a meaningful relationship with a live-in lover, and this after a seven-year, failed marriage, so ammunition about relationships was both poignant and plentiful. The character of 'Flo' in 'Once in Doubt' was based upon both those women, and her dialogue with 'Harry' was derived from destructive lovers' quarrels that had left indelible memories. The slashing of Harry's wrist to spray his blood onto the fourth wall to create a painting is viscerally connected to the trauma of forgetting my lines at McCarter Theater at the age of twenty-three and a certain healing in that, creating positive from negative, so to speak, making art from life. The entire play was deeply personal, and I was finally playing the role of an artist, 'Harry', whose paintings surrounded him. All of the paintings on set were mine, four large paintings, seven feet high and four feet wide, large enough to dominate the pure white stage, while the action of the play unfolded. Even the set design was personal to me.

At the play's opening, Harry contemplates suicide with an opening monologue:

"My enthusiastic, suicidal plunge; seeking a new birth, a bowel elimination, an intestinal shitting, shedding, "Out," I say, and I die. I sit here transfixed, planted for a moment, silent, and slowly I recoil, as if to attack with my fangs any slight movement. . . (FLO moves her foot. HARRY stops and then continues) . . . movement . . . in my immediate surroundings."

(HARRY points his finger to his head)

"If I do it with a gun, will it hurt? If I do it with a gun and spray the wall with my brain cells, as a genius painter would do, will it hurt? Will there be a buyer for my aching cry for help, a collector of wall murals, who will pay a fantastic price for it. I, the

131

devotee of abstract expressionism, will pull the trigger in my own art gallery, flinging pieces of my brain onto the wall and with line, form and color create an abstract celebration of the moment. (HARRY turns to FLO, who reads her book). I, then a corpse, will wave to you, "Goodbye," blowing soft kisses for your green eyes to catch, as I die. My lips will touch your eyelashes, as I wave again from the other side, where bodiless souls bounce against one another, an entire community of souls, their brains shot out, spewed onto walls by the beings who owned them.

(HARRY holds up a small piece of glass)

"This is the way, not a gun; more process involved, more process. After all is said and done, I'll still be conscious. I'll see what is happening . . . But it takes courage, it does; that is, to take the glass and cut. I'm trembling, I am. It will hurt. I know it will hurt.

(HARRY pantomimes slashing his wrist and sprays imaginary blood upon the fourth wall)

~~~

'Once in Doubt' deals with a chaotic relationship between 'Harry' and 'Flo', and a visit in the second act from 'Mr. Wagner', their working-class neighbor. At the opening of the play, to create his final masterpiece, while contemplating the meaninglessness of life and relationships, 'Harry', a painter by profession, slashes his wrist and sprays the fourth wall with his blood *(blood does not appear in the play)*. With a visible piece of glass, the slashing itself is pantomimed. Throughout the play, 'Harry' creates a collage on the fourth wall composed of imaginary objects in his studio, mixed with imagined sprays of blood from his wrist. The actual painting process on a white stage is a choreographed, pantomime dance, executed continuously by 'Harry', while dialogue between him and 'Flo' is spoken simultaneously. After a furious first act, 'Mr. Wagner' enters, wondering what all the noise is about. Suddenly we have a threesome on our hands, at which point 'Harry' manipulates 'Flo' to seduce 'Mr. Wagner' into making love, while 'Harry' watches from a ledge above. Their love affair, contrived by

'Harry', is another of his original 'works of art', a modern day 'happening' of sorts.

~~~

All day I wrote into the darkness of night. The phone rang incessantly. I didn't answer it. Answering machines were still a luxury then. I didn't have one. Later I was told a casting director had been calling about a commercial. Screw commercials. Writing a play was my obsession. The outside world was unimportant compared to my absolute need to write, to express myself, to keep the pen going. My identity as a writer was a non-issue. I happened to be writing and no more than that. The source of this compulsion is still a mystery to me. Healing my mind had something to do with it, purging myself back to health by means of a rigorous session of writing, 'pushups of the brain', so to speak. My medicine for the day was putting words onto a blank page.

Thirteen hours had passed. I'd written the entire first act of a play that would ultimately change my life *(not aware of this at the time)*. 'Playing like a child' was the ingredient that allowed me to write with absolute purpose long hours into the night. *'Once in Doubt'* had been written, as a little girl might play 'mother' to a doll, or a little boy might pretend to be a cowboy with a toy gun. 'Child's play' was the ingredient, the ability to enjoy the work, rather than worry about it. Writing a play to satisfy my troubled mind was the whole of my motivation. More importantly, the play was worth performing. Its characters and their dialogue were rich, deeply personal, and artfully shaped. When my pen was laid to rest, I was sure in my heart it would be performed. Of that I was absolutely certain. Without question, the actors would be cast; the scenes would be rehearsed and the play would be performed in a New York theater, where I lived and worked at the time.

A playwright without a plan, I left my loft and walked to a local SoHo bar where a beer was nursed. Too often a somnolent condition overtakes any man, half awake and going through the motions to live out his days. But *'Once in Doubt'*, regardless of the tribulations the play offered in producing it, awoke me to life at its

133

fullest. The hours spent writing had nothing to do with a career. Writing had been enjoyable, albeit ardent work for the sake of itself. Writing *'Once in Doubt'* had been my conduit for survival during a period of despair, when my life hung at a precipice. I was living alone at the age of forty, after two failed relationships. Forced to write in order to heal myself, I did just that, wrote most of the play in one, long session from morning well into late night. Having never written a play was not an obstacle. After twenty years on stage, theater was familiar territory to me. Writing for the theater came naturally.

After *'Once in Doubt'* was completed, a theater had to be found to perform the play. La Mama on East Third Street was run by Ellen Stewart at the time; henceforth the name *'La Mama'*. During the sixties, seventies and eighties, Ellen was the mother of Off Off-Broadway Theater in New York City. Originally I met her through my work with the *'Open Theater'* and later with *'The Talking Band'*. Ellen Stewart didn't pay actors, and she didn't pay for the expense of the set, but she provided box office, performing space and lighting, and *'La Mama'* was a well-known theater in the Lower East Side of Manhattan. Numerous New York artists had worked there, until they became well known enough to expose their work to a broader audience. Directors and writers like Sam Shephard, John Vaccaro, Tom O'Horgan and Joseph Chaikin had begun their careers at La Mama.

Obsessed with performing *'Once in Doubt'* as soon as the play was written, the next day I met Ellen Stewart in the La Mama lobby, adjacent to the box office.

"Ellen, I want to do my new play at La Mama. Would you give me a run?"

"Oh, I don't know, baby," she said with a downward inflection in her French accented voice. "I know you as an actor, but I don't know you as a playwright."

"Please, Ellen, let me do it," I begged.

Something in me was willing to humble myself to get my play up on the boards. I begged her in front of a few actors entering and exiting the lobby, something I wasn't used to doing. As embarrassed as I was, doing the play was the single, most important event of my life. I simply would not be refused.

"Please, Ellen, please let me do it at *'La Mama'*! Please!

I reduced myself to my lowest level of humbleness; even tempted to go down to my knees. I'd never begged for anything before, never. Begging wasn't in my genes. Throughout my career, I'd always been invited by directors or producers to work with them. I'd never begged for work or for anything for that matter. Ellen Stewart forced me to beg, and I was a willing partner in that theater lobby, begging in full view of passing actors, each one observing me belittle myself as they walked by. A few lingered for a moment and watched me plead for Ellen to do my play, wondering why I was so desperate, wondering what could be so very important. They'd never seen me behave in such a manner, and how weak I must have seemed, how undignified. I didn't care about appearances. My play was all that mattered.

Finally, after what seemed an hour and realizing I wasn't about to surrender, Ellen offered me a late night slot at La Mama. She gave me permission to do *'Once in Doubt'*, after another production's curtain. Both plays would be performed at different time slots on the same nights and on the same stage. *'Once in Doubt'* would begin at ten o'clock at night with our curtain coming down at eleven-thirty.

'Once in Doubt' would be performed for the first time at *'La Mama'*, as a two character play, between *'Harry'* and *'Flo'*. The neighbor's role, *'Mr. Wagner'*, would be added for the *'Cast Theater'* production in Los Angeles and all productions thereafter. After we opened in New York City, even at that late hour, we still managed to fill the house. Performing the lead role of *'Harry'* was a turning point of my career. Audiences saw me for who I really was, a passionate, somewhat clumsy and fully emboldened artist hopelessly in love. On stage, I could move well and functioned from the deepest place of my soul, a hidden place where the 'secret me' had dared expose himself both as an artist and as a lover. Performances elevated me to heightened awareness night after

night with all of my resources fully ignited, having created the play and also playing the lead role. Performances were grueling, requiring every ounce of physical strength. The character was I, after all, so my commitment was total. Since *'Harry'* was constantly dancing across the stage, as he sprayed imaginary blood onto the fourth wall from his slashed wrist, the performance required physical endurance. Completely exhausted every night when I walked off stage, sweat poured off me in buckets. I was finally playing an artist, *'Harry'* the painter, a man who thought as I did, an artist who created paintings, as I did, and loved a woman from a place that I fully understood, since I had experienced all of it.

Theater found its deepest meaning when I became 'the playwright', as well as 'the lead actor' of my plays. *'Once in Doubt',* enjoyed approximately four hundred performances over a period of fifteen years in various cities; Chicago's *'Remains Theater',* *'Stark Raving Theater'* in Portland, Oregon, New York's *'La Mama',* Yale University, University of South Dakota, Los Angeles' *'Cast Theater',* *'Los Angeles Theater Center',* the *'Odyssey Theater'* in Los Angeles, *'The People's Light and Theater Company'* in Philadelphia, *'The New Theatre'* in Dallas and Michigan University. The play is published by *'Chicago Plays'* and also appears in my anthology, *'Mother's Son and Other Plays'.* It won the *'Los Angeles Drama Critics Circle Award',* four *'Los Angeles Dramalogue Awards',* one for playwriting and a *'Maddy Award'* also for excellence in playwriting.

~~~

It has never been difficult to deny my maleness, but 'macho' does not represent the whole picture of who I am. I wrote a part for myself in *'Back When/Back Then',* that required the character of the macho, violent *'Father'* to wear a dress, which I did unabashedly in New York City, Colorado Springs, Los Angeles, Dublin, Ireland and Edinburgh, Scotland productions. The dress I wore in *'Back/When-Back/Then',* contradicted the *'Father'* character's homophobic brutality and hard masculinity, punctuated by his unmitigated violence. Not to overlook the costume's appeal

136

to my senses, his feminine garment revealed his unexpected, female side that I suspect exists in all men.

According to my play, *'Back When-Back Then'*, after the *'Father's'* wife is discovered in bed with a woman, the *'Father'* beats her to death *(modeled after my father's violence during my youth)*. I was drawn to the idea of playing a violent, homophobic, masculine father adorned in a dress, to play the main antagonist as an uneducated, physical male in lady's garb. The cross-dressing *'Father's'* costume suggests how unadulterated violence often compensates for latent, hidden softness, the feminine side, if you will, of any man. There is also something theatrical about a so-called 'man's man' in a dress, something colorful about it and surely provocative to audiences. The *'Son'* in *'Back When/Back Then'* is more self-critical, more introspective and represents a part of me as well.

Both characters were based upon the environment in which I was raised by a violent father and a gay mother. Upon clearing out the mother's things, after her death, the *'Father'* picks up one of her dresses. Immediately his dead wife's voice speaks to him the moment he adorns her dress. The *'Father'* decides to wear the dress to continue a dialogue with her. Only he can hear his wife's voice. The *'Father'* seems to be talking to himself, while his son is in the same room.

Jack Black played my son brilliantly, while I portrayed the exaggeratedly macho *'Father'* character, wearing a lady's dress. The character represented brutal masculinity, a man who dealt with the world by means of physical force. The combination of a masculine man wearing woman's clothing and painting his face like a tropical bird created a monstrous 'father figure' in drag, vivid and striking with a grotesquely lined face, dark mascara and bright red lipstick that offset the gnarled bones of an aged lantern jaw, protruding like a rhino's horn, as if to say, "Here I am, folks! Take me as I am, whether you like it or not! You have to accept me out there, ladies and gentlemen! I am unavoidable! I am unavoidable! With an oversized male body dressed in woman's garb, I challenge all brutes who think they are men by virtue of what they wear, and, above all, I challenge their unmitigated violence."

Men seem an odd bunch with their need to swagger and brag, beat their chests and push their weight around. Politicians are the worst of the lot with their false virtue that too often reeks of wanton corruption; Donald Trump, the narcissist, is a perfect example of a repugnant, chest-pounding male. Yes, men at times, but not always, repel me and disgust my sensibilities. There is no other way to describe it. Men start wars that slaughter women and children and afterwards, when the smoke clears, the same men nobly stand before us to justify the random killing they've caused.

I prefer to be separate from these types of men, realizing in the same breath that I've committed the same violent acts that I describe. I too have punched men, bloodied their noses; broke a jaw once and not proud of that. At the time of my youth, I dealt with conflict like my father did; with fists, like clubs carried by the Cro-Magnon species, who knew no other way to solve conflict. I learned from my father, who learned from his father and so on down through generations; one man teaching another how to fight and how to win battles. Today violence is repugnant to me, but more than that I have grown tired of waging war. I left the violence of my teenage years, when I didn't know any better. The savagery of one man hitting another plainly paralyzes me, not to mention committing acts of violence upon a woman. It frightens me, this violence business. Men frighten me, and yet, I am a man, who must deal with other men to survive in a brutal world.

These personal truths are the root of my play, *'Back When/Back Then'* and a gallant attempt at reconciling my conflict about being a potentially violent, heterosexual male. This is a complex issue for me, stemming from my relationship with my father. I do feel urges to strike out at smug, self-righteous men who claim to be patriotic when perpetrating mayhem in Iraq. To put it bluntly I have urges to wring their necks. Nothing would be more satisfying than getting my hands on Donald Trump or Tom De Lay or Carl Rove, or Paul Wolfowitz, or Richard Pearle to show them first-hand what violence really is. But if they stood before me I would be tongue-tied, frightened to speak. They would be men, after all, and all men represent in some way my father, whom I once looked up to as a boy, while fearing his unmitigated violence.

Having initiated the destruction of an entire nation, the twerps I mention are more violent than my drunken father, who limited his attacks to the barroom and occasional assaults upon my mother. But these monsters in the government are lethal, responsible for the deaths of hundreds of thousands without a hint of conscience. They're capable of deeds that will affect the lives of my sons and daughters well after I'm gone.

As a boy, males too often showed themselves to be untrustworthy. This fact registered subliminally in my subconscious when any man stood before me, and I was challenged to stand up to them in my own defense. They represented everything that was violent from my earliest memories of my father and at times to the present day. If it is possible to destroy the universe, it will be done by a man or a group of men. But, and I repeat, I am a man too. True, my essence is soft, perhaps more woman than male, not homosexual, but I prefer soft things that are beautiful, like children and beautiful paintings, architecture, sculpture and anything that elevates the dignity of life itself. My toughness today takes the form of tears that well up in my eyes when I think of my father's violence, and the toughness that goes hand in hand with the recognition that those vulnerable feelings are a great gift that allows me to investigate my relationships with my four children and subsequently to write *'Back When/Back Then'*. Behaving like a macho fool would block that exploration.

It would kill life before actual death.

It is clear to me why I have written the characters in *'Back When/Back Then'*. The cruel homophobe, cross-dresser *'Father'* character is derived from my boyhood experience. All the characters are outsiders, all total renegades, ostracized by the normal American majority that so often has played the role of the intolerant oppressor. My mother was a brave woman in the face of her husband's oppression. She was so very different than most women, not only gay but creative and spiritually independent at a time when women were relegated to the kitchen. She married a man from whom she denied sex. Their difference in intellect, their lack of empathy and inability to communicate were the destructive foundations of their marriage. They withstood all of it for twenty-seven years in the face of rejection, suspicion and in her case, staunch oppression of her creativity.

Throughout those years, she bravely maintained her relationship with a woman named Mazi. She insisted upon writing and painting with the kids at school and her husband at work. Her paintings leaned against the living room walls and at nighttime were routinely destroyed during her husband's drunken rages. You couldn't blame the man. Sexually deprived as he was, the smell of oil paint infiltrated the house and was offensive to him. The man had no use for art. Mother's destroyed paintings and her broken nose were the result of her rejection of him that led to his loneliness and subsequent violence.

The root of both the *'Father'* and the *'Son'* characters in *'Back When/Back Then'* is both animal and intellectual, both poet and beast. In order to write the play, I was forced to embrace both my fragility and the unfeeling brute that lies within me. I've identified with both. Each is fully within my reach and affirmed by the characters I've played. Oh, yes, I am indeed familiar with how an unfeeling male behaves, how he speaks, the guttural tones from his throat that define his insensitivity. That male, 'animal part' has from time to time been the so-called 'real me' too.

Today I write plays by habit. Habit alone is enough. 'Work for the sake of work' makes absolute sense to me. Regardless of lack of financial profit, writing characters, who think as I do, is a truly creative way to spend time. Earning a living from television and film has always been a side-effect. I never wanted only money. Films and television support my obsession to write, providing income enough to support my family, while I incessantly write words that have been locked in my soul for decades. Instead of operating within a 'sleep mode', writing plays alerts me to my personal crisis that have both defeated and inspired me. Writing and performing words based upon poignant, life-altering crisis have given me purpose to continue my work, more so than public approval, more so than handshakes from strangers, who might recognize my face from a television series they may have seen a year before.

140

Descartes once claimed, "I think and therefore I am." I embrace that idea. "I write and therefore I am," describes a similar truth. Originally written from a continuous flow of thought, a play records the playwright's consciousness within the boundary of a specific theme. Performing the lead role offers heightened self-awareness. Once on stage, my entire being becomes a conduit for self-expression. The message created from my life becomes a visible, tactile experience absorbed by an audience that expects something special. A state of emergency accompanies each performance. Trepidation is a part of the experience, absolute fear of failure, fear also of exposing secrets. That fear locks me into a heightened state of alertness. I am truly alive when I act in my plays.

Since I perform my plays myself, along with a talented cast, I take full responsibility for every word, every sound, every gesture, as well as the entire theme of the play. Simply said, I become the words. When I'm acting one of the play's characters, my writing is worn on my sleeve, 'in the flesh' so to speak, leaving me susceptible to audiences' judgment and very much 'alive' in the fullest sense of the word. A feeling of completeness is the sole justification for all the hours of diligent work. My fellow actors experience something similar, I'm sure. Otherwise they wouldn't engage themselves so fully. A cathartic paroxysm on stage is the final outcome night after night, after rehearsing for months, sometimes years, before opening to audiences. This ultimate satisfaction, derived from perfecting both the play itself along with the performances of the actors, is reward enough. The work alone is indeed healing, the intensity of it, the catharsis of it, the pure emotional release of expressing what is inside my mind and physicalizing that ineffable part of my being into a theatrical experience. When the performance is finished, a quiet satisfaction is its own reward, pure, unadulterated pride in what I have accomplished both as a writer and as a performer. One could argue that both the performance itself and audiences' approval interrupt the monotony of daily life.

~~~

For decades I have been writing plays and have performed them all: *'Once in Doubt', 'Mother's Son', 'Back When/Back Then', 'Foul Shots', 'Pornographic Panorama', 'Awake in a World that Encourages Sleep', 'Foreclosure or Yelling at Women Walking Their Dogs' 'Back Home'.* All are published and have been performed in Dublin, London, Ireland, Edinburgh, Scotland, *'The Theater Project'* in Baltimore, Colorado Springs, *'Stark Raving Theater'* in Portland, Oregon, *Los Angeles Theater Center',* *'The Cast Theater'* in Los Angeles, *'The Odyssey Theater'* in Los Angeles, *'Theater for the New City'* and *'La Mama'* in New York.

These works not only provide continuous opportunity to perform major roles before a live audience, but they also offer a steady diet of rehearsals, two hours a day, five days a week, often for a year or more before I finally bring a play to an audience. That daily two hour, morning session has become a daily 'tune up' for me, a way of starting each day by practicing the craft of embodying characters I've written. That is how it is, if I'm to take myself seriously. My skill is dependent upon a daily diet of good, healthy, rigorous rehearsal. Acting is what I do, so do it! Don't wait for a job. Make my own job!

As I have stated, my life is the subject matter of my plays. This is true of any playwright. By focusing upon what concerns me most, my writing keeps me in touch with who I am. Writing plays has allowed me to probe subjects that define me as a man – issues of maleness, creativity, homophobia and political injustice in various forms, as well as conflicts that arise within relationships. All are personal fodder for writing plays. My knowledge of how to construct a play is derived from hundreds of workshops I shared with the famed *'Open Theater'* under Joseph Chaikin's astute direction, from whom I learned to harvest a performance piece from an original, fertile idea. Choosing a richly personal subject, writing the words that best express that subject, casting the play, rehearsing for a year and performing it before an audience offers the great privilege of staying in touch with my world and with my inner connection to that world. By the grace of Gods, the writer/actor in me has found a voice that sings the music of my soul. That music is indeed my lifeline.

142

Writing plays requires a solitary stand, away from the public, alone in my studio. Literary work is a marvelous thing to awaken the mind to one's thoughts, to brighten the brain and to alert it to ideas that would lie dormant otherwise. Thoughts are part of every man's existence. We have thoughts moving through us continuously. A writer has an opportunity to state what he thinks, by putting his words into each character's mouth to communicate personal ideas.

"Hamlet", Role of Laertes, Rip Torn,

Geraldine Page

1982

Rip Torn invites me to meet his wife, Geraldine Page, the great actress of stage and screen. On the day of our appointed meeting, I arrive on time. Once inside their apartment, 'ceiling high' stacks of books border a three foot wide passageway to an open space where Geraldine sits and quietly greets me. Conversation is held to a minimum. She observes me briefly, says a few forgettable words, and that's it. I don't talk much. Rip provides conversation. Geraldine listens, while she observes a young man in his thirties built like an athlete, shy as hell, socially inept and in a state of wonder as to why I'm a guest in their home that seems to serve more as a warehouse for books than living quarters for two acclaimed actors. I've been acting professionally for maybe fifteen years by now, both Off Broadway and Broadway, and I'm still a bit unsure of myself.

Apparently I pass muster. With Geraldine Page's sanction, Rip Torn casts me in the role of *'Laertes'* to Rip Torn's *'Hamlet'* and Geraldine Page's *'Gertrude'*, a worthy role that any actor would covet, especially with such an illustrious cast that, aside from Rip and Geraldine, is composed of a cross-section of New York City eccentrics, most of whom are connected with the Actors Studio, along with numerous so-called 'downtown' actors, like Taylor Meade, who has appeared in numerous Andy Warhol films and who considers himself an 'underground' movie star. The man is flamboyantly gay and lovably odd. Then there is Jerry Ragni, who has written *'Hair'*; Amy Wright, an excellent actress, who is Rip Torn's lover, playing the role of *'Ophelia'*. Rip cast himself as *'Hamlet'*, while his wife, Geraldine Page, plays *'Gertrude'*, Hamlet's mother; a notable threesome if there ever was one. Geraldine Page is fully aware of Rip's affair with Ms. Wright, but that never interferes with the work. Jane Haynes, Ron Faber and I represent the *'Open Theater'*. Of the rest of the cast, I know only Taylor, Jane and Ron. The others are somewhat familiar acquaintances, some of whom I've seen through my work at Joseph Papp's *'Public Theater'*. I feel a bit out of place, except for Rip, who apparently likes me. Regardless of his notorious drinking, I respect him inexorably, admire him for his sincerity, for his courage, for his willingness to put himself on the line and take the blows that will accompany the risk of playing such a complicated role as *'Hamlet'*. Rip is always a touch mad, and I love him for his madness.

'Laertes' is a plumb role, full of compassion for his sister *'Ophelia'*, a role that could easily propel me into the New York theater limelight. The character's passion is easily accessible; perhaps too much so. Nothing can dissuade me from learning all the lines immediately and showing up for the first day's rehearsal 'bright-eyed and bushy-tailed', eager to perform fully to an empty rehearsal hall. My overriding obsession for a so-called 'finished result' during the entire, six week, rehearsal period merely to impress this illustrious couple is my unconscious goal. Meanwhile, both Geraldine and Rip take their time examining Shakespeare's words, meticulously probing their meanings, their intentions, carefully investigating each line and patiently waiting to perform fully in front of paid audiences, when it will really count. On the day of dress rehearsal, Geraldine is still on book, still exploring Gertrude's inner life, while I'm performing my ass off.

We opened the following night to a full audience.

'Laertes' appears in both the first and fourth acts of Shakespeare's *'Hamlet'*. Under the impression that both Geraldine Page and Rip Torn are so-called 'Method actors,' every night I habitually cloister myself for a full two hours in the dark corner of a stairwell of the *'Greenwich House Theater'* before making Laertes' second entrance. There I sit for two hours, while the play is being performed, mulling over the inner life of *'Laertes'*, intensely concentrating and fully aware that passing actors are witnessing my nightly purge. The purpose of my pensive brooding is not only to gain Rip's and Geraldine's approval, but to establish

145

before the entire cast that I'm 'really feeling it' and how earnestly 'Method' I really am. Most importantly my nightly brooding pose will hopefully deliver the full emotional terrain of my character and demonstrate that I am as great a 'Method Actor' as Rip Torn and Geraldine Page. The so-called 'work' takes priority over informal interaction with the cast.

'The work' is a common phrase among 'Method' people, as if 'the work' were a religion of sorts, understood only by the 'chosen few' who have studied with the infamous Lee Strasburg at the Actor's Studio. Surely the opposite is true. My affectation is committed, however. I will suffer off stage, as *'Laertes'* suffers, in full view of the entire cast. In my innocence, I'm sincerely in search of my character's emotional life but haven't the vaguest notion what could possibly bring that result. Stubbornly maintaining a sulking pose on a stairwell is the whole of it. And what a show I put on for the cast. What a laugh I must give them all. 'Method actor' my ass! In truth, my best performances are off stage - purging *'Laertes'* motivation in the dark corner of that stairwell night after night, meditating upon *Ophelia's* suicide, guarding myself from evil forces lurking within Shakespeare's so-called 'kingdom'. It never occurs to me that mingling with the other cast members in the dressing room and saving all that stored up, manufactured passion for the live audience would serve me far better. Also, a little humor would help, but I'm unaware of this at the time. Impressing Rip Torn and Geraldine Page takes priority. Such was my foolishness at that time.

Acting on the same stage with Geraldine was never comfortable. Everything I did on stage, every inflection of my voice, every gesture were executed with her approval in mind. Yes, I'm ashamed to admit that 'aiming to please' was still my primary intention at that time of my career, a fatal flaw in any actor's development to be sure. Meanwhile, Geraldine Page's Gertrude imagined an illicit, flirtatious, sexual relationship with *'Laertes'*. Every time I caught her eye on stage, she gave me a knowingly wicked and lecherous grin from ear to ear, as if wild sex in some nearby darkened corner had taken place between us. In my awkward state, I became somewhat frozen by her salacious

146

advances in my direction. Her fame and reputation were intimidating enough without our alleged, illicit affair plastered across her face. The absolute wickedness in her eye was daunting. My overwhelming 'shyness' before her sexually implicit glances resulted in a slightly halting, insecure *'Laertes'* with proverbial 'egg on his face'; that is, whenever I was forced to relate to her throughout the play. Geraldine Page's sexuality literally threw me into a tailspin, when our illicit relationship could otherwise have been rich ground to explore; that is, if I had my wits about me.

Today would be a different scenario with the two of us dueling it out on stage as equals. Alas, what is past is past and nothing to be done about it. The effect of her illicit glances might have brought rich emotional reward, but unfortunately the time was not right for brilliance on stage. I was still restricted by inhibition, a battle that would be won one day. Avoidance of her advances at all costs became my strategy, if only to catch my breath.

Weeks passed and I carried on agreeably, doing my very best. Audiences appreciated the work, I suppose. One never knows. They were forced to sit through four and one half hours of Shakespeare with one intermission. Rip insisted upon doing the 'Old Quarto,' rather than a shorter, more modern version of Shakespeare's script. The man is a purist, insists upon being true to what Shakespeare originally intended centuries before. But we were performing to a modern audience conditioned by a steady diet of one hour television shows, while smoking a joint. For a modern audience, it must have been an arduous wait for the play to end.

Things were going reasonably well; that is, until late in the run, when I made my usual entrance, after *Ophelia's* drowning and knelt before Geraldine Page, feigning a magnificent condition of grief by burying my head into her lap to disguise that I was not really crying. Geraldine knew truth when she saw it. She also sensed an absolute 'lie' on stage. The brilliant actress had been on to me from the beginning, having witnessed my nightly purge in the wings. The week before, while I was sitting alone backstage, waiting for my entrance and purging myself for God knows what purpose, she gently patted my head and sadly commiserated, "Poor Laertes," her sarcasm clear as ice. I was the butt of her joke, but more than that, an air of annoyance accompanied her remark, astutely aware, as she was, of the show I was making. By this point of the run, I'd faked bereavement for my sister's suicide night after night. Geraldine had enough of my phoniness, upon which, with a burst of sudden strength, she furiously grabbed my big head from her lap and ruthlessly lifted it with force enough to make her point. Pent up with anger, Geraldine riveted her eyes directly into mine, as if to say, "How dare you risk the integrity of this production!"

Shakespeare cheered from his grave at that moment, exposed, as I was, for all my false posturing on stage, not to overlook my ambition to impress. I wished so very much to please Geraldine Page, and was so very willing to fake the 'truth,' for that purpose, when simplicity would have sufficed. Unfortunately I didn't know what 'emotional truth' was at the time, especially while performing side by side with such illustrious talent in my midst. I wasn't used to being on stage with famous actors and felt I had to do something extra to match their alleged, brilliant performances. Perhaps that could be my excuse. Indeed, this 'acting business' has been a profound discovery for me.

Today I know exactly what 'emotional truth' means. Believing the words fully is, of course, a necessary ingredient. Anything I do or say is the real 'me' anyway, so might as well leave the question unanswered and get on with it without laboring to be 'truthful'. Saying the words accurately and meaning them fully has brought good results for some time now - hard to remember when a certain ease began on stage, but the process did take place gradually; that is, once I understood that acting and 'being accepted' by the likes of Geraldine Page and Rip Torn aren't so damned important in the overall picture of things.

~~~

My memory of Rip Torn and Geraldine Page is a fond one, however. 'Hamlet' ran for three months and was well received by consistently full audiences, although Rip's portrayal of 'Hamlet' was criticized as "too petulant" by the New York Times reviewer, after which he toned his performance down and received excellent praise for his work. The man is a very skilled actor, handling Shakespeare's verse with grace that few actors can manage. Rip's insanity I loved, as well as his passionate commitment to theater and to the craft of acting itself.

Last I heard of Rip Torn, he had broken into a bank while drunk, thinking it was his apartment building. He doesn't do much acting anymore in his late eighties. I hear his body shakes from old age and excessive drinking. Geraldine Page is dead. Both affected me profoundly not only with their superb talent but also with their integrity and willingness to take risk, both of which I later implemented when I struck an independent chord by writing and performing my own plays. Rip Torn had the same sense of 'taking the bull by the horns' and striking out on his own. We both understand that an actor has to invent his own projects in order to grow as an artist. His gallant attempt at playing the difficult role of *'Hamlet'* to a New York City audience parallels my writing and performing my play, *'Once in Doubt'* to audiences all over the country. We both struck out on our own for one reason, to stretch our talents, to broaden our artistic horizons. Perhaps I absorbed Rip's courage by rubbing elbows with him and Geraldine in his production of *'Hamlet'*.

~~~

Tomorrow I'll shoot a complicated film that will involve a loving father and son relationship and business with food and cigarettes with a hug and kiss at the end. I will be 'me' without knowing for sure what 'me' is. Relaxation has something to do with it. I've been searching for the answer to that question throughout my career. Actually finding the real 'me' has been part of acting, painting or writing. What I am writing at this moment is part of that search. What thought am I thinking? I write it down, as if it is a clue towards finding my essence, my character and my integrity to see this thing called 'acting' through; in fact the essence of 'life' itself.

The two are intertwined. Life feeds art and in my case art feeds my life. I am an actor by profession, but that's not the point. The point is to continue the search, regardless of how much a fool

I make of myself to the great Geraldine Page. I'm still working and still pondering the question of "Who am I?" in the context of my so-called 'work'.

Or is it rather an obsession?

How Was Your Flight?

Written in Barcelona, Spain, Shooting 'Drug Wars' June 13, 2002

The shouts of a child and pounding feet on the floor above threaten the intimacy of the moment. Moldy wetness flirts with my taste buds; more banging of doors, clanging toilet seats, smashing garbage cans, a plane passing above, the neighbor's television drifting up, faint sound of voices and music; rich noises herded together and mooing like cows in the rooms and hallways of a raging four-story tenement pastureland. All interfere with a quieter ambience of a father's devotion towards his daughter. I walk into her bedroom, watch closely the light glancing off my little girl's forehead, a pretty forehead. My daughter opens her eyes, looks at me, so plainly innocent, sitting in silence.

"Love you, daddy."

There are sounds everywhere. It's raining sound. The streets are composed of sound. The entire four story, New York tenement building reverberates with sound. Birdseed falls from the window above down to ours - the sound of love. The world is composed of love. Oh my! Oh my! My little girl! The world is love. My heart beats to the rhythm of the streets outside, sending a series of dots and dashes that apologize for any time lost between us. My child sees her effect upon me. A daughter knows everything by some mysterious intuition. She sends the warmest of smiles to her father. Becoming more the parent than I, her tender hug follows, loving me more than anything in the world, comprehending only what a little girl can.

The room evaporates soon to silence. The refrigerator motor's whining song is all that is left, along with the sound of hands clapping outside, applauding some event. Boulders fall from my throat to my stomach, standing numbed before my little girl,

151

staring up at me. Each word from her child's voice hangs like a small feather, floating above our heads. Each fluttering vowel from my little girl's mouth gracefully registers its meaning. It is God's poetry, spoken by a Greek muse and prophet of love's magic between father and daughter through the ages. Her warmth lifts the weight from my shoulders. I softly smile and absorb what she says, but her words choke me. A cougar has taken a bite of my throat and has left me groveling for something to say. Words I would otherwise utter turn into indecipherable bursts of air in place of sound, indistinguishable stoppages that cannot be translated. My heartbeat vibrates through my ribs. Nothing to grab onto. A gaping jaw suggests my dumbfounded condition, as I mumble something about "loving her too". But my words are inaudible. Unable to free my voice, I manage to look into her eyes, if only to hide my clumsiness.

~~~

Scheduled for an audition today - a film, called *"Grace"*. Haven't worked in two months. Would be nice to land this job. One of the assistant producers, Kritzer his name, a real loud mouth, my manager briefly – obnoxious man. Got rid of him quickly, an assistant producer on this film. Doesn't bode well, even with a good reading. Holly Hunter, a close friend of mine playing the lead role and producing. Did Sam Shephard's *'Buried Child'* together in St. Louis, great cast and a great run. She wants me in this film but might be too complicated with friends. We were lovers too. Yeah, too complicated.

Never mind. Don't talk myself out of a job. Just do a good reading, no, not just good, brilliant. I want brilliance. Why not brilliance? I have the time to prepare. It's been a long time since I've been brilliant. I forget what it's like to be brilliant. I've been mediocre lately. Not a good feeling, middle of the road, not good enough to get the job. Forget it. This one will be different. I can be brilliant. But I must do more than try. Insist! Don't just try! Go for it, dammit, go for it! Haven't worked in two months - would be nice to land this job, a great part that could put me back on the playing field, impress people in high places. More work would follow.

Actors are warriors, constantly asked to prove ourselves. The question is whether I can still claw my way into a paying job and care enough to put myself out on a limb. Any actor has to come up with creative truth, not a comfortable process. Seems ridiculous to a grown man. I seem absent from my auditions lately. Phoning in my auditions has become the norm. Maybe I'm burned out; not sure what's going on.

My daughter's needs come first. The audition can wait. I drive her to school, preparing for her world history test. It's actually fun, but difficult at times, asking questions about the 'Paleolithic Age', otherwise known as the 'Ice Age' and also the 'Neolithic Age' when temperatures warmed and agriculture had its beginnings.

"What were the years of the 'Neolithic Age'? Who were the hominids? What was the Homo erectus known for? The Neanderthal? The Cro-Magnon?"

She explains the natural progression from man's 'hunting and gathering' stage to the development of civilization. A good kid, but her heart isn't in it. The little girl is resistant, doesn't like being force-fed information that doesn't interest her, prefers swimming or ballet or playing with her dolls. I don't know what I prefer doing. Movie acting? Stage acting? Something normal perhaps? Meanwhile, what's better than taking time out for my daughter? Another test in English vocabulary, we go over that too. The words under her belt, she'll do all right. History is more complex, her delivery halting. She knows enough, recites the information for her tests on the drive to her school. It'll earn her a good grade. The ride takes about forty minutes. We use every second. We arrive. Our work comes to a halt. I walk her to the school's entrance, tell her I love her, wish her good luck and drive away.

My audition is next. That's a different story.

~~~

Today I'm in serious trouble, hit with a serious anxiety attack; fear of the future, my life on a precipice, about to fall off,

153

stranded, no job for months, feeling down, brushed off to the side. It's all my own doing, trying too hard, struggling to get back in the mix, hard pressed to do anything right; botched up auditions. I need help from somewhere, from someone. Help must come from within. Tension in my brow, along the side of my head, I'm floundering, trying to regain composure but frazzled. I've been through this before and managed to hang on during the difficult times by working at it, always by working at it, whatever 'it' is. Still standing and making a living. Thank God for that.

Stop for a red light. This feels different – always feels different, isolated and stranded - if only to create something out of nothing; if only to function happily. But who knows what "happily" is? I'm out of the mix, the rejection, the cruelty of no longer being needed, that useless thing, expectations so very high at one time, so very high, perhaps too high. I tried. Oh, how I tried and good things did come, but now, such languor, such lack of a future. Driving again, not too fast. Where am I headed? That question again. The answer is spiritual. I'm sure of it - not completely sure but somewhat sure. "Just be yourself". Must remember that. "Just be yourself." Time spent playing with my young daughter, the goodness of that, always careful not to lose patience. That's what anxiety does. Makes a man lose patience. My mind is exploding.

Something spiritual, something of the soul, some definition of who I am, what I saw, staring at myself in the mirror this morning. The figure stared back with a look of wonderment, staring at me - a large figure too with broad shoulders and a swelled belly from eating. I think it was me. Yes, eating one thing or another. Devouring might be a better description, that act of consuming fully, so as to satisfy an appetite refusing to be quelled. Nothing satisfies anymore, except the child. Oh, yes, the beautiful children, whom we bomb in other countries and resulting loss of limb, such an act without thought, such an act without shame. What more to look upon? Holding on. Holding on. Oh, goodness! Where is the goodness? Where? Goodness within the numbness. I smell something sweet. Or is this another pleasant emanation that characterizes the sadness of passing time? Forces have overtaken me lately, strange forces that leave me unaccepted amongst my

154

peers. I haven't the old "get up and go" I used to have, the unbounded energy of youth. Then I accomplished objectives without complaint. My objectives meant everything then. Now things are vague, less defined.

~~~

Coffee and a cigarette at a sidewalk table where two women talk incessantly on their cell phones. Mine is in my breast pocket, useful for telling the time. One drag on my cigarette and then another, then a sip of coffee to settle my nerves; mustn't be late for my audition. I'm about to be judged. Actors are judged. It's their way of life to be judged, impossible to avoid, perhaps rightfully so, as I often judge. Judging is human, a necessary evil that goes with living. Yes, I'll be judged, but above all, don't panic and behave like a pro, whatever that is.

"Just be yourself" is too often repeated. "Just be yourself," a phrase lacking proper definition; nervous and doubtful. Plenty of time to prepare - if I can't pull it off in two hours, then I'll never pull it off. The words are well-written, easy to learn, first one page at a time and then two pages, and so on, until three of five pages are under my belt. The text is easily absorbed. Finally, I recite the scene under my breath word for word. Things seem to be running smoothly, working on the long monologue that tells the character's story. Maybe I'm not cut out for this work - a little late for that. I've been auditioning for thirty years. So far I've survived; reciting lines while smoking, drinking coffee and listening to the women chatting in the background, all part of the business. That's how it is. I've dealt with anxiety a million times and today another nerve-racking test in a list of thousands. I want this one. The character is too young, a thirty-eight year old, 'on the wagon' alcoholic. I'm a sober forty, perhaps a bit of a stretch to be believable but it would be too simplistic to call myself old. "Old" is a title. I'm not old, an old man, an old, doddering man, who drools from the lips. No, I am not that; still strong, still virile.

Finish my coffee - a splitting headache getting worse. Coffee makes me nauseous. Finish the cigarette, not much pleasure in smoking. Don't know why I do it. Don't know why I act. It's a habit too, I suppose. Don't need a reason. Never mind. Just land this job. Get work. Maybe my career means too much to me. The wife and kids more important than any job. On the other hand, it takes money to raise children. Maybe I don't want to act, the silliness involved, the vanity, the press, the gossip. But enough, I need this job. Don't talk myself out of it.

Nine-fifteen - time to put my hand into the fire. I walk down the stairs, traipse to the car and embark, reciting my lines; the emotional fullness of that first read vague by now. Tears flooded my eyes when I first read the character. Only one requirement now, "to remember," or maybe two, "Get the part!" What about the horror of the character's story, the blow to his boss's head and the subsequent loss of his high-paying White House job. What would it feel like to lose a job in the White House, to hit my boss and send him to the hospital? The question never asked; a fatal mistake.

~~~

Driving again, saying the lines out loud. Practicing my lines, while keeping my eye on the road, apologizing the way I would if I were talking to the President of the United States, which I never have, except for Bill Clinton who was Governor of Arkansas at the time. Spoke to him while I was making a forgettable film in Arkansas with Charlie Sheen - small talk about Yale, our alma mater. Stayed at Yale for only one year, but didn't reveal that detail to Clinton. The President of the United States will be played by a famous actress. At one point she was very attractive, but not so much now, makes it easier; that is, if we work together. But I'm getting ahead of myself. We're not working together. Not yet anyway. Put that out of my mind, haven't gotten the job, setting myself up for disappointment I can do without.

Must find another agent - another audition on Monday. Agent and manager still sending me out; thought they'd given up on me. I'll leave my manager someday too - lost faith in me. A casting director mentioned I gave a bad audition, useless information. My manager repeated the remark, sent me into a

156

tailspin for a couple of weeks - still recovering - my manager an insensitive man who has never performed. Doesn't have the need; I have the need. Maybe I'll always have the need. It's a pride thing, not to be put on the shelf, not to be rendered useless. I refuse to be set aside, refuse to be pushed into the background to make room for the big shots. I am a big shot. We're all big shots. Every last one of us is a big shot.

Driving a bit too fast; slow down and maintain calmness. Damned headache still hurts. This part! I'm right for this one. If only I didn't want to please quite so much. If only I weren't so willing to jump through hoops for a job. If only I didn't feel the need to pretend I'm at ease when I'm not. Acceptance from strangers too important, my dependency overwhelming, totally impressed with what they have to offer me, namely an identity, so I might feel like a person. But, no, I exaggerate. My life is enough – my wife and children and my dog; mustn't forget my dog. My dog is part of this audition too. She contributes something to my presentation. When I walk her at six in the morning and clean up her mess, I'm a person who cares for his pet and takes time out to walk the animal. Walking and feeding the dog are part of me too when I audition, a man kind to animals. The character would be kind to animals too.

Better go over these lines.

Drifting again, lack of definition, lack of self, I don't need definition, don't need to know who I am, don't need boundaries, not to get this role. I am that person I saw this morning, glancing into a mirror at his swollen face, brushing his teeth, a habit, brushing my teeth, applying skin products to disguise what lays inside. I see myself in so many roles, playing them at whim; a memory of what once was me in a different setting, wearing a cowboy hat and standing before a restaurant table of celebrities. Was I thinking straight? I think not. There was never much by way of thought before action, too often reacting from blind impulse with no thought behind it, the result a horrible mixture of foolery and shame in the aftermath. Oh, God, paid a terrible price for little thought before action.

I'd better go over these lines again.

"How was your flight?" the President says to me.

And I say, "It was fine. It was fine."

But should I think of a real flight that I've taken? Or it's a throwaway maybe, like really casual, like I don't care very much about the flight, like the flight was uneventful. We have more important things to talk about. Yes, that's how it would be. The scene isn't about my plane flight, so I'll underplay to allow the scene to go somewhere. "Go somewhere!" Yes, that's it. But where to go? Apparently the President wants me as her running mate. How flattering that is. How flattering for her to want me. But it's not me she wants. I'm just an actor. She doesn't know me. She wants a character that's been written into the script and not me - mustn't confuse that if I land the job. No! There I go again putting the horse before the cart. The audition! The audition! Stick to the audition. My God, how easily I slide into the result. Must go over my lines - remember the lines and half the battle will be won. It's all in the words. Just say them. But, no! There's a trap in that; must bring words to life. Life must be brought into my reading, vitality and life – not deadpan, lifelessness without heart. Yes, that's what I've always had, lots and lots of heart!

This drive is too long. I'll be there soon, never mind. There should have been a plan, but there was a plan; remembering that plan I once had, trying so very much to be different, when all along I was one of them out there, milling about in the same groundless fashion. So alone, all of us actors, foraging ahead so bravely with nothing to depend upon, aside from breath. I breathe. There will be more breath to come. My children come to mind, my children I dutifully raise in absence of something better to do. But nothing better to do, I'm sure of it, so little that's worth caring for. Bombs dropping in Iraq; I know everything. I know nothing - nothing to know, nothing to concern myself - empty space of mind, past blunders. Future blunders I can do without.

~~~

Approaching the lot, Twentieth Century Fox - auditioned here before for some television thing but wasn't cast. No use thinking about that. That was then. Now is now. Stomach churning, my God, I'm nervous. Actors in the distance, all dressed in suits. Oh, God, we're a well-dressed bunch. I park on the fourth floor where guests park. Ask the guard where the building is. He points. I follow his finger, dressed in my fancy suit I was married in, with my little scene tucked away in my hand. Walk to building number forty-one, high, triangular- shaped with a small alcove in back, framed with steel girders and slapped together with large, dark, fitted panels. Once inside, the lobby gives the impression of expediency, built to serve an anonymous public without the use of first names. I wait in the wrong room, until I realize it's the wrong room and go to the right room. Walk past some actors, the oldest one of the lot. They wait nervously for their turns to read, eyeing each other without being too obvious - enter the office to sign in and wait, hoping not to fail, determined to be brave. I'll play the hell out of this alcoholic Presidential advisor. His dysfunctionality will be mine. The character is mine. Yes, he must be mine.

"Keep everything simple," I tell myself, seeking a chair, dressed to the nines, clean shaven, pretending confidence. The chair I choose is adjacent to the audition room, a form-fitting canvass number that hugs my behind like the arms of a warm grandmother, allows me to observe each actor's entrance and exit as they begin and end their auditions. Keep my head buried in my script, pretending to study but examining every one of them, curious to discover a secret that might guarantee the job. One actor swaggers into the room, completely on top of things, greeting those inside, as if he knows what he's doing. "All the world's a stage" for some. Others make jokes, filling the room with fake laughter. I'm quiet and nervous compared to them, not as confident. Don't know why, sitting, quietly go over the lines. Is it time yet? Do I know the scene well enough? Too easily distracted, what are the others doing? Repeat the words five more times, the words, the damned words, my obsession. What about the character's complex emotional life? No, save tears for the reading, mustn't waste feelings, as if emotions are stored in a quart bottle and can only be doled out in small doses.

Across the room, the nimble tapping of a secretary's fingers on a keyboard sends facts into a data bank - perfect for the job, tall, nervous, her hair neatly pulled into a bun, face barely visible through her dark, plastic glasses that obliterate the shape of her eyes, the contour of her face. The arched shape of her body suggests long hours sitting at her desk, insisting that everything is in order, everything in its place. Her head turns, jitters about. Has she missed something, any details left unfinished, anything left undone?

I'm part of her process. Without actors like myself, her job would come to a halt, but that doesn't warm her to me. Communication between us might slow up her busy pace, small talk held at a minimum. Little interest in talking, my thoughts are private, not comfortable in a casting hall, clinical place with its white and yellows, hard white walls and everyone ready to audition. I sit motionless and obedient as the secretary lady works, indifferent to her sterile surroundings, highlighted by a hard-metal desk whose impenetrable surface is so cold, so impersonal that I wonder how it feels to be bombarded every day by its steel flatness. She seems adjusted to her fate, "twitting" about in her world of paper clips and pens that she settled for long ago. I wonder, as I sit in this tense environment, if she has any idea how anonymous she has become, as if she were hatched from the desk itself, fully matured, and already running her corner of the universe from the moment of her birth. Her efficiency is mesmerizing, every minutiae of her routine under control, every detail perfected by the quick, sure movements of her hands and arms, the subtle twists of her torso, as she moves above her desk - the confidence of her glance to each, exact location, when she needs some object within her reach. Staples, pens, rubber stamps, paper clips fall to and from her fingers as if pouring out of her arm. She takes her tools for granted with the concentration of a good mechanic, uses them with the expertise of a master craftsman, expecting maximum production from her efforts.

Meanwhile someone is drilling outside; a workman doing a real job, lucky guy to have a real job. I barely hear it, barely hear anything. How long I've been in this room. Seems half my life has passed in an instant. No, it's been minutes and not years. No matter,

160

illusion is part of everything, leaving its nasty bite. Somehow I'm not cut out for this work, but the dye has been cast. I'm doomed to see this through. How often must I make a fool of myself? How often must I forget my original vow to find freedom through my work? That's what I wanted once, what I set out to do. The rhythmic clicking of the secretary's computer lures me to coffins of hopelessness. Wish I were stronger. But I am who I am, too willing to cooperate, dressed in the suit I was married in, lines memorized; the role, the role - a clone like all the rest with no real talent. Good memory though, partly tired of it all, partly excited too.

Eyeballing the pages of the script to familiarize myself with the light; won't use glasses for this one. But why risk losing my lines? What the hell, I'm brave today, centered but nervous and care too much about landing the role. Quietly I memorize my lines again. Lines have become everything to me. Reciting my lines, as I greet the secretary, reciting my lines, as I sit in the hallway, waiting for actors to finish their readings; always reciting my lines, always focused on the words, while we all wait nervously for our auditions, eyeing each other without being too obvious, pretending not to care – a dangerous state of mind when in fact I do care. Care so much that I could die if I fail. I've told myself, "There is no failure," but that's a lie. 'Failure' has become familiar territory and a bit too often; even now struggling with failure. The other actors, from the looks on their faces, are as anxious about failure as I.

Meanwhile, contrived smiles and oodles of charm ooze out of me to an empty, white wall - practicing mechanics, a smile here, a pause there, followed by a sad expression. Whew! What a day it's been. The blank wall would surely hire me. Thoughts drifting, various challenges of late, having to do with the wife and constant nagging about having another baby, like three aren't enough. Why am I bothering myself with this right before my audition? Another way of undermining myself, destructive fool that I am. Haven't come through in months, haven't shown my toughness, my ability to act well under pressure with producers and directors watching. Best thing is to show up. But I've done that. I'm here, but somewhat absent. Don't feel things. Don't worry about it. Feelings are constantly changing from moment to moment anyway. My head progressively getting worse and anxiety building - there won't be any excuses for this one.

Wonder who will get this part? It won't be me for sure. No, stop that! Focus more! For God's sake, focus! Another actor enters the room - laughing. This one is a joker, one joke after another, as if he's a cool guy, joking under pressure. Joking shows how calm and collected he is, joking away with others laughing, and meanwhile my wife plans to impregnate herself - all this laughing in the room, a pain in the ass. The actor walks out with a big smile on his face, like he's pulled the wool over their eyes. Probably has. The mood inside the auditioning room is happy, people making a forced effort, much laughing when nothing is funny.

Wandering thoughts, calmness, even-temperedness, the utter relaxation I project. The audition will be any minute now. Not really thinking clearly. What am I doing? Merely sitting and waiting? Should be preparing, I recite my lines again. I know them. Except for once when I check to see if it's "gonna give you" or "giving you". It's the latter version. I've been rehearsing it with "gonna give" instead of articulating the word "giving." That can screw a guy up, if I let it. I won't let it. I'll close my eyes and fall asleep, which I never quite manage to do - difficult to sleep in a chair. My closed eyes avoid conversation with William Sanderson from the Bob Newhart show. I've known him for years, nice guy but don't want to talk. William Sanderson enters the audition room. Time passes. William Sanderson walks out of the audition room. Two other guys do the same, walk in, time passes, and walk out. Don't look too happy. They probably didn't know their lines. I know my lines. Maybe I shouldn't know my lines. Too often I've known my lines and blanked out - mustn't blank out with this one. No, hold it together, center myself and be a man about this. No, it's got nothing to do with manhood.

The guy with dark skin and a square jaw next. He goes in like he doesn't care much. Who is he kidding? Leaves the room quickly - doubt he got the part. A few minutes later another guy with a blue dress-shirt; talks with too much breath, as if he's experimenting with his voice. A bald-headed man in front of me, uttering short 'oos' and 'ahhs' before it's his turn. I've tried that -

162

doesn't work. Those sounds show he has a voice, as if he'd suddenly lose it. We're all crazy actors, all figuring out how to deal with fear; my wife on my mind again. The bald-headed guy is reading for my part. He's making those sounds, short 'oos' and 'ahhs' to prove he exists. Who cares whether one exists? The sound of my voice won't prove I exist. I'll try it anyway. I make a little "oo" sound barely audible for the bald guy to hear. My nerves don't go away. I used to talk too much at auditions. Not anymore. Talking isn't good. It never was. Too much energy wasted. But absolute silence isn't right either. Talking is a way to listen to how I talk, so I can imitate how I talk during my audition.

~~~

The casting director comes out and blows me a kiss, suggesting how fond she is of me. I smile in return. Her positive energy won't help me through this, but that's not the point. The point is that she's on my side. If there's any help to bring the part my way, she'll come to bat for me - nice to have the casting director on my side. Nice lady. Much older than the last time I saw her. Much older with capped teeth, too white for her red skin, aged from hard living. She was a good-looking woman once but not anymore with her flattened butt that's lost its shape. I'm getting older too but there's some remnant of an ass left. Hers has disappeared forever.

She escorts me into the room. Kritzer isn't here, thank goodness. Holly Hunter smiles when I enter the office, gives me a big hug. We like each other. She wants me to do well. I'm introduced to the executive producer, a nice enough gentleman about to become a millionaire; that is, if he isn't one already. That's what producing offers, piles of money. They pretend to their mothers they're artists, when they don't have a creative bone in their bodies. Money is king. These men could be bankers or stockbrokers, and it wouldn't matter, as long as there's money to be made. This producer is one of them, I suspect, not that it bothers me really. I've been conditioned by decades of involvement with producers. I'm not cynical – just realistic. There is little depth in this frivolous world of capped teeth, facelifts and dyed hair, a world of silly writing that imitates what sells to the general public. The dollar is what counts here and the question of whether I can generate an increase of volume sold of products advertised. Will more folks buy their sponsor's gadgets because I'm on their show? That's part of their thinking, aside from my acting, which at times is nothing to brag about. Other times I'm good at what I do, a crap shoot as far as I'm concerned. Am I a good actor or a bad actor? Do I sell the words in the script?

Holly Hunter is on my side. I suddenly feel confident and sit, ready for action, in a cloth folding chair that has been provided in front of a video camera. The aging casting director is reading the part of the female President of the United States. I'm somewhat confident, not completely. My voice is inordinately deep today; not used to its deepness. Wish it were less so, but I'll go along with its resonance, as if I'm a Marlboro Man or something macho. Remember the words. That's the important thing.

We're about to begin, all geared up. Wish I weren't quite so limited by this camera in front of me or quite so bounded by this chair - the smallness of the room another pain in the ass. Told a psychiatrist that once; he wasn't impressed, sort of noncommittal. So neurotic in those early days, now I'm better. In some ways I'm better, still capable of irrational behavior – like walking out of this room right now – just picking my big butt up and leaving; if only to have the freedom to do that. I could also leave my wife and start a new life somewhere; that is, if she keeps pushing this thing about impregnating herself, the absurdity of it all too much really, driving me to think independently of marriage.

Maybe I should leave. Yes, I could leave this room happily, if I so desire, disappear into the sunset and never return. That would be a big mistake, walking out like that, leaving Holly Hunter in the lurch. What would Holly think of me? I pretend I don't care, but I really do.

No, I'll begin the scene.

"How are you, general?" the casting director reads.

164

"Quite fine, Madam President," I answer in my deep voice. The producer is looking at my credits on the back of my eight-by-ten photograph, not paying attention to me.

"Was your flight okay?" she asks.

"It was fine. It was fine," I answer, following the words on the page to the best of my ability. So far so good, the producer still reading my resume; hasn't looked at my acting yet. There's not much to look at really, with my voice locked into this muscular, deep-toned stance that refuses to vary from line to line, a monotone from one sentence to the next. "Being here now" has always been difficult for me, wishing to prove I'm worth a hill of beans, which I am not, unless I land this job, which I won't, or maybe I will. My mouth is moving, reading with glasses, another impediment but difficult to see without glasses that block eye-contact with the casting director. I'm still searching for my voice.

"All the polls indicated that the nation thought your ticket should have been reversed - you at the top and Symington underneath," the casting director reads.

"Yes, those polls went over very well with the boss."

Damned if I know who 'Symington' is - a mortal sin in this business.

My God, where is my voice, my tired, overused voice from drilling lines all night and half the morning right up to the time of this audition? Hardly any voice left after so much drilling. I've defeated myself, floundering before these professionals - must wonder if I've ever acted before, when I truly have, kind sirs, all my adult life, Broadway too, making a good living too. God knows how - sent my oldest daughter through college with television earnings. God knows how - sent my son through a fancy private grade school, middle school and a fancy college too. Can't believe I managed that - sent my seven-year-old through a fancy-assed kindergarten, another small miracle, but getting back to my voice, can't find my damned voice. Where is my voice? Where on Earth is my voice? Hello out there. Are you out there? Can you hear me? I'm inaudible, my voice outside my body. Words are not my own, no point of view, inadequate. I am inadequate, trying so very much to be heard.

"Loosen up, goddamnit." Or be doomed to stay in this mental prison. Impossible to unlock myself, my voice won't enter its upper register where most of my expressiveness lies. High notes are better than low ones. Extreme tension controlling me - my chin locked down onto my throat. Won't budge; feigned relaxation, pretending confidence. I might explode; can't help myself; makes no sense to blame. Punishment would be irrelevant. I'm not doing this on purpose. One failed try supports the next, until failure becomes a fixed pattern throughout the reading. Everything I'm saying, references to "polls" and a man called "Symington", I have no idea what or who they are, and been acting for decades; should know better; ought to be ashamed of myself. No, it's beyond that, paying the price for laziness. No, that's not true. I worked hard to prepare. But I have no thoughts - merely scrambled waves of feelings with no way to escape myself, no way to allow real thoughts - too late to think clearly, a robotic word machine, imitating a human being, a bad imitation too. Nothing good can come of this.

The producer is watching me now. Room for lightness here, I smile, as if I'm aware of the humor, not truly moved; jack hammer on the street pounding away, that guy again with a real job. My heart would imitate the sound, if it hadn't stopped minutes before. I hold my head up straight so as to show off my face. Why am I thinking about my face? My face is the least of it. The reading is what counts and the connection I have with myself. But I'm thinking about my face, not breathing; not open to sensations; not here in the room, barely visible to myself let alone to others. Is this what it's come to? Must make logical sense of this, clarity of sorts, some explanation as to why I'm locked, but no time for that. Jesus God Almighty, don't have presence of mind to think clearly, might as well fake it. Faking it is all I've managed up to this point. It would be jarring to suddenly do something 'real' but must hurry, mustn't hold up the works. Actors wait in the other room - producer watching me on the monitor. Important moment has arrived - time to be sincere, the next line a real test of truth – an apology of all

166

things. What could be more fitting? I try my best to soften, to humble myself before saying the words.

"One night I did something. I didn't see it coming. I meant to push the guy. I didn't do that. I hit him . . . He felt light as a feather . . . flew backwards, landed white as a ghost, not conscious. I'm so sorry, really, I'm sorry. I didn't realize I hit him."

My voice is drowning in monotone, little more than a feigned naturalism with contrived self- pity, shuffling feet and self-conscious concern, mostly mechanical with the emotional underpinnings of a brutal attack against my colleague missing. I've plainly lost the job. But I plod onward for the sake of finishing. Somehow it's important to finish. Don't know why. Maybe they're not quite sure how badly I'm doing. Perhaps I'm acting better than I think and don't know it. Or the producer doesn't know the difference. No, fat chance of that.

"I went to the hospital," I recite. "They told me I wouldn't go to jail but not to come to work the next day. They fired me."

Tied up in knots, my voice locked into my chest, if only to relax. If only my very future didn't depend upon this part; if only to speak softer to allow simple communication; if only to breathe for once; if only to drop my shoulders for a brief second to think real thoughts. But no, all these contrived inflections, every reaction programmed at the sacrifice of discovery. I'm surely lost.

Where have I left you, mister me? Are you out there? Or have you disappeared altogether, never to be found again. No, I'll find you. I'll search behind the barricade built between us and find you hiding. I'll lead you then, 'I' leading 'me' by the hand and bringing myself into rays of sunshine. There will be an awakening then and my lungs will start breathing deep breaths, and the words that come from my mouth will finally make sense.

That will happen on some courageous day.

The producer gives no sign of support, rather shakes my hand. Thanks me for coming. We're both embarrassed, trying to be nice. I hopefully look in Holly Hunter's direction for a few words of encouragement. She seems embarrassed. Aren't I good, after hugging me the way she did in front of everyone, as if we were close friends, as if she trusted my talent would prove itself? Aren't I good? I'm beginning to doubt. Did I do it right? Was I too willing to comment, rather than actually becoming the character? Holly seems mortified. I'm mortified. The tension in the room is palpable. My mouth, my loud mouth; expressions on their faces of disappointment, as if they expected something more, at very least an actor who knew what he was doing, an actor worth being hugged by Holly Hunter, the lead actress and one of the producers of the film.

~~~

Once out of the room, gasping for freedom, off to my car with a forty-five dollar ticket on its windshield. I'm only a little pissed. Parking tickets don't matter. Immediately out of the fancy suit I was married in, allowing cool air to tickle my sweating armpits. My true self has been masked for hours. My essence has been hiding. Tough business, this 'acting thing'; letting an opportunity slip away like this, freaking absurd - little 'Goodie-two-shoes', thinking I'm fully prepared when I'm not. Don't feel proud of myself - outright ashamed and tired of being judged. "Is he a good actor? Is he a bad actor?" I'm both good and bad and not ashamed of either. To succeed, one must fail before strangers. It bothers me too, overacting or generally phony, unconnected to the words. When I'm completely off, it embarrasses everyone, including myself, proving my worth and all, a disaster waiting to happen. There must be a way to get back on track - haven't figured it out. Something must be done, don't want to be shelved as useless, an over the hill "has-been," a forgotten warrior of the acting profession.

Wonder how my little girl did in her test.

~~~

Upon entering my home, I allow myself to unravel in the presence of those I trust. In truth, it is 'I' whom I don't trust and not the abstract 'them'. There is no enemy and no battle other than a

168

deep, internal struggle within. My wife sits in her underwear on our bed, observing me. Inertia grips me in its fist. My body is still. The room is silent. How very attractive she is. No attempt to remove my clothing. No need to move, sitting sprawled on a soft chair, shirt buttoned, shoes laced. It would be logical to undress. In my youth, I responded well to ladies sitting on beds in silk underwear. But silence is enough for now.

My wife observes me. We've been through a great deal together, all of it good, in the process of raising two lovely boys, ages twelve and eighteen and our seven-year-old girl, not to overlook a grown daughter, whom I love so very much. We've managed a good life. Remarkably income has been plentiful to survive. We own our home; the mortgage paid off, the kids' schooling paid from money earned by acting. I sit motionless, impenetrable stillness between us. She knows not to ask about my audition. Her naked thighs are inviting, forever my dear wife.

The wall's lovely yellow ochre is sponged to its surface by hand – my wife's touch. Yellow ochre was her choice. Plain, cold white would've been mine. It's a custom job done by a Spanish house painter with an artist's sensibility. He did an excellent job painting the interior of our home, although he was attracted to my wife and made that point clear. I wasn't jealous. We have a history of being attractive to outsiders. They aren't a threat to us. We'll outlast them all. Meanwhile the walls are sponged an elegant layer of yellow ochre. Without her, I would be staring at an empty, white wall, thinking about my botched audition. There would be no sons to look after, no little girl to keep my heart warm. The wall would be cold, not warm yellow ochre. The room would be bland and empty, in place of my wife's greenish eyes and smooth white thighs.

She stares at me and I at her. The message from our eyes is a loving one. It's impossible to move. I avert my eyes for a moment and stare at nothing in particular; another day, a botched audition and barely able to lift my hand from my chair. My wife speaks. Words from her mouth are kind, aware of my fragile state. After so many years, her ability to read my mind is uncanny. I love her gentle spirit.

"Do you want filet mignon for dinner?" she asks.

She speaks with a touch of concern. My wife cares for me. That is important – to be cared for. Perhaps I deserve to be cared for. But then everyone deserves to be cared for.

"Filet mignon is good," I say.

She's already having it delivered. I'm hungry for filet mignon, mouth slightly salivating. I remove my shoes and socks, then wiggle my toes - freedom in that gesture, having to do with the bondage of heavy shoes, heavy leather that weighs down my feet when I walk. Shoes enclose the heat, and my feet sweat uncomfortably, but when I remove my shoes and socks my feet breathe freely. As a sign of surrender, my shirt is removed, my naked shoulders bringing immediate relief. Breath comes easier. The movement of removing shirt and shoes breaks the room's stillness. Things are happening, my body responding to the thought of eating filet mignon, also to my wife's naked thighs that run smoothly into her hips - hips and thighs and filet mignon all possible in one evening.

I'm a happy man.

The bed sits high above the floor. My wife's legs dangle somewhat, slightly parted. She's a beautiful woman. I can't help myself – my feelings for her, my dependency upon her. Without her, life would be solitary and barren, a world of botched auditions sprinkled with a few successes. Somehow it all works for me. I stare again directly into her eyes. Filet mignon is in the air, other things as well - my inertia for one, my reluctance to move. At very least my tie and shirt are off and later my pants, a beginning at the end of a tough day. I appreciate what is available, the prospect of steak for dinner, sitting, both of us with the children at the table, eating filet mignon, the harmony of family at dinner.

I'm at ease here. The room's splash of color is bright and sunny, bathing my wife in a background of ochre - a feast for my eyes. Her body glows against the pale of our bedroom. It is private here, silent and private. No one is nearby. We have each other. That is enough. We are enough. It is not necessary to move. My tie is off as well as my pants. That is sufficient. I'm more at ease in silence, nothing but stillness; her beauty a gift to me, more than sexuality, the intimacy of our union perhaps, our life together. This is our marriage – the trust, the sacredness of privacy, the closeness of that, staring into each other's eyes, neither of us feeling pressure to speak – simply being together. We are in love, and we are married. In our bedroom, there is nothing to want. It isn't necessary to move, or to do anything. The two of us is all that is necessary. How fortunate we are. Filet mignon is in the offing for both of us. What good fortune to have filet mignon in my immediate future with my wife sitting on the edge of our bed.

More relaxed now; everything in this room appeals to me, including my naked feet and my wife in her underwear. Our souls are naked as well. No requirement to speak. My bungled audition an event of the past. Filet mignon waiting for us. Life is good, our marriage good, our lives good, my wife's skin, her eyes, the soft bed, the surrounding clump of pillows all spell one thing – home. This is our home and our bedroom. Later we shall be eating filet mignon in our dining room. We shall feast to our heart's delight, after sharing intimate moments in our bedroom, thoughts of steak, love, family and security. We are safe here. A botched audition is overshadowed by this private moment with her.

~~~

Later that evening, I tiptoe into the room where my delicate daughter lies. As I approach that sleeping, helpless form, clutching her red doll, her blonde head is visible through a haze of darkness, dreaming of lollipops and horses and toy trucks with rubber wheels. In the grip of my arms, I see in the darkness the details of her angelic face. My child keeps me sane - her innocence. In the morning, this little girl will prance into my arms to greet me with kisses, demonstrating enthusiasm that only children can offer, a wide eyed expectancy that her daddy is by her side, and that will be great fun, and together we will play with a new toy, together with old toys and invent new games that will be fun, and her daddy will offer his little girl sweets and toys and soft dolls to squeeze. My animal voices will make her squeal with laughter, and she will wear her new sneakers, and she will walk around the house with her shovel and pull the cat's tail, and life will be good with her mommy and her daddy taking care of her, and they will be nice to her, and they will be nice to each other, and the world will be a big toy for her to play with a big handle on it too, like her shovel, to swing around and bang against her sandbox, and life is so much fun, so much fun, so much genuine fun! A big daddy too is so much fun! My steady hand upon her shoulder will avoid stumbling from heights too steep, as she gropes her way through her formative years without time for rehearsal. Indeed, any little girl needs her dad.

I fall to my knees, careful not to wake her, and like a knight returning from a Crusade, lean over her resting head, planting a tender kiss upon my child's brow. It's a father's kiss for his daughter, full of the deepest love I can possibly summon and protective in its deliberateness. Then I relax into the soft rug and dream of tall flowers and high grass. My daughter runs happily through acres of yellow sunflowers. "That's what life should be," I vow, as the rug swallows me up, eyes closed and secure with the little one next to me, confident I will protect her from harm. She believes in me. My spirit is filled by her glowing warmth. I will never let her down. Successful auditions will be for her sake, not for mine. My powerful wish for her well-being will guarantee a successful career for my family's sake and not for mine.

Next time, I'll land the goddam role.

Film Vs Theater

Essay Published in the 2018 edition of 'The Storyteller Anthology'

In between unemployment checks I'm a part time plumber's assistant. My boss, a big, fat man, pays me off the books, fixing toilets, connecting pipe, putting in sinks; nothing complicated, so that my time is filled and I don't have to think, and my hands are busy, and my eyes are on the mark, and I'm busy, busy, busy, and my back is bent, and it hurts, and it's sore, and I'm useful, and my lack of purpose isn't an issue. Things are getting done, after all, but there has to be an end to this "no hub, pipe" business with "quarter inch, half inch, one inch" jargon every day, but probably I'll continue at the same frantic pace, and my hands will thicken, and my body will strengthen, and there will be a little bit accomplished every day. But I'll always wonder what it is I'm heading for and why I was born to begin with.

Activity doesn't seem to solve my basic yearning for something unidentifiable, and when I'm confronted with empty time, I wonder who it is I am supposed to be, which has nothing to do with sweating copper that leaves me with these thickened, plumber's hands, and they will always be my hands, and the thickness of them will stay with me forever, and the roughness of their skin will always be me too, as I am the product of all the things I have done, but large, open spans of time frightened me, and my tendency is to fill them quickly.

~~~

A memory of a vacuous fellow around 1980; I forget his name. Years before I'd heard from a mutual friend that he'd been left a formidable inheritance from his parents, before becoming a part time 'social worker' to add 'meaning' to his privileged life. Money wasn't an issue to this 'jerk' and neither was his need to work for a living, as I'd done for much of my adult life, either by performing roles on the New York stage or doing manual labor when I was broke.

In my early-forties, our paths crossed in New York City. He noticed my graying hair and asked, "Are you sorry you're an actor?"

Totally dumbfounded by his condescending tone, I thought to myself, "The nerve of this 'sonofabitch' to ask such a question, as if Hollywood movie stardom was required to be a successful actor." My impulse was to punch him, but didn't. Not the violent type, I guess.

Not being a theater goer, the fellow was unaware of my resume of some forty New York theatrical productions both on Broadway and off, not to overlook years of performing all over the world with the *'Open Theater'*. Regardless, the guy pissed me off, but I tried my best to remain calm in the face of his challenge, aware also that he'd struck a sensitive chord. My meager income and uncertain future had characterized me as a failure in his eyes, and I didn't like it. The freshness of my youth was gone by then, and some inner voice suspected he was right. I should've been a "movie star" or something like that. That's what he was implying anyway.

174

"You think I should be a movie star?" I answered, as if he didn't know what he was talking about.

"I'm a New York stage actor, man. Haven't done much film," stated firmly with a touch of contempt, as if Hollywood were beneath my high standards. The fellow detected I was annoyed by his comment and backed off the subject, but I persisted.

"You want me to go Hollywood?" I asked him directly.

I looked him straight in the eye, as if the prospect of going to Los Angeles to achieve 'movie star' fame was at best frivolous and beneath me. The urge to present myself as a so-called "serious New York stage actor" was firmly established, as we stood uncomfortably before each other. New Yorkers often condescend to Hollywood; 'movie star' superficiality is somehow "less than" the mad scramble of New York City. For New Yorkers, "living in the city", as they call it, is the height of 'being real', while Hollywood represents phoniness. That's the usual take anyway - the 'fake world' of Hollywood compared to the grit of New York.

I tolerated the fellow enough to swallow my pride and share a cup of coffee with him, while he served tidbits of gossip about a mutual friend.

Another time in my early forties, an acquaintance of mine suggested that I was "afraid of success". We were sitting at a table in a coffee shop at the time. I left immediately, vowing to show him and the rest of the world that I would prove myself to him and others like him. Maybe my father might have had something to do with my reaction. That guy's impression of my failure was similar to my father's, whose approval meant so much to me. The profession of acting was a mystery to my old man, and since my career was lacking in film visibility, he had no idea what I was doing for a living before he died too soon to witness my current film visibility. To my father, acting wasn't 'real work' that a so-called 'real man' would do; that is, unless I were in the movies, which would be public enough to prove my worth in his eyes.

"I will show them," I'd promised to myself. The 'invisible them' was unspecific then, humanity in general, I suppose, that seemed so much more attuned to the ways of the world than I. My career originated from chaos, anxiety and the suspicion that I did not quite belong. In spite of this, once the original choice was made, becoming an actor became a question of pride and my unwillingness to surrender to defeat. There was no higher cause in my need to perform, aside from proving I could do it, possibly to compensate for something lacking inside, some invisible, integral part that seemed missing. Performing for audiences would heal that void, or so I thought, and it did to some degree. Creating characters almost, but not quite, established a sense of 'wholeness' within a murky sea of doubt. Avoidance of the profession's hazards was never a viable alternative. I was too naïve to avoid, until the struggle became an unconscious habit. On the positive side, for twenty years acting had provided a modest income for my family and fulfillment enough to carry on to the 'next chapter'.

I would not quit. No, I would never quit. Quitting wasn't in my nature. I was too naïve to quit, or lacking in common sense, one or the other. I hesitate to use the word 'stupidity', but there might have been some of that as well. Of course, I am not stupid, but certainly prone to ramming into brick walls to prove something I'll never know. But, boy, that blind willingness to continue against all odds left its imprint, the willingness to battle it out, to discover who I really was in the world of theater, whether it made sense or not - such a difficult profession, acting in front of audiences, finding the truth of a play; people observing an actor blundering about on stage, such vulnerability for anyone willing to try.

Another time, when I was having a beer in Manhattan's Broome Street Bar, where I'd worked for a brief period as a bouncer, one of the regulars exclaimed, "You've been an actor for years, but I've never seen you in a movie. What's wrong, man?"

There was nothing I could say. Justifying my stage career seemed useless. Again, I was bothered by this layman's comment and determined to do something about it. None of my critics were theater aficionados. Having never seen my work on stage, my lack of film visibility was translated into unequivocal failure. My need to pursue film work became urgent. Film had always attracted me, but the security of the New York stage had limited my horizons.

Shutting my critics up for once and for all became a priority. Acting in film had been part of my original motivation for becoming an actor from the time when I was a kid with my mother at the 'Arcade', the both of us watching the brilliant performances of Marlon Brando and Vivien Leigh in 'Streetcar Named Desire'.

New York City represents a vivid memory of hanging by my fingertips for survival, like so many actors, living hand to mouth, entrapped by theater's minimal income and prejudiced by the notion that Hollywood was basically for movie stars. The West Coast represented another world that seemed not only foreign but also superficial, as if film actors were sell-outs of sorts, closely aligned with all that was tacky in America. New York actors enforced that viewpoint. It never dawned on me that they might have been envious of film stars. Until I turned forty, I didn't much notice my paltry income. Survival was enough, as long as I was acting. But working continuously in theater and gaining little recognition beyond New York City audiences for a modest income began to take a toll. I was at a standstill career-wise. Both fame and money were missing from the equation.

Twenty years earlier, my decision to become an actor had cemented my fate. By my own 'free will', I'd bitten into the 'forbidden apple' in the proverbial 'Garden of Eden'. What followed my 'original sin' has been a life of washing dishes, bouncer at Manhattan's Broome Street Bar, longshoreman on Pier Twenty-eight on the Hudson River, digging ditches to lay drain pipe, waiting on tables, busboy, hundreds of nerve-racking auditions, followed by enough roles to make a few bucks and gain more experience. My burgeoning skill as an actor had always been the measure of my success, not money and certainly not fame. During this trial and error period, I'd earned an average income of eight thousand dollars per year, a paltry sum for a Brown University graduate. In fact, I was a struggling artist with a modicum of skill developed by twenty years of stage work. One production always followed another, and during more lucrative periods, I rehearsed a downtown play during the day and performed an uptown production that same evening, which provided two weekly paychecks to catch up with living expenses. For my entire adult life,

I fully embraced every aspect of that original choice to be a professional actor; all the part time jobs, all the failures, not to overlook numerous successes.

Oh yes, over the years, enough roles have come my way to continue the struggle, not to overlook that acting in front of audiences is both euphoric and addictive. Nothing else gives me such absolute pleasure. Nothing else provides a sense of wholeness, of being a fully creative human being. The stage has always provided a unique place for my creative soul to ignite. An audience of expectant strangers has always shocked me into a state of heightened alertness that has become addictive over the years. An adrenalin rush kicks in, and I am on automatic pilot to offer my innermost, best self. Inspiration and an uncanny vitality overtakes me that is in sync with life itself. Every fiber of my being, every nerve and every muscle functions with maximum intelligence. Life itself is intensely magnified. My entire being vibrates with quiet joy for what I am privileged to express. Everything I do and say is engulfed by a magnificent spark of life. The fire within burns to full flame, and I can do no wrong. Every move, every vocal inflection, every gesture has meaning, and I become a full human being, a complete man, totally confident and totally capable.

It is no wonder I've became addicted.

The money I earn for survival is irrelevant. I act because I need to act, no other reason. Always I've insisted upon greatness in my work, and often I've failed gloriously. During rare performances, a sublime state of Nirvana arrives on stage, and the tiny kernel of that from which I am made is briefly uncovered. The question of, "Who am I?" is clarified by the profession of acting, regardless of results. Theater has expanded me into a conscious being. Anxiety about my future is part of that consciousness and perhaps the source from which awareness is born.

~~~

After two decades of living from 'hand to mouth', I'd performed in approximately forty New York productions but only three small film roles in Paul Mazursky's *'Unmarried Woman'*,

178

Joan Miklan Silver's *'Between the Lines'* and *'Goodbye Girl'*. My stage work had been exposed to a select New York City audience familiar with the works of the *'Open Theater'*, the *'Living Theater'* and the *'Wooster Group'*, along with dozens of plays both on Broadway and off Broadway, mostly at Joseph Papp's Public Theater. I'd faced failure, fear, frustration, lack of funds and humiliation on numerous fronts, until in my heart, I could truly call myself a professional actor, a pro's pro, a guy who could do a good job performing varied roles on stage.

~~~

It was time to pursue a film career. Becoming more visible to the general public meant roles in films. For the longest time, I'd refused to admit this, having been somewhat brainwashed into believing that so-called 'movie' work was a shallow pursuit compared to theatre. In the cloistered setting of the New York theatre with its arrogant impression of itself, I assumed the stage offered the best training and not film. New York actors were so haughty about their so-called 'calling' in life, as if what they were doing was a religion of sorts. I almost believed them, not that I cared about the depth of theatre. I was deep enough, all right, more than willing to go the extra mile to withstand unlimited hardship, if only to stay in the mix. But films would expose my talent to larger groups of humanity, and I needed that exposure for success in my critics' eyes. Once I turned forty, playing major roles in movies attracted me more than ever. To be known to the general public, to be recognized for my skill and to be paid well from film work became a priority for me.

The possibility of 'fame' spurred me onward, a ridiculous goal really when I think about it. Lee Harvey Oswald is famous for committing a despicable act. Anyone can be famous by shooting a President, but regardless, some abstract desire within me wished for public approval from a very young age. In truth, I was seeking my father's approval, longing for validation from a man who barely noticed me when I was a boy. Some abstract need for approval had always been a source of 'blind willingness' to continue the struggle, although I wasn't fully aware of this. College athletics had guaranteed a certain degree of notoriety: picture in the paper, winning the game, the honors involved, the all-star teams, the championships, but being in the movies surpassed all of it. Actors don't wear helmets. Their faces can be seen and magnified to huge proportions. Their voices are magnified too. Audiences concentrate upon the actors, as their story unfolds for the duration of the film, and people leave the theater with an indelible impression that they know each actor personally. I wanted audiences to know me in that intimate way, but more than that, I wanted my father to perceive me not only as his son but also to respect me as an actor. This was somewhat unconscious to me.

In short, the most visible medium to the general public was film. Something had to be done. A choice was made to 'sell out', to 'cash in' by pursuing a film career. To be cast in a major film with a major role became my goal. But it had to be a sizeable role. The first step was to plant that goal firmly into my head.

~~~

The year is 1984. My agent has scheduled an audition for a Michael Cimino's *'Year of the Dragon'*, written by Oliver Stone and starring Mickey Rourke. The audition was for the film's second lead role and could transcend my career to another level. Michael Cimino had recently won an Oscar for his direction of *'Deer Hunter'* and Oliver Stone for writing and directing *'Platoon'*. Both men seemed a bit out of my league, but that wouldn't dissuade me from reading for the role. By that time, I'd auditioned for dozens of parts unsuccessfully and had developed a rather thick skin from frequent rejections during my career. Nonetheless, I would give it my best shot and take it from there. At the time, a plumbing job provided income for survival.

"Do the reading and forget about it, then back to my plumbing work," was the plan.

I was a plumber's assistant at the time for an ex-con, named Ken Wayland, who had served time in San Quentin for armed robbery. His nickname was *'The Troubadour Bandit'*, a tag he'd acquired from his habit of singing, as he went about the business of robbing people's apartments; that is, after tying them up at gunpoint. He'd been caught and convicted and had served his time. I'd met Ken while working for an organization called 'Street Theater' that ran acting workshops for Grasslands County Jail inmates. I was hired as the director of those prison workshops, while Ken's function was to book performances of the plays created by ex-offenders released from prison. The men, mostly black, were paid a humble salary to create and perform their plays under my direction. At some point, funding for those prison workshops terminated, at which point Ken and I became plumbers for survival.

Ken and I liked each other. Both of us were suited for plumbing work, but in my case, a career as an actor was my ambition, not plumbing. My audition later that afternoon could be the start of a legitimate film career and would change my life forever. That morning I was nervous about my reading. For the greater part of the day, I dug trenches in the basement of a New York City loft building to replace drain pipes as old as the building itself. The pipes had eroded from being exposed to moisture for a century or so. Working with my hands was familiar territory for me, and Ken was a skilled plumber. We talked while working, *(when not going over lines for my audition)* mostly about theater and his experiences in prison. Women were discussed too. I'd been married and divorced, after my daughter, Oona, was born. He'd left the love of his life years before, and no one had replaced her.

My audition was constantly on my mind, while Ken performed the more skillful tasks, welding pipe and fitting joints seamlessly to avoid leaks. As he welded pipe, I did the brute work, which I preferred, breaking the cement basement floor with a sledge hammer and digging with a pick and shovel three feet into the exposed dirt beneath the cement. I didn't mind the work and even enjoyed the physicality of swinging a sledge hammer onto bare cement, until it cracked and could be removed manually. The heavy work suited me; something about the strength required, the muscularity involved and the awareness that crushing cement could only be done by a man who possessed such strength. I've always savored physical exertion, useful both for the task at hand, as well as for earning my keep.

We worked well together, Ken and I, our friendship bonded by a mutual goal to complete the job, after which we'd eat hamburgers at a nearby SoHo restaurant and discuss whatever came to mind.

But on that particular day, the plan was to work until three in the afternoon and then leave for the audition for *'Year of the Dragon'*. The physicality of the day's labor might exhaust me, but I needed the money and couldn't let Ken down by not showing up. I doubted the role would be offered anyway. Hard work beforehand was of little concern. Hours were passing fast. The lines from the scenes I'd be reading were quietly mumbled, as I dug into the basement floor, the muscles in my back taxed by the ensuing labor. The work was physically more strenuous than I'd expected - my body overheated from swinging the sledge hammer, from digging holes with a shovel and pick. Exhaustion distracted me from the pending audition. So be it. The chips would fall where they may.

~~~

By the time Ken and I parted ways, I had little energy left. Apathy towards the world at large best describes my condition. Finishing the day was more important than actually landing the role. Along with that surrender, came relaxation. I was too tired to worry; a brutal day's work had taken its toll. My body exhausted, the ultimate goal was to return to my apartment and sleep in a warm bed. The reading had to be done, one way or the other, but my mind was empty, no nerves to speak of and little by way of fear. Too often I had been rattled before an audition, especially an important one. But on that day, "Get it over with," was my attitude, "Finish, get the hell out of here, go home and drift off to sleep." I forgot about being judged; forgot the role could change my life; forgot that I might never have to crack cement again or dig ditches for a living, if only to be cast in the damned role.

~ ~ ~

The subway brought me to Union Square where Michael Cimino, the illustrious, Oscar-winning director, would be holding court. I approached the building, a 'ditch-digger' transformed into an actor foraging for a career, a legitimate profession that could possibly replace a back-breaking plumber's job for an hourly wage.

"First climb the stairs to the floor where the audition would be held. Then read for the role and go home," was my mantra.

When I walked into the room, people seemed friendly enough. That was usually the case during auditions, a room full of friendly and welcoming people. I appeared before them in my work clothes, script in hand, wearing a striped polo shirt dirt-smudged from a grueling day. My hands were dirty from the hours of handling the tools of my trade; patches of tar on my forearms, stinking sweat from my armpits, work clothes covered with dirt and mud-lined boots completed the picture. My attention wasn't focused upon appearance. Looking back on it, this was a blessing of sorts. Preoccupation with 'how I looked' had too often led me astray while being judged. Thoughts of how I came across to others and, "How should this line go?" and, "How should I perform that phrase," had too often been the preamble to failed auditions. Thankfully my thoughts were focused upon a soft bed at home and not upon my appearance.

They spoke as if they knew me; that is, the casting directors, two women, whose names escape me, nice ladies, one young and one middle-aged. Michael Cimino sat among them, quiet and non-committal, his round face fixed with intense, dark eyes that absorbed everything in the room. The man was obviously an observer of human behavior, a student of life and not a talker. He certainly perused me intently, waiting for the reading to begin, as I stood before him, eager to get on with it.

The women made small talk, mostly complimenting me for my work with the *'Open Theater'*, the avant-garde theater company that had dominated Off-Off Broadway, Europe and the Near East during the sixties and early seventies. And there I was, standing before one of the most talented film directors in modern history; dirty clothes, scuffed boots and tar-covered arms and hands, dirt on pants, under fingernails, and totally unaware of my appearance. The young casting director, from the way she spoke, favored my talents on stage and seemed to be rooting for me before the reading began.

She even mentioned my acting skill to our famed director. My career had humbled me by then. Struggle had been too much a part of my history to allow myself a bloated ego. But I was indeed flattered. It's always flattering when someone speaks favorably about my work. Acting is an elusive skill, depended upon one's state of mind. Give me a pick and shovel, and I can kick ass anytime, but acting has always been a crap shoot.

It was time to read. Michael Cimino knew his craft. He knew a good actor when he saw one too. I was in that room because the casting directors had recommended me. My artistry would be proven in the next few minutes - or not. I sat down. The older woman remarked that my hands were dirty. Barely making eye contact, I answered with a brief, "Yeah, just finished a job," and immediately focused on the script. I barely lifted my eyes when I responded; nothing overstated, nothing elaborate, only a short recognition that my hands were indeed dirty and so what? Embellishment was unnecessary. I was too tired to elaborate upon my need to earn a few bucks by digging trenches. No explanation was offered beyond, "Yeah, I just finished a job," leaving the subject in limbo. I wasn't in the mood for talking. A soft bed and sleep were in the back of my mind.

The reading began. The younger casting director read with me. My voice was surprisingly strong, nothing compromised about it, nothing weak, and I spoke confidently, as if I were the character, who had finished a day's hard labor and didn't care much about what happened next. My body was relaxed, muscles loose from the strain of swinging a sledge hammer for seven hours without a break. There was nothing left in me, no resistance, no awkward shifting of the body that might interfere with the delivery of the words, no tightness, no tension, just the sound of the character speaking, as if he meant what he was saying. Brutal, physical labor of laying sewer pipe in the basement of a New York City building had left me at home with myself. 'Pick and shovel work' had submerged me into my own skin without my knowing it.

I noticed that I was oddly at ease with myself. In the true sense of the word, the character embodied the 'real me.' As I say, my voice was strong and resonant. When I spoke the lines of the character, self-assurance penetrated the baggage that had weighed me down so often in the past. The day's hard, manual labor had brought me closer to myself, something having to do with being useful, something about being exhausted to the point of 'not caring'. When a man does an honest day's work with his hands, he does feel useful. His purpose in life is defined by the sheer effort involved. Dignity for a man is interlocked with the physical effort necessary to earn his keep and the pride that comes from doing work that few men would be willing or able to do. My bricklayer father would have been proud of a job well done, and I was proud to some degree. The day's work had grounded me; primal satisfaction of a breadwinner earning his keep to pay the rent and my daughter's school tuition had done the trick.

Michael Camino cast me on the spot in that room. I couldn't believe it. The way he offered me the role was so simple. "You can play the role of 'Lou'," he stated quietly, calmly. At first I wasn't sure what he said. "You mean I'm in the film?" I asked to be sure I was hearing right. "Yes, you can do 'Lou' in my film, *'Year of the Dragon'*, he stated a second time with a slight smile on his face. He seemed to be aware what the role meant to me and enjoyed my reaction to his offer, which was a mixture of pure euphoria and delight. I was immediately uplifted and overjoyed, although I tried my best to hold it in. At that moment, both my life and my career had been automatically raised to a new plateau of visibility; no more guys asking me, "What's wrong, man? I never see you in movies." No more laymen asking if, "I was sorry I was an actor?" I left the room as if in a dream and remember running out to the street with a huge smile on my face.

The day's hard, physical labor had a strong influence upon my winning the role, possibly related to my father's influence, who always glorified tough work, "to put food on the table for the kids and a roof over their heads." He was a strong one, my old man; drank too much but strong as hell. Similarly physical labor offered me stability in that audition room - the confidence that no matter what happened with the acting, I would always be capable of feeding that beautiful daughter of mine. That's a strong emotion for a man to feel, whether he's a working actor or not, to be a

185

dependable provider for his child. If I hadn't been given the role, I would have been fully capable of taking care of my daughter. She'd be fed with a roof over her head. That's for goddamn sure.

~~~

When we began shooting *'Year of the Dragon'*, I'd rigorously prepared for the role. Michael and I were on the same page in that regard. "Total commitment" was our unspoken promise. Mickey Rourke was afraid of failure. So was I. That fear bonded us. We were both hampered by insecurity derived from our dysfunctional youth. This was never spoken, but we sensed each other's insecurity. We pretended to be on top of things, but beneath that outer layer of macho behavior, we were two fragile men feigning confidence. Both Michael Cimino and Mickey Rourke were aware I hadn't much film experience, but Michael was an inordinately kind man, sensitive towards all his actors. Since I was less experienced in the world of film, I took the lower birth in the pecking order on the set, partly to please Mickey Rourke. Playing a major role in *'Year of the Dragon'* was enough for me. I didn't need more than the work itself; to play a major role with Michael's guidance. Our director was able to assuage my insecurities, always with a gentle tone, always encouraging, always supportive. I still feel love for Michael Cimino, almost thirty years later. He cast me in my first major film role, for which I'll always be grateful.

Mickey Rourke never learned his lines, so I consciously felt the rhythm of our dialogue to sense when it was time to speak. The cues he delivered were seldom the same, so I was always on high alert, paying absolute attention to what he was saying. Mickey wrote the words on his hands, on a nearby wall, on a table or anywhere that suited his fancy. He was very skillful at maneuvering his body to read whatever came next, usually paraphrasing the lines, but, aside from that, his acting was superb. He is a talented man, a good man, although tortured in his own way; his life a series of mishaps, growing up without a father, running the streets of Miami as a boy, his older brother serving time in prison. It was a wonder he had survived, not to mention become a movie star. His accomplishments surpassed imagination, given his upbringing. The

186

man's talent was exemplary, in spite of his proclivity for self-destruction.

At first, I was a bit too aware of Mickey's film reputation but quickly learned to trust our bond. From all appearances, Mickey enjoyed working with me, and I needed his support. *'Lou'*, the character I played, was both Mickey Rourke's best friend and his boss. Mickey played the role of *'Stanley'*, a good detective but undisciplined. Our film characters loved each other as close friends and partners involved in dangerous police work. Since my character was his boss, I disciplined him on the job whenever he messed up. *'Lou'* and *'Stanley'* maintained their affectionate bond throughout the film with a few bumps along the way. Their friendship is best described as 'tough love' between two macho cops trying their best to do an important job.

Mickey and I had a few things in common, which helped cement our union in the film. He'd been offered a full football scholarship to the University of Alabama, but since he'd flunked out of high school, he'd never attended college. I'd won a football scholarship from Brown University with some measure of success. Football was the subject of numerous conversations, maybe for both of us to maintain our macho image, although I sensed there was much more to his soul, as there is to mine. In my case, macho football talk came easily enough, and Mickey responded well to the male image of guys tackling each other and ramming them into the ground. In my case, 'football talk' was expedient, useful for our characters' friendship in the storyline of the film. I listened attentively to him expounding upon the game, mostly to please rather than any genuine interest. We related to each other closely through our understanding of the game. Any football player has pungent memories of the physical collisions of blocking and tackling, the bruising contact of muscular bodies banging into each other and subsequent injuries ignored during the following week's game. We respected each other for having endured the sport's brutality. But we seldom revealed our softer sensibilities, the more fragile parts that men often disguise for the sake of their alleged manhood. That disguise served well our characters, along with momentary hints of repressed love between us throughout the film.

The wish to do everything perfectly still plagued me, while we worked. My thinking was flawed. I was unaware of what I know now when I shot *'Year of the Dragon'*. I believed during my tutelage with Michael Camino that, aside from hours of sense memory exercises executed in privacy, hard work and determination were the main ingredients required. The work was taken a bit too seriously, as if the outcome was all up to me. A sense of humor would have served me better and confidence that things would fall into place naturally without trying so very much. I isolated between camera takes and concentrated beyond what was necessary. The work was too important to me. On the other hand, how could it not be so? *"Year of the Dragon"* was my first shot at visibility in the world of film.

'Year of the Dragon' was a successful chapter in my career as an actor. In fact, the film completely changed my life. I'd finally 'made it' when I saw the film at the premier. At least that was my impression from audiences responding positively to my work. Perfect strangers passing me in the street expressed their appreciation for what I accomplished in the film. My performance was rather well done, I daresay, at the risk of braggadocio. More importantly, I found entrance into the world of film, which made it possible to earn a decent living. Seventy thousand dollars was the sum total of my earnings, far more than I'd ever earned on any job. It was time to arrive at a new level of income and make life easier, possibly even to be known for my art. Public notoriety hadn't been fully vented. Fame as an actor still attracted me, perhaps my Achilles Heel; such an evasive notion, fame.

~~~

Oliver Stone, Tom Cruise

'Born on the Fourth of July', 1990

The filming of *'Born on the Fourth of July'* brought me to the most public of arenas, namely the world of Hollywood, in a major motion picture no less, where adoration was potentially as prevalent as public ridicule. None other than Tom Cruise and Oliver Stone were the lead actor and director respectively, two heavyweights, enormously successful. I was a pro too, but I didn't quite know it. By some fortuitous stroke of luck, I was given the opportunity to rub elbows with them socially and collaborate with them professionally. Oliver Stone knew my work in *'Year of the Dragon'*, a film he'd written but directed by his Oscar-winning

189

friend, Michael Cimino. Casting me in *'Born on the Fourth of July'* had been Oliver's response to my performance in *'Year of the Dragon'.* He was convinced both from my work in that movie and from Michael Cimino's recommendation that I would be right for Oliver's film. In fact, the man barely knew me.

Mr. Kovic, Tom Cruise's shy, working-class father, was the role I played. The character's greatest obstacle was his inability to communicate with his son. My habitual shyness matched the emotional life of the character. Although I'd performed in numerous New York stage productions by then, my deepest self-image was that of a manual laborer, derived from the numerous part-time jobs I'd dutifully performed when acting work had been scarce. I hadn't changed much since my days of washing dishes at Tortilla Flats in New York City's Greenwich Village. "Once a dishwasher, always a dishwasher," although hauling ass as a longshoreman on Pier Twenty-eight on Laight Street in downtown Manhattan was equally a part of my history. Essentially, at that point of my career, after performing in some forty New York stage productions, I still had a laborer's mentality, a guy who worked with his hands. A 'beast of burden' is the best way to describe it, whose natural bent was lifting, pushing and hauling like any old workhorse did. In truth, I'm still a purebred 'working man' at heart today and not much of a 'thespian type.' Tom Cruise was definitely out of my league. Or so I thought. Mr. Kovic, the character I played was also a blue-collar, working class guy and would surely have been intimidated by Tom Cruise's celebrity. But I was unaware of that parallel between me and my character at the time. Mr. Kovic personified my working class father. Subconsciously I absorbed my father's personality within the psyche of the character I was playing; shy, self-effacing and willing to do any manual job to pay off the thirty-year mortgage and get the kids raised.

~~~

Oliver Stone is an intimidating, determined man, who plods onward when filming, crushing all obstacles in his way. Something about his legendary reputation confused our relationship in the beginning. That confusion may have been his intention. I'll never

190

know, but his dominant presence off-camera definitely interfered with the natural flow between actor and director. In short, I wanted very much to please Oliver, but plainly I was intimidated by the man's notoriety. He'd recently won an Oscar for *'Platoon'* about his experience in Vietnam; that is, after he'd dropped out of Yale. Afraid both of failing him, as well as not fulfilling the important message of his film, my shyness haunted me, too much so. I felt personally responsible for the film's message and the daunting prospect of failing all bereaved parents of wounded and dead victims of Vietnam, but most importantly I was afraid of failing myself.

My silence was the norm in the presence of mindless chatter of the cast. Tom Cruise, Tom Berringer, Willem DeFoe and Oliver Stone were all so 'happy go lucky' on the set. They had worked together while filming *'Platoon'*, and with that film's success, they behaved as if they were part of a 'good old boys' club, from which I was excluded. Excluded from their comradarie, I had to do something special in Oliver's film to come up to their level. How to pull it off was the question. Delving into my character's psyche was certainly part of the task, unaware, as I was, that so much of my natural insecurity already fulfilled the essence of Mr. Kovic's character. Both I and the character were painfully shy. Inadequacy permeated my mental state. 'Silence' was my characteristic way of dealing with the world from the time of my youth. My mouth was permanently sealed in their jovial presence. Speaking meant bullshitting, of which I had barely a modicum of skill, not that I didn't learn eventually. Today people can't shut me up. But in the presence of an all-star cast and an Oscar-winning director, my silence became an impediment. Fortunately the fit between me and the non-communicative character I played was seamless without my realizing. Perhaps my taciturn persona was the reason Oliver hired me in the first place.

The first day of shooting was scheduled after a brief rehearsal period of one week. During that period, when I wasn't on call, I stayed in my Dallas hotel room, totally isolated. Confined for hours in that tiny space, I drew pictures on large sheets of paper with carbon pencil and paper, both private and relaxing. 'Emotional recall' exercises were also part of the daily routine, executed painstakingly, almost religiously and in complete isolation. I imagined my daughter, Oona, whom I love deeply, paralyzed in a specific environment that I detailed audibly to a blank, hotel room wall. I certainly took myself seriously in those days. This image of my paralyzed daughter, recreated in my mind, paralleled Ronnie Kovic's life-altering injury and his father's reaction to it. Mr. Kovic loved his son, as I do my daughter. The parallel relationship of father to daughter accurately instilled my character's inner life, or so I thought, which became mine as days passed. My emotional reaction to my son's crippling war injury was revisited every day by means of those 'emotional recall exercises'. In fact, the exercise was a bit muscular with lots of forced crying and all the accoutrements that accompany the cliché of sadness. Of course, Oliver Stone knew none of this. I worked in my hotel room's solitude. For all he knew, I was in one of my avoidance modes, isolated in my hotel room, completely apart from him and the cast and not particularly interested in mingling.

Once after my nightly ritual in the hotel room, I happened upon Oliver's table in the downstairs restaurant, where he was sharing war stories with Willem DeFoe, Tom Berringer and some other well-known actors from *'Platoon'*, also cast in *'Born on the Fourth of July'*. As I was passing, he rose from his chair and introduced me as a "great actor I want you all to meet," at which point two or three tall Texans passed between us, and I slipped behind them away from Oliver's table. I completely left Oliver in a lurch. What the hell. Some demon within me had no choice but to get the hell out of there, away from all those so-called 'famous actors'. Actually I'd worked with Willem DeFoe in Arthur Miller's *'The Crucible'* performed by New York's *'Wooster group'*, of which he was a member, and later I worked with Tom Berringer in that *'Charlie Valentine'* film with me playing the title role. Big deal, playing the lead. I don't know what to think sometimes. At any rate, I split from that table, got the hell out of there and isolated in my room, did my 'sense memory' exercises probably; don't remember anymore. But it was important to be alone, rather than bullshitting with a bunch of actors in the hotel bar.

What Oliver failed to realize was that I actually had become Mr. Kovic and wasn't merely playing a role for some random movie I didn't care about. Substituting my daughter in my hotel room with 'emotional recall' exercises had miraculously allowed me to enter the complexity of both the character's pain and his shyness. Oliver's introduction in the hotel bar was sincere, but I couldn't handle a table full of celebrities. Mr. Kovic would have taken the same exit. Both the character and I were leery of most people, especially famous ones, and since I actually was Mr. Kovic and not merely playing him, I took my exit to avoid being trapped. There was no choice. I just reacted and took my exit. The character would have done the same to avoid a group of famous actors. "They were better than me" was my thinking or some such nonsense. Or maybe I didn't want to hear a bunch of actors expounding war stories about shooting 'Platoon'. Whatever, it doesn't matter now. I did what I did and escaped the scene, away from the famous people. Today it would've been different but 'avoidance' was my natural inclination then.

Admittedly it was bizarre behavior on my part. My director must have wondered what the hell was going on in my mind. Oliver was forced to endure my eccentricity for the duration of the shoot. So what? Big deal. I had to do what I had to do. Both Oliver and I were similar in our commitment to the quality of our work. That's what really mattered. He would understand my eccentric behavior, if we were to discuss it today.

~~~

During the morning of first day of filming, we shot an opening scene, when Tom Cruise persuades his family that it is his moral duty to join the marines. Tom spoke all the lines, while my wife, played by Caroline Cava, and I listened attentively. As the scene was shot, I sat on a couch very still next to Ms. Cava, listening to Tom plead his case. With one line to say, it seemed superfluous to move randomly, if at all. With dozens of New York plays under my belt, it could be argued I was more skilled than that. As I say, the character of Mr. Kovic, written by Oliver himself, was habitually quiet and extremely shy. I was also shy on that fancy-assed movie set with Tom Cruise and Oliver Stone parading around like movie stars. Plainly I didn't belong. Unwarranted or not, that's how I felt.

On that particular morning, after we finished the scene, Oliver cornered me away from cast and crew, claiming I hadn't "done enough" in the scene. He chided me for my "stillness". What was I supposed to do? Do a dance or something? I had only one line in the damned scene, and told him so.

"Why didn't you give me more lines?" I said in my defense.

His remarks had stung me, as I stood before him, like a kid about to be spanked, a grown man, big and strong enough to kick his ass, but I took his abuse stoically. He carried on about my not having "done enough," and that most of my performance would "end up on the cutting room floor" and that I'd sat like "a bump on a log" and "What did you think you were doing? Couldn't you scratch your cheek or something?" That remark pissed me off to no end. Scratch my freakin' cheek? Was he kidding me? Screw "scratching my goddam cheek!" Screw Oliver Stone! The scene had been shot already, a dozen times if not more. Why hadn't he given me that direction while we were shooting?

Oliver claimed I wasn't the same actor he'd seen in *'Year of the Dragon'*, wasn't a mature 'man' or some macho bullshit. That really got to me, the bastard. The film was shot in macho Dallas, Texas, where "men are men". Needless to say, I wasn't one of them, nor did I want to be, although I looked the part. I've always looked like a so-called 'real man', as boring as that may sound. Big deal, 'big man', I've never been quite taken by the notion of posing as a "real man". 'Macho men' bore the hell out of me frankly. Willem Defoe, Tom Berringer and Oliver Stone were so-called 'real men'. They seem so full of themselves and yet so frightened of being found out – bunch of nonsense if you ask me.

Already our relationship was a shambles. That morning Oliver transformed me into a little boy, looking desperately for his daddy's hand to hold onto, his arms to wrap me, his love to engulf me. Surely none of the above would ever happen on a movie set from any director. Why should it have, after all? I hadn't been hired

194

to find my father's love. I was there to play a leading role in a major motion picture. That point was sorely overshadowed by a neurotic relationship with my director.

"Scratch my cheek," my ass!

At any rate, I was crushed by his assault, totally devastated. Mr. Kovic would also be devastated by his son not able to walk again. This emotional connection with my character hadn't dawned on me at the time. I was too hurt by Oliver Stone and too pissed to think about my character, which might have been a blessing. In fact, I actually 'was my character', although my acting that morning felt at very best mediocre with the illustrious Oliver Stone's betrayal that had cut me to the core. My respect for the man had been to the highest degree, and his apparent distrust had deeply wounded me. His macho approach I respected enough to tolerate, but his aggressive sense of purpose had overshadowed our trust. Oliver didn't know much about acting, but he was sure of what he wanted, and his political point of view was exemplary. I trusted him on this front. Actors laid themselves bare for this filmmaker's intensely committed political message; the Vietnam War, America's imperialism, and the hypocrisy of our nation inflicting violence upon the world.

Either way, I was completely shattered by his comments, completely dumbfounded by them too. His remarks had destroyed me. Then again, the character I was playing, Mr. Kovic, was also a destroyed human being, shattered by failure in life, augmented by his son's crippling injury. Both I and the character I was playing were both distraught and confused. Meanwhile, I internalized his remarks and simmered quietly. Hurt and pissed, I licked my wounds, vowing to prove my worth to the man. Beneath my rage, I had ultimate admiration for Oliver's political awareness and for his talent. That's what hurt the most. I had to do something special in my work, if only to settle the score with my director. The question was "how?" Acting skill perhaps? There wasn't much of that left in me. Manliness and all of its silly ramifications? Bullshit. Who the hell knew?

~~~

The greatest stroke of luck came that same afternoon, when the shooting schedule was altered by a downpour of rain. We were forced to shoot indoors a highly emotional scene that hadn't been originally planned for that day, when Ronnie, again played by Tom Cruise, comes home for the first time from Vietnam, paralyzed from the waist down. And Mr. Kovic, played by yours truly, witnesses his son again for the first time, wheelchair-bound and surely a heart-wrenching situation for any father. As I say, my original purpose was to please Oliver, but that hidden agenda was already a destined failure. He'd literally knocked me off my pins that morning. But Mr. Kovic, my character, would be off-balance too at the sight of his crippled son. The character would be in a state of absolute loss, the shock of seeing his kid in a wheelchair, unable to walk, wounded by senseless war that his father had given him permission to fight. What situation could better match my frame of mind, after being diminished by my director only an hour before?

~~~

In my emotional state, pulling off the emotional depth of the scene wouldn't be easy. I didn't want to fake the acting. No, I wanted to be 'real', whatever that meant. But since I didn't much care anymore because of my director's comments, nothing really mattered beyond finishing the damn job. It was a logical follow-up to relax about the whole goddam mess; a few more days and I'd leave Dallas and return home, where I'd pick up the pieces and restart my acting career by shooting my next film with a new director. I was already completely disoriented by Oliver's comments, but my vulnerability turned out to be a perfect fit for Mr. Kovic's state of mind. Who knew? I didn't. Who cared? In truth, my director had put a match under my ass to do what I was capable of doing, the son-of-a-bitch.

I accomplished just that. In my fragile state, both hurt and ashamed, it was a logical follow-up to relax about the whole goddamn mess. I willingly surrendered, threw my hands into the air, convinced that the film and my work in it were a lost cause.

"Just say the words quickly and get the hell out of here," became my silent mantra. Oliver Stone *(my surrogate father)*, was disappointed in my work, so nothing really mattered. I simply didn't give a damn. My surrender was complete. 'Not caring' was a perfect frame of mind for ultimate freedom in the work, especially after caring so very much. 'Caring' was what had inhibited me in the first place. 'Caring' so very much had tied me up in knots. When an actor doesn't give a damn, he has a shot at entering his own skin, a chance for total freedom. The wish to please is no longer a part of his thinking. 'Not caring' can be powerful, not caring and willing to try anything, simply because each momentary impulse makes logical sense, relaxation that comes with apathy.

Tom Cruise and I began the scene, and the result was a small miracle.

The most magical unleashing of courage overtook me. What was about to take place surprised everyone, I'm sure. Disheartened by Oliver only an hour before, my despair was palpable. There was no way of hiding it; no reason to hide it either. I didn't know it at the time, but Oliver might have chastised me with this in mind. He might have had a purpose. I don't know, but in my vulnerable state of mind, I simply said the lines; Tom Cruise paralyzed in his wheelchair and I, his broken-hearted father, both trying our best to communicate in the kid's bedroom with high school wrestling pictures and all the room's memorabilia from a healthy, athletic kid's past, knowing he would never walk again.

The unexpected happened. I was in touch with the situation immediately, first by hugging Tom Cruise, which I would never do in real life.

"Nice to have you home, Ronnie," came from my lips, a line improvised.

When I hugged Tom Cruise, I truly loved my son, as if the horror of my son's injury was really happening, my kid paralyzed in a wheelchair, the result of some stupid war, and since I didn't care much about what I was doing, everything just flowed out of me, emotions, tears, everything. During the entire scene, I loved the kid deeply. In truth, Tom Cruise was my son, my crippled son, and the horror of his injury from a stupid, senseless war had broken me. I turned my face to the wall when tears flooded my eyes, so my son wouldn't see his father crying. Words that hadn't been written in the script left my mouth. The lines simply said themselves, as my paralyzed son listened from his wheelchair. To adjust to each detail of the situation, I improvised more lines, each one spoken from the heart. It didn't matter that my improvised lines weren't Oliver's written words. I said what was necessary for Mr. Kovic to survive emotionally in that tragic situation. The pain of failing my director gave birth to whatever made sense in the scene. Oh, yes, I said the words from the script, but my improvised responses embellished the writing perfectly. Emotions were inspired by Oliver's nastiness and enhanced by my son sitting before me in a wheelchair, paralyzed by war, the tragedy of that, the hopelessness of that.

In my surrender, the father figure I was playing was in a state of profound loss from his son's injury, as I was in 'real life'. Faking emotion would have been impossible. I had no choice but to feel what I was feeling, so I simply felt what came my way and left it at that. My feelings had more to do with Oliver's comments than with my son's injury, but an audience wouldn't be aware of the difference.

Ego was not part of my performance on that rainy afternoon, obliterated as it had been by Oliver's nasty tirade and leaving only the character's unabashed innocence. Or was it my innocence? Didn't matter. Mr. Kovic was barely able to speak during the scene. He managed to substitute words of 'love for his son' with "I built some handles for you in the bathroom, Ronnie," to help his paralyzed boy go to the toilet, again improvised. I said whatever Mr. Kovic needed to say and the hell with it. My mood was such that I didn't care. And yet I did care so very much.

In my state of absolute surrender, I became a raw nerve on that rainy afternoon, vulnerable to every nuance the scene offered. My original purpose of pleasing my director was irrelevant. The quality of my performance was irrelevant too, as well as Oliver Stone's disapproval of my work. The words of the script didn't concern me, nor the direction in which the scene was going, nor the litany of accomplishments associated with Tom Cruise's glorious

198

acting career. I didn't care that he was a gigantic movie star. I didn't care that I was performing in a major motion picture either, and most importantly I didn't care what I was feeling. In fact, nothing mattered. I could do anything, and it wouldn't change Oliver's opinion of me. My son concerned me and not my acting ability. What could be a better state of mind?

This miracle continued for every take of the scene. What father wouldn't be sensitized by the fact that his son would never walk again? Fortunately I was unable to control myself every time we reshot it for three hours. This was a good thing. The horror of the entire situation was enough to arrive at Mr. Kovic's vulnerability. Once the cameras were rolling, the character could do no wrong; my body followed commands without question, without struggle, a condition that could be best described as a kind of 'non-thinking'. More tears flooded my eyes. I withheld them as much as possible, as any father would. In the presence of my paralyzed son, a supreme intelligence instructed me to communicate a father's love at a time of life-altering crisis, his boy permanently crippled by war. Whatever was happening was not the result of 'making it happen' but rather the result of some invisible muse's wish for it to happen. Every feeling flowed with ease, emotions, tears - everything I'd held within me for the duration of the shoot, maybe for the duration of my life. The situation before me was all I needed. I was perfectly at home with whatever emotion came and went. My fragility was enough; no need for more. My son's paralyzed legs were the horrible reality, along with his high school wrestling pictures and all the accoutrements of the boy's previous, promising, high school life, strewn throughout his bedroom.

Indeed, divine providence was with me on that fortuitous, rainy afternoon.

For the first time, I was completely at home with myself. Maybe 'outright pain' is required to "feel at home" with oneself. Who knows and who cares? The insecurity that had gripped my soul had given birth to a beautiful character stuck in his life, as was the case with Mr. Kovic, who had never accomplished much beyond holding down a job in a supermarket. Tentativeness characterized the man, as it did me on that fortuitous afternoon. My instability, related to Oliver's alleged low opinion of me, personified a common, working-class father intimidated by the world at large. My anxiety, my wish for perfection, my paralyzing shyness and outright fear flowed freely through the persona of Mr. Kovic. The horror of his son returning paralyzed from the Vietnam War was branded upon my entire being. There was little confidence in my work, but Mr. Kovic lacked confidence as well. I was unable to communicate with Oliver Stone, similar to Mr. Kovic's inability to communicate with his son. My inhibition and the character's inhibition were one and the same, not because of some acting skill I had suddenly acquired, but rather the result of supposedly having failed the illustrious Oliver Stone.

The work in *'Born on the Fourth of July'* was not derived from a sense of 'knowing' what I was doing. On the contrary, it came from 'not knowing'. Unexpected vulnerability came from a confused relationship with my director, more than from any preparation I could have mustered. A determined wish to prove my worth to Oliver Stone, who had betrayed my trust, was what submerged me into utmost grief for my son. Heightened sensitivity was born from being thrown off balance by his harsh statement that, "I hadn't done enough" and why hadn't I "scratched my cheek or something". The remark still irks me, a bullshit thing to say to any actor, but it worked, and I must thank the man someday. The emotionally complicated love bond between a father and son became crystal clear between Tom Cruise and me at the right time and place, thanks to Oliver's disapproval. The man opened my soul, yanked a great performance out of me, and I thank him for that.

Or was it his wisdom?

In fact, Oliver Stone is a superb director, on the same level as Joseph Chaikin, Tom O'Horgan, Michael Cimino, Neil Burger, Antoine Fuque, Liz LaCompt and Julian Beck. Oliver's political viewpoint parallels mine and often delves into the most unlikely of places to bring desired results, even if it means probing an actor's insecurities. Upsetting me that morning was his intention, I'm sure, if only to serve his film. I had been 'played' by my director, even tortured to some degree, in order for me to arrive at the proper level of vulnerability during an unexpected rainstorm that altered our filming schedule. Fortunately his conscious manipulation prepared me for the 'homecoming' scene. Fully aware that our schedule would be altered by rain, he consciously led me into the fragile state of mind so necessary to embody Mr. Kovic's life-altering situation. Today I'm grateful to the man for pushing me into unfamiliar, risky, emotional terrain at the sight of my paralyzed son, helplessly confined to a pitiful wheelchair.

I didn't mind having been being 'played' by Oliver. His manipulation was necessary to probe my sensitivity when cameras were rolling. As a male in a repressive society, I am often shut down to some degree. If left to my own devices, no doubt tension derived from 'fear of failing' might have blocked me. Oliver Stone's direct punch into my 'emotional gut' freed me from myself, exposed tormented feelings that might have otherwise have been locked. My son sitting in a wheelchair, paralyzed from the waist down, did the rest. Without Oliver's harsh words, my reaction to my son's injury might've been a contrived 'sadness' with a trembling lower lip or grim, stone-faced forbearance. I'm able to fake either easily. Maybe I'll always need an Oliver Stone to kick my ass for the sake of emotional freedom.

Self-imposed repression is a bitch sometimes.

Generally 'the unknown' is difficult for me. For much of my earlier life, I'd been programmed to cut off feelings, which is a useless stance today in my profession. Oliver knocked me off my pins on purpose, and he was right to do so. A few minutes of his scolding opened my soul to emotional truth appropriate for the scene between father and paralyzed son. Rather than trying so very hard to be 'real' by forcing feelings, he gave me the gift of emotional accessibility, thereby opening the floodgates that lasted throughout that afternoon shoot.

However, I wouldn't say the excellence of the performance was only a matter of luck. True, a rain storm had altered the shooting schedule immediately after Oliver's reprimand, but one must remember that for my entire adult life, thirty years of continuous performances had prepared me for the role of Mr.

Kovic. During those decades, I'd been searching to embody characters fully, continuously exploring the puzzle of acting. No, it wasn't just a matter of luck. Yes, my performance was derived from Oliver's manipulation for a specific result, but I too was expert at my craft enough to embrace the outcome of his manipulation, and rather than crumble, I moved through the scene with the grace necessary to allow a beautiful scene to unfold. What happened was 'pure gold' in the end. Intuitively I knew what to do once the cameras were rolling, in spite of my outrage with Oliver or maybe because of it. I'm not sure, and again, it doesn't matter.

The right set of demons did overtake me on that rainy afternoon, the result of which was one of my finest moments in film. The bedroom scene with Tom Cruise is in perfect marriage of caring and vulnerability rooted in a daunting family crisis. The stillness in the performance, the character's inability to express himself, his pain for Ronnie's injury all portrayed a man victimized by daunting life. The character's pain is palpable throughout the film - Mr. Kovic, a sensitive 'common man', frightened of the world at large.

As I say, Oliver Stone's tirade about my "not doing enough" was more effective than any preparation I could have mustered. His harsh comments motivated me to get off my ass and do what had to be done. Oliver knew my capabilities. That's why he'd hired me in the first place. He knew my talent and sensed the depth of my connection to his film. I'm grateful for the precipice from which I fell, grateful also for my director's wisdom to push me over that precipice into unknown territory and surely worth the price. As mentioned earlier, the man doesn't know much about acting, but he intuitively coaxes the best work from his cast, as was the case with both Carolyn Cava and Tom Cruise, who also gave their finest performances in *'Born on the Fourth of July'*.

~~~

After finishing shooting for the day, another actor in the cast, Ed Lauter, mentioned in front of Oliver and we had attended the same school. Thinking Ed was referring to high school, Oliver

202

was baffled by Ed's remark and asked, "What high school?" Ed interjected that we both had attended Yale University, at which point Oliver did a double-take and exclaimed, "You went to Yale?" as if it couldn't possibly be true. "I thought you never went to college," he gasped without thinking. Apparently, he'd been under the impression that I was afflicted with the same disadvantages as Mr. Kovic, a shy, uneducated man, barely making a living by working in a supermarket. From Oliver's view, I had fully personified Mr. Kovic's 'working class', uneducated persona and not only when acting the role.

When we finished shooting *'Born on the Fourth of July'*, Oliver placed his hand on my shoulder in a fatherly fashion and complimented my work. His comments were genuine, and they were appreciated fully. I was living in the skin of the character by then, and I valued his sincerity, after which we both went our separate ways - twelve weeks well spent for both of us. I saw him once again, but that's another story.

The film was a huge success.

After *'Born on the Fourth of July'* was released, the stakes became higher. Playing a main character both in Michael Cimino and Oliver Stone films validated my film career. I opened myself to the world more and achieved a little here and there, one film upon another, *"The Chamber" with Gene Hackman, "Falling Down" with Robert Duvall "Training Day," with Denzel Washington, "The Ref," "Flubber" with Robin Williams, "Walk Hard" with Susan Serandon and Sean Penn, "Interview with the Assassin,"* in which I played the leading role. Success became enjoyable. I was an actor to respect. Strangers knew my name and approached me to shake my hand, telling me they were fans. After twenty years of struggle as a New York stage actor, I was in the movies, mingling with the stars, rubbing elbows with figures who were bigger than life, Tom Cruise, Oliver Stone, Gene Hackman, Michael Cimino, Mickey Rourke, all accomplished actors. That gave me the strength I needed to delve into unknown areas. Performing was less foreboding. I was one of the normal folk, a man like any other man but different too, considering my profession that exposed me to vast audiences. Finally I was a legitimate film actor after twenty-three years of stage.

How naïve I was.

Twenty years after I shot the film, a woman stopped me in an airport after recognizing me from Oliver Stone's *'Born on the Fourth of July'*. I'd achieved fame in her eyes. But I was no longer a young actor eager for approval. Notoriety didn't affect me much, although I appreciated her kindness. I was a seventy-one-year old man with a fifty-year acting career behind him and somewhat inured to the notion of fame. She didn't know who I really was, having never read or seen any of my plays.

John C. Riley, Walk Hard,

The Wrong Kiiiid Died

Published March 2020 edition of 'Rosebud Anthology'

~ ~ ~

Four o'clock in the morning before the world wakes up; freshness in the air, the light beginning to peek through the darkness of night, headlights on, radio off. Mumbling my lines, I drive reasonably fast. Sixty miles per hour is reasonably fast; no tickets for me. Wind tossing my hair, gray by now, slight elevation of spirit, a sense of purpose in the air, driving to work, not any kind of work, film work, the movie business, so different from the usual notion of work, offers a certain degree of adventure that most jobs do not. Meanwhile, plenty of time, nerves aren't frazzled. That's a good thing; no worries on that front, not a chance of caving in on this one. No, sir, when it comes to the movie business, I'm good under pressure, always come through in a 'pinch'.

The drive a bit long, all the way to San Pedro, a drive to remember at four in the morning; a certain calm with being on time, an important part of the creative team; nice to belong. Never was one to rebel, except when it came to this acting thing; insisted upon a profession that guaranteed personal freedom. That took strength; lots of part time jobs and bouts of self-doubt along the way; oh, yes, plenty of strength. Drilling these words early this morning just to be sure. Won't be much to this day, just look John C. Reilly smack in the eye, as the character would, say the lines and smile once in a while; shoot the scene and go home, nothing out of the ordinary. A good time will be had by all.

"All right, I'll bite. Whatchawanna talk about?"

Mumbling words as I drive with the rural accent of the character I'll play. I know the words, but that's my way, the endless drilling; useful to a point; always know my words.

How did this happen? How did I, of all people, become confident in the face of movie work? Patience with the world is the answer, patience with the world and forgetting about Marlon Brando. All actors imitated Brando during the fifties, myself included. Would Marlon do this? Would Marlon do that? But no more Marlon Brando for me; living in my own skin is enough.

Zipping by cars, following trucks, watching for signs - the bridge, the bridge, must turn at the bridge, still The hammering away at my lines that I'll never forget and finally arrive at the Los Angeles waterfront, where we'll shoot. People greeting me warmly, nice people, including the director, Jake Kasden, a nice guy. I respect him - nothing I wouldn't do for this guy. We'll make a great film, working as a team. It was different when I shot *"Born on the Fourth of July"*. Worry controlled me then of not being up to the task, of not having the goods, too much doubt about pleasing Oliver Stone and wanting so damned much to do everything right. Probably the most vulnerable work I ever did in a film, when I think about it, played Tom Cruise's father and executed one brilliant scene that I'll never forget. Yeah, my work was excellent in that film. What a miracle, considering the struggle involved.

Today things have changed. My own man today, stable and balanced. I actually feel good about myself. Oliver Stone was tough. But Jake Kasden is comfortable, and by luck, this waterfront reminds me of Manhattan's Pier Twenty-eight years ago, when for a day's pay, I unloaded boxes of fruit off barges on the Hudson River; a longshoreman then and tough to the ways of New York City survival. Made it out of that situation too, unloading fruit from boxcars with black men built strong as hell for the work. White guys too, guys like me, hippies trying to find their way. I found my way. Here I am, playing a great role in a John C. Reilly film, *"Walk Hard,"* wind blowing my gray hair - made it out of the docks, raising four kids with money in the bank, money in my pocket. Two of them graduated from college so far with two more to go. Yeah, I'm my own man today, my own man. I was my own man when I worked on the docks too, had a dream then that actually came true.

Eating ham, cheese and egg on an English muffin Sitting on a pillowed couch in my Winnebago next - about to act in a scene with John C. Reilly, just the two of us, tired but in pretty good shape, a day like any other, no, nothing different here. Simply do the work and have done with it. Yup, a working actor, well-prepared and fully balanced in a business riddled with insecurity, but nothing to fear today. I know the scene inside-out, having studied it with an acting coach. Confided everything in that kind woman, nervousness, fears and the whole nine yards; took a load off my mind. My wardrobe finally arrives, while chomping a delicious ham, cheese and egg sandwich on an English muffin, still going over lines by rote, loudly practicing the rural accent of the character with hints of emotion. Seems unnecessary to drill the lines when I know them so well, but no, drilling is my way and my way works up to a point. I'm even skilled at times, not like the greats, of course, but definitely relaxed when I do a role, yup, absolute professionalism and always sure of my lines. The complexity of the characters I play is usually a crap shoot, but that's alright with me. "Do the best I can" is my motto nowadays.

"The wrong kiiiiiid died!" comes out of my mouth for good measure with a thick southern accent.

Instructions come soon enough from a pretty 'assistant director', who walks me to "makeup and hair", where I gotta listen to endless chatter from the makeup lady, who has her own set of problems. Everyone has problems. Finally I'm placed on a set for the first scene, sitting next to a black guy from *'Saturday Nite Live'*, quietly delivering my little speech under my breath that I'm about to shoot with John C. Reilly. The director, Jake Kasdan, talks about the scene before we shoot. John C. Reilly and I run through the lines. We both know the words, won't be a problem with the words, well-written too. Both of us take to the scene immediately. John and I talk a little, getting to know each other type stuff, "How old are your kids?" "Where do they go to school?" – nothing intimate, a few 'macho' comments passed between us to show we're not gay, just to make that clear, since we have to hug in the scene. Men do what they have to do to maintain boundaries, to show they're 'real men'. The whole thing is a bore. I had a gay mother once, whom I loved very much, so we don't have to go through that nonsense, but John doesn't know anything about my mother. No, mother won't be brought up in this setting.

John and I have no difficulty along those lines anyway, both of us totally focused on the work. He's a perfectionist, whereas I come well prepared but will accept any result that feels right - more lenient, perhaps, maybe because I'm older. Age has its advantages, can cut myself slack, rather than pushing all the time - more comfortable with myself than I was when I was young. John is riding high right now, so he wants his work to be great. He's a talented man, doesn't have to worry. God bless him. I like him. He's a good man. When he sees my sunburned bald spot, he calls for an umbrella to cover my head. How nice. How kind of him.

The sun is coming out fully all of a sudden, so I get rid of my thermal shirt. Don't want to be hot, but my microphone is connected to the damned shirt, so I mess the whole thing up, the embarrassment of the moment smoothed over by the sound technician, who allows me to put my outer flannels on with the reattached microphone, but not before I've exposed my spreading waistline that I try to suck in; hope John and Jake don't see my little belly, a fat movie star, not too impressive. With the bald spot already noticeable, my little fat belly would be the end. Then again, what the heck, I'm too old to be embarrassed by stuff like that.

John C. Riley is the star so they shoot him first. I'll be last when I'm drained of energy. That's the way it goes when you're not the star. I don't mind, don't hold it against him, trying to cooperate in every way possible. Playing his father is enough glory for me. If they ask me to pick up cues, I do it. If John wants the scene to be more emotional, I show a little feeling. I'm flexible. The sun is hot, but tolerable. We begin John's half of the scene, run through it without a hitch. John seems unhappy. I'm cautious not to interrupt his train of thought between takes. He's a perfectionist. I'm simply happy to be acting to the best of my ability. The best of my ability seems enough. Why ask for more? John is pushing for something better. He's a good actor, so I go along with him. More personal, he wants his work to be more personal.

Meanwhile the sun is draining my energy. My scalp hurts by now; the makeup lady spraying sun-block onto my bald spot. I'm definitely getting weaker. Hours of shooting, all of it with the camera on John C. Reilly, none of it on me; I don't mind; energy still strong enough to maintain a solid front. I'm more than willing and refuse to show signs of weakness in between takes. John is pushing by now. Again, "coming to tears" seems the issue, complaining that we should be shooting the scene on a sound stage without helicopters and passing motor boats interfering with sound quality. The seagulls make too much noise. Stopping every minute for passing boats, John seems upset. The crew's movement bothers him, interruptions, one after another, stopping, starting from the top of the scene. Our star finally does come to tears, after pushing over and over again for a deeper emotional connection. I'm off camera, so I'm not pushing, simply trying my best. That's all I care about, old and happy just being here and working with this guy. He's nice to me, very considerate, the sun hotter than hell on my burned bald spot; energy seeping out of me like blazes.

~~~

Finally, after our tenth take, John C. Reilly turns in a brilliant performance, so we take a lunch break. My end of the scene will be shot after lunch. I've gotta be ready for that. The seagulls are still making a lot of noise, and I sit next to the young, handsome black guy on *'Saturday Nite Live'*, and he's trying to be cool, and I'm still drilling my lines quietly, so he doesn't hear, but it's hot and I'm tired and trying to be professional, mumbling my words and never missing a beat, not one beat and a little bit pissed about the heat and worrying about my performance after lunch and stuff. Got to remind myself that I have as much going for myself as anyone here, but sometimes I don't see it that way, as much as I try to appear healthy with therapists and acting coaches and what have you, trying to get through it all with anything available that might bolster confidence, and meanwhile the lines are too familiar now for any kind of freshness. I've said them too goddamn much with this cool, calm and collected fella, eating lunch next to me from *'Saturday Nite Live'* who's completely unflappable *(I like that word unflappable)* with my little attempts at being funny, saying at one point, "I'm wasting my youth on this goddamn scene," which is funny, because I am sixty-eight years old and my youth is obviously gone. The *'Saturday Nite Live'* guy laughs a little, but has this quizzical look in his eye, as if I were really imagining myself to be young, which I am at heart, but certainly the *'Saturday Nite Live'* guy must realize that I'm aware that I'm relatively ancient compared to this young *'Saturday Nite Live'* guy, who slightly condescends to me on the basis of our age difference, and I'm feeling all this 'stuff' about this guy, as I'm acting out my lines to myself a little too loud and with a bit too much muscle going on with gestures and everything, all the time delivering the words quietly to myself.

With all this going on in my head, we talk about New York City; that is, I and the black guy from *'Saturday Nite Live'*, and he tells me he bought a house in Tarrytown, New York, which indicates he's made some money, which is truly an accomplishment, given how few roles are available for black actors. He must be awfully talented; that is, on *'Saturday Night Live'* and all. Of course, I can't help but to compare my career with his. It's

210

inevitable that would happen when I think about it. We're both actors. "Who is more successful?" type of thing. It's hard to say, and who cares anyway? He's an actor from *'Saturday Night Live'*, so the guy has an identity, which I didn't at his age. At least I think I didn't. I probably did. But being on *'Saturday Night Live'* at his age is really something, compared to where I was at his age. Why at his age, I was completely unknown to the general public, had no money and little, if any success and was completely out of it, as far as a career was concerned. I resisted success when I was his age, while he's embracing success, and I'm fascinated by what he thinks of me. Does he respect me? Does he like me? I imagine he's completely unaffected by me, so superior when he looks at me, as if he's already sized me up. I could care less. Haughtiness is a bore.

After John C. Riley turns in a brilliant performance, the sun has taken its toll; the effects of dehydration are showing. My energy is waning, but I'm determined to perform well after lunch, when the camera will be on me. The words don't feel fresh after saying them so many times, and I'm tempted to ask the *'Saturday Nite Live'* guy if I'm believable, which wouldn't be right, since people are paying me to do a job and not to ask some *'Saturday Nite Live'* guy how to act. Besides, I don't want to tip my hand that I don't know what I'm doing, which I do, but every passing minute brings new questions about the words I'm saying, and meanwhile the *'Saturday Nite Live'* guy next to me has no words and sits in the heat calmly, as if he really knows what he's doing, which may be the case, and all the time I'm trying to be a liberal and definitely not a racist, which I suspect we all are without knowing it, to some degree anyway, even in the *'Saturday Nite Live'* guy's case, but, as I say, it's hot, real hot, and I have white skin, very white that burns in the sun, compared to the black guy next to me, who's on *'Saturday Nite Live'*, so he must be very talented. At least he seems calm compared to me, but what do I know; that is, aside from my lines that I've drilled into my head like a Russian KGB.

I don't know why I said that. Just had to, I guess.

~~~

My lunch is finished and it's time to shoot my end of the scene. Giving it everything I have, everything at stake here, my career, my life, my heart, my soul, my kids and my wife, all expect the best from me. I really want to come through for them, for me too, but mostly for them. We've already been directed, so I have some idea about what to do during my first take, after which. Jake says, "Great!" as he always does, supportive guy, encouraging me to feel good about myself as a man, not just as an actor, but as a man with thoughts and feelings that count. I do everything possible to make him happy. The wind is blowing my hair every which way but can't worry about that. I'm a movie star for a brief moment, not Bert Lancaster, but plain old me, attempting my best under these circumstances with the sun beating down on my bald spot. I don't make a fuss about it. Creating a fuss over my sunburned bald spot wouldn't do much good anyway. Doing the work well and not my bald spot is what counts to make a good movie, which would benefit all of us. That's enough, isn't it? I'm not asking for more than that. The wind is tossing my locks and the vast space out there of sea, miles of sea bordered by an enclave of harbor where the water is deep enough to accommodate huge cargo ships that I don't have to unload, as I did in my youth. The sun on my bald head, sunburned; energy draining out of me, half-cooked by the hot sun, half-cooked and still fighting for my career, still fighting to fulfill the best of who I am, still fighting to say the words the way Jake Kasden thinks they should be said.

Struggle slowly turns to joy, as John and I work in unison, focusing intently to create a brilliant scene between father and son under the hot sun. Energy is draining out of me.

"I love you, Dewey!!!"

Now that I'm on camera I say the words with all my heart and soul. What a cliché. Nonetheless, it's true, and yes, indeed, I really do love John C. Reilly at this moment, while we're performing our father and son scene. I do love him as a father would love his son, more than anyone in the world, at least for the moment. Love has become a major part of our work together, a solid bond of love based upon our mutual wish to create a film that is beautiful, to make something glorious that holds together in the public eye as viable art. We are unified, John and I, in a mutual endeavor of creating a relationship, the universal father and son for every audience to share. We are the clay, from which our director will mold a beautiful metaphor of family relationships, while the hot sun beats down on my bald spot, sapping energy out of me, but who cares about that? We actors are fulfilled as we create. Freedom of spirit abounds. Life runs fully through our veins. We are truly alive.

"The wrong kiiiiiiiiid died!"

My southern accent rehearsed hundreds of times, letter perfect, and then a moment to notice how tired I am and how the wind is blowing the unruly ends of my gray hair. I'm completely drained, but the scene isn't finished yet. I still have to be cut in half by some freak accident involving the sailboat's boom or a line of cable or something. My body will be severed, leaving my upper torso separated from my lower torso, and then deliver another speech about how my son shouldn't feel guilty about having killed three relatives.

"Don't go beating yourself up because you killed three relatives!!!"

It's a comedy, so the audience will laugh at that line.

I'm weak from the sun, while the special effects man builds an apparatus for my lower half to be hidden beneath the deck of the sailboat, giving the impression that my body will be cut in half. The apparatus is simple enough, a hole cut through a wooden board that resembles the floor of the boat. Only my upper half will be seen, bordered by fake blood. Next to me, my severed legs stand upright on the deck, as if the cutting was clean and crisp, severed like a lean slice of baloney. The position of my legs is uncomfortable beneath the deck, forcing all of my weight to lean heavily against the edge of the wooden board. I don't let on though, as long as we get this 'cutting me in half' business over with quickly.

God, what an adventure this acting profession is!!!

The relentless heat of the sun really getting to me, after ten hours of shooting. John is generous, as he has been all day, making sure drinking water and an umbrella are available. Our work stops again. Another freighter passing through the harbor, and I wonder where it's going; a tourist cruiser, a gigantic ship, designed for pleasure - ship cruises always a bore to me and prefer to be in this hole, pretending I've been cut in half. It's more fun, and when it's over, I'll be visible to the public, a little bit famous, just a little bit, but now my body and mind are exhausted from shooting for ten and a half hours and show no signs of weakness, although my bald spot is completely red, according to John. Too late, the makeup artist sprays more sun block on the patch of bare skin to prevent more severe sunburn. I recite my death speech over and over, ten times, twenty times, the sun having taken its toll; the effects of dehydration showing, energy waning, but I'm determined to do the damn scene well.

Yes, back to the scene again; I mumble my words over and over again before we begin.

"Don't you feel guilty about this, Dewey? I still love you."

And I do love you, John C. Reilly, just as I loved Tom Cruise when creating the homecoming scene in *'Born on the Fourth Of July'*, seeing him for the first time paralyzed, and Ashton Krutcher for our father-son scene in *'Just Married'*. I'm Hollywood's father of movie stars, the paradigm of fatherhood for middle-America, the man who fulfills the image of a model, male parent, according to all the directors in Hollywood. Well, maybe not all, but three or four or maybe even seven or eight; Tim Olaphant's father in the TV series, *'Justified'*. Brad Pitt and I worked well together. I was his father-in-law, which is almost like being his father. Charlie Sheen, Mickey Rourke, Robert Duvall. He's a great one, although I wasn't his father. I forget the rest. The wind is blowing what is left of my hair and observing this expanse of waterfront that empties into a vast sea that extends all the way to China. Maybe I'll shoot a movie in China someday with John C. Reilly and Oliver Stone, who will pull my best work out of me by telling me I'm "not doing enough", whatever that means. Oliver Stone, John C. Riley and I have chemistry and mutual respect enough to create a great film in China.

"I still love you, Dewey!!!"

214

The line finishes the scene, and I climb off the boat that feels like a freaking trampoline, start talking to a sharp-looking girl for a few minutes, lovely girl, but too young for me. John C. Reilly cries out, "That was awesome," a bit of an exaggeration, but he's a kind and generous man. Hope we did something good together for both of our sakes. Maybe we're both perfectionists, after all. I'll probably be recognized from this picture in the gym or somewhere. Maybe this will be my last movie. Maybe I'm not so good in this one. I gave it my best shot, but maybe that's not good enough. To know what I'm doing is the real issue, to be a professional. Sometimes I'm too eager, too enthusiastic, and I lose the forest for the trees. Mustn't lose sight of what I'm doing. Must be truthful in my work, must be truthful.

I wonder what 'truthful' really means.

Steel City Premiere

2009 Independent Spirit Award *Nomination*,
Best Supporting Actor

My cleaned and pressed sport coat crinkles in the back seat of a limousine that rolls elegantly through the Los Angeles streets; a chauffeur, no less, with a British accent to add a touch of style. Anything more that might come my way is icing on the cake. A good book by Richard Wright to read on the plane finishes the picture. The producers paid for the flight and a room at a Las Vegas hotel. My work in the film, *'Steel City'*, has garnished me an *'Independent Spirit Award'* nomination for *'Best Supporting Actor in a Feature'*. I ride on the crest of the wave like a Hollywood movie star. Not a star really, but at very least a respected, journeyman actor who knows his craft and, "Don't bump into the furniture while you're at it!" The game is about over with so few years left. I've made peace with gray memories of youth, resulting in a solid position in my profession, and subsequently 'making it' by the time I was middle-aged. I've done it all, slowly but surely in my dysfunctional, bumbling fashion that almost ended before it began.

With my limousine approaching the airport in record time, the chauffeur has accomplished his mission. He is rewarded by a sizeable tip of twenty dollars, and I, bouncing into the terminal, followed by a short wait, after which I embark. Southwest Airlines offers a glass of apple juice and a bag of peanuts before landing an hour later.

Once off the plane, I'm picked up by another driver and whisked to the Palms hotel, arrayed with slot machines, fast food and an assortment of goodies that I dare not indulge. Life is good with a Visa Card stashed in my wallet in case of emergency. I'll avoid the pitfalls of having wads of cash in my pocket. I'm not in Las Vegas to spend money. I check in and bed down for an hour in front of the television that floods the room with news reports of bad things happening in the world. Closing my eyes, I drift off to sleep, and upon waking a short time later, all seems a dream, having forgotten where I am.

My cell phone; must not forget my cell! Call a friend perhaps to announce my nomination. Not many friends left to chat. Life is more private than it was in my youth. No matter, the fire is still there. I'll carry on regardless. A film premier in Las Vegas suits me, after living barely above the poverty line during my twenties and thirties. No sense dwelling upon the past. Las Vegas waits for me with all of its glamorous trappings.

Up then and quickly downstairs. Brightly lit décor of the main lobby suggests the promise of instantaneous wealth for an eager tourist population with its assortment of protruding bellies and wide asses. Chain-smoking mannequins operate an array of one-arm bandits, eagerly eyeballing the line-up of little pineapples and peaches - always one missing and throw another dollar into the slot. They're willing to bet it all on machines that give nothing in return. The entire city promises fortunes that will never be won.

I wait for six-thirty when the red carpet event will take place in front of photographers and reporters gathered on the other side of a golden rope; nerves on edge but experienced enough not to rehearse, hoping to present myself favorably, seasoned, as I am, to the publicity game. Words will come when the time arrives on the red carpet. I'll pose for reporters' cameras like an old pro. It's necessary to arrive well-dressed, my suit well-tailored with a favorite silk tie, given by my father-in-law. Shoes click when I walk, and I've lost weight lately which bolsters confidence. Plainly I look great, a sharp contrast to my character in the film. What more can I ask? It's all good, my arrival on time and a decent film that portrays me in a leading role.

"Mr. Barry, look over here." "Give us a look, Raymond." An interview in front of a video camera follows, explaining how excited I am, "to appear in such a great film with great direction and great acting and marvelous writing *(a word I never use)*," as if I really mean what I'm saying. I'm expected to tell the reporter that I love the frills of Las Vegas when I really do not, that it is a great place to visit, when it really is not, and that I cannot think of a better place to have a premier of a movie, which I certainly can, namely, New York City and not Las Vegas with its promise of a sharp headache and an empty wallet at the end of the night.

I don't 'make nice' to the interviewer when it comes to the city of Las Vegas and admit that I have no plans to party but expect to call my wife before going to bed soon after the event reaches its end. After a few moments, the woman who interviews me seems resigned to that fact that I'm going to say the truth, regardless of her prompting, avoiding my reaction to her 'fair city' with flashbulbs popping and constant yelling, "Mr. Barry, over here." Shyness is not an issue anymore, nor is fear. Those days are over. All obstacles in my life have been met face to face. Self-pride is intact from taking the hits and repeatedly returning for more. I've had enough punishment to last a lifetime. Well-being and health represent who I am today and can't ask for more.

218

Meanwhile, the talented director, Brian Jun, who is slightly drunk, invites me to dinner in a restaurant some thirty floors up, along with another actor in the film, who seems full of himself, not to overlook his overweight wife, who has bourn him two children. The poor kids apparently are home-schooled by the obnoxious actor and his fat wife, which may mean they are not schooled at all. Both parents are remarkably stupid and unaware of how limited they are, trying so very hard to give the impression of God knows what.

Upon perusing the menu, the couple seems shy about ordering food. That should give me a clue to leave the restaurant at once. The menu is expensive to be sure. I cannot read the prices without my glasses. After eating their share of the meal, three of their party *(including the blow-hard actor)* skip out on the bill, claiming they have to attend a "question and answer session" before the screening of the film. They leave me sitting with his overweight wife and a stranger, who seems knowledgeable about astrology. Of course, I'm the 'big spender from the East', picking up the tab to the tune of one hundred and ninety-six dollars, plus tip of forty dollars, which is only half the bill, since the astrologer guy pays half as well. The rip-off amounts to two hundred and forty dollars for a lobster salad and three glasses of mineral water. The wife of the blowhard actor, who, as I say, has skipped out on the bill, pays nothing, but she does offer a "Thank you", when meals are paid.

After leaving the rip-off restaurant, I proceed to the theater. I see myself in the film, *'Steel City'* and almost come to tears twice. The film's depiction of human pathos, failure, misunderstanding and cruelty in the face of humanity's harshness touches me. Brian Jun is a hell of a director and writer. He's created the entire film after writing and casting it. My hat's off to the young man. I'm the old guy in the film, as I am the old guy in my current television series, *'Justified'*. Playing the so-called 'old guy' brings me back to the time, when I was a young 'stud' not quite ready for success and too concerned with 'doing it right'. I wanted to be 'good,' whatever the notion of 'good' meant. 'Good' to whom, after all? I am 'good' in *'Steel City'*, but it makes life easier to simply watch and forget how I come across. Judgment doesn't add much to the experience, having done my best, and once the work was finished, nothing more to be done. The work or art, whatever one may call it, is enjoyable, especially when I don't give a damned about what folks think. My colleagues, who go through the same nonsense, generally will say whatever is necessary to please anyway, so who cares what they say?

As I watch the film, I realize that acceptance of myself came without announcement at some invisible point during a fifty year span. Self-judgment simply evaporated suddenly. I cared too much earlier in the game and gradually cared less, until relaxation followed. Oh, yes, waves of anxiety bombard me occasionally, bringing me to my knees, helpless, defeated and wondering how I got there. Defeat is profound for its ultimate surrender and subsequent state of relaxation. Suicide never enters the picture. I'm so close to death anyway. Why hurry the process? It will arrive in due time. Surrender is what fascinates me, surrender that involves not caring so much, as is the case when I watch the premier of *'Steel City'*. I see myself performing and refuse to judge the tightness in my jaw, the flaccid dewlap on my neck, the baldness on the back of my head or the beginnings of jowl formation hanging from my cheeks. None of it matters. It is all me, and all of it is acceptable.

The skill of the other actors and Brian Jun's direction at times overshadows mine. They are highly watchable, whereas I'm not particularly interesting to myself. That disassociation is perfect. Their performances take me on a sensitive journey of love, loyalty and rejection. The lead male, who plays my nephew, is absolutely beautiful, both physically and emotionally. I care for him as I become more engrossed in the plot. I love him as I watch and care about what is happening to the boy. He becomes my hero, and I wish for his return whenever he leaves the screen.

Contrarily I see little of interest when I appear, although my skill is visible. That's fine. I don't need to be top dog. I've been nominated for an *'Independent Spirit Award'* for my performance. That's enough. The other actors deserve the attention. I don't need attention. Attention is available without trying. 'Trying' is no longer necessary. I shall not try. Being is enough. From 'being' comes enjoyment of all life. Being at one with the world is enough. That so-called 'oneness' with life has not been fully accomplished in my case - almost but not fully. But at least, I seem to deal gracefully with whatever confronts me.

When the film ends, I take an early exit, meeting the director's lawyer, who compliments my performance and offers pleasant conversation. Feeling liked and accepted for my work, I leave content, somewhat fulfilled, well respected and even honored by people's reaction to the artistic accomplishment of Brian Jun's film, as well as to the quality of my work.

The evening is topped off in a discotheque on the ground floor, a human zoo with music so loud and girls half-nude dancing on raised platforms above a drunken audience below. I'm getting the VIP treatment with industry people shaking my hand, offering their cards to get in touch and a host guiding me to a table, as if I cannot find it myself, which I probably couldn't with the thick press of so many bodies. I smile too often, careful not to reveal how desirable the waitresses are with their brown-tanned bodies created for love. My enjoyment is all I have to offer with my diminished sexual prowess. No argument there. I had my deserts along the way, nothing to complain about, take what is available and be satisfied. Meanwhile the dancing girls with their wiggling behinds display themselves for my pleasure.

The director's parents sit across from me, absorbing the atmosphere like voyeurs in Dante's Inferno. This is a Catholic couple about my age, who seem to arrive at the most unlikely of occasions, at bacchanalian parties mostly, when their director son is celebrating the success of his film. They also appeared at Sundance where Brian Jun's film had been accepted as part of the competition. That too was a mob scene, designed for the young at heart, preoccupied with getting laid and smoking crack cocaine. Needless to say the director's uninvited parents were out of place then, as they seem to be tonight. The threat of their boy losing himself to a world totally alien to 'Catholic family values' no doubt have something to do with their unexpected arrival at this nightmarish mob scene, the so-called 'premier' in Las Vegas, where prostitution and gambling are an integral part of everyday life, and half-clad girls dance their hearts out to the rhythm of heavy metal rock played so loudly that conversation is obliterated by its pounding reverberation.

Talk of any kind is useless in such a setting. Sex and dance and getting high are the commodities valued here. The director's parents bear expressions of total bewilderment. They seem paralyzed to some degree, their stone faces expressionless, while bombarded by visual and auditory assault from every angle. Their faces scream out for a graceful exit, but they dare not desert their beloved director son, who is drunk by this time, embracing his girlfriend, equally as drunk, both of them sticking their tongues into each other's mouths beneath the gyrating disco dancers above, who pump the air vigorously with their neat little crotches barely covered by a scant pair of panties revealing an ample view of flesh.

The Catholic couple hovers in the general vicinity of their son. They appear lost in a crowd that has nothing in common with sixty-year-old Catholic parents of a son, who makes films about sex and drugs. If I were in their vicinity, they would have someone to communicate. In the case of Brian Jun's father, the fellow is a bit younger than I and often rails on and on about the construction business, a subject about which I know little, aside from the memory of a part-time New York City laboring job that provided sustenance during my thirties. That memory leaves me with little interest in the subject. Fortunately, the music is so loud and the closely packed bodies create a barrier between the director's parents and me. Communication of any kind in this throng of disco music and shouting voices seems futile, and I am grateful for that.

Meanwhile, I entertain myself by fantasizing about the tanned waitress with her silver skirt and brown, bare stomach, evenly muscled up to her full breasts scantily covered by a halter that barely hangs from her shoulders. She is clad for the pleasure of her customers, who rarely tip for her efforts. So crowded and so loud is the room that the prospect of tipping is ignored in this anonymous zoo. Waitress and crowd blend into one, each body the same as the next, one gray shape no different than another. The waitress can barely distinguish one tipping customer from a non-tipping customer. I represent the latter category. In fact, I order nothing. Having been beaten for two hundred and forty dollars for a shrimp salad and three glasses of mineral water, I've already donated an ample sum to the establishment.

An enthusiastic expression is plastered on my face, as I observe the panorama of bodies, inundated by loud music and voices shouting to be heard. I'm drinking mineral water and appear satisfied, as if the celebration appeals to me, which it doesn't really; that is, with the one exception of the waitress's lithe, nubile body now bending toward the table, serving drinks below the dancing, scantily-clad girls on the platform above. From appearances, the director's father lusts for the waitress in the middle of this bacchanalian scene. He's ashamed to tip his hand, while sitting next to his overweight wife of some thirty years. The visual assault of the sexy waitress' round rear-end thrust into his face, when she leans over to serve drinks, is too much ass for the man. Caught, as he is, by sheer lust on the one hand and responsibility towards his homely spouse on the other, what is he to do but politely stare, and perhaps record a few savory fantasies?

After retiring to my room by midnight, I watch television and gradually fall asleep with the beginnings of a headache over one eye. I didn't win the *'Independent Spirit Award' for 'Best Supporting Actor'*.

Next time maybe. It's okay. My nomination was enough.

Stanley Kramer, Legend Award

Los Angeles, California, August 2009

I stand on stage embarrassed by the applause. My wife and daughter are here, thank goodness. One can't go far without a wife and a daughter backing me up. Their presence matters. I've dressed for the occasion. That was the least I could do. The director is a little pissed that I'm not particularly enamored with his film, *"Charlie Valentine"*, a cheapened version of Tarantino's *"Reservoir Dogs"* with too much shooting and far too much killing. The film bored me, as I watched it, and also bored with the director right from the beginning of the shoot, a self-congratulating man with little by way of imagination. But I can forgive him for that.

Thank God for my daughter and my wife. They both look beautiful. Think of it, *'The Stanley Kramer Legend Award'*. I'm presumably a 'legend' now. Bathed in applause, I am both embarrassed and frightened of saying the wrong thing. The applause is gratifying. Then again, maybe anything I say is appropriate when receiving the *'Stanley Kramer Legend Award'*. The audience stands up in my behalf. How impressed I am; the size of the crowd, the mass of bodies before me, and I am expected to make a speech, a few words of appreciation for selecting me as their living 'legend'.

"I've been doin' it for fifty years," I say.

The crowd again applauds. When they do so, my heart jumps up into my mouth. It wouldn't be beyond me to bolt out of the room at a moment's notice. Somehow I'll be fine beneath this blanket of trepidation. Things won't get out of hand. I'll be all right under the glaze of lights. I give my short speech, after thanking them for their applause, explaining that I am grateful for their generosity. A few words are necessary to smooth things out a bit, to show I am humbled by the occasion. The more the audience applauds, the more I am willing to speak. I feel more confident. A rush of thoughts come to me - what to say? What to say? I open my mouth and words are formed. I don't quite realize what I'm saying, although the words are audible, phrase by phrase.

"Actors are a strange bunch and performing itself is a 'weird' thing to do," I say. "One day a professor at Brown University asked me to be in a play. I did the play without knowing what a play was, let alone act in one, which I did badly."

The audience laughs.

"But that didn't matter. I was oblivious to what I was getting myself into, oblivious to the complexities of acting; that is, what was involved to act, the nerves, the fear, the satisfaction involved when things went well. I didn't know what real struggle was then. I had little fear during those innocent days, but now, when receiving this award, I'm scared, particularly about what to say to you all."

The audience applauds again.

"Actors love trophies, plaques and framed certificates that have written on them the celebrated actor's name, as well as the year and words that describe the title of the award and so on," I say. "The actor hangs the award on his wall to be reminded that he or she is a so-called 'legend', whenever there is doubt about his purpose in the world. Awards never mention the general angst with which an actor lives on a daily basis. Awards are a means of pretending that things are normal when doubt is always prevalent. But doubt is part of the job."

"There has never been an award for 'doubt', at least not as far as I know."

The audience howls with laughter. The night is a grand success.

~~~

My career began in one place and arrived at another by daring to stay the course when things were going badly. I refused to surrender. That's how it is with actors who stay in the so-called "business". For those who stay the course, there is no choice. There certainly was no choice for me. I was going to live my life as an actor regardless of the outcome, regardless of whether the profession would accept me. Thoughts of rejection, never entered my mind, and when rejection came, I had to make a buck. I opted to do part time jobs to survive, as if it were an anomaly, as if it were not I who was being rejected by the world of theater. That technique of pushing aside the 'lean times' whenever it came into the picture and relating to failure as if it were not happening to the so-called "real me" has served me well.

I endured adversity. It would have been so easy to do something else with my life. I could have been a professional painter or sculptor, certainly an occupation I respect, but I preferred acting. The process of buying and selling my art work did not suit me. Neither did proselytizing my art to galleries that might do the selling part. I have painted for decades, since that dark period when I was twenty-three, living in a storefront. I enjoy painting but not for a living.

Why acting has become my unequivocal identity when I respect writing and painting as much remains a mystery. The unassuming nature of the artist, who prefers to retreat to his studio for work, away from the public, away from the cheering crowds, away from approval of others, intrigues me. I respect the visual artist's solitary stand, but I refused to make that my occupation. My need to be in front of audiences

I cannot explain, a need I've always had, from the time I was very young and competing in front of cheering crowds in various athletic contests.

I chose immediate approval from audiences' applause and flattering comments after a performance. Compared to the depth of solitary painting and writing, I admit the superficiality of film premiers. After fifty-nine years of acting, I might even say that my career has brought with it enormous depth and this for one reason alone; I was forced repeatedly to perform in front of crowds of people, when I wasn't fully confident emotionally nor spiritually to fend for myself. Today the isolation and loneliness of writing or painting serves to compliment my public life. That isolation and the concentration that accompanies it suits me more than pleasing an anonymous public with clever usage of words. As years have passed, I've become less enchanted by my image upon a screen and by how a newspaper reviewer responds to my work. Perhaps I have become my own man. I don't know for sure, but acting has become easier, as I have cared less about my effect upon the world and how I am perceived as a performer.

Surely I've screwed up a few performances in my time, and to be fair with myself, I've been at the top of my game other times. Earlier my career has been riddled with fear, but finally my full talent has managed to emerge. To admit that I am a skillful actor is not easy. Bragging is a plain bore, so I won't. On the other hand, so much is uncertain in the profession that one must learn to enjoy success, not to overlook the backdrop of my work, which is my life and the people in it. A support system is necessary to function within certainty, a steady support system that will not disappear when things go awry. In my case my wife, Robyn Mundell, provides that support. I am fortunate to have this fine woman in my life for thirty years. I wasn't ready for a healthy relationship before we married; too much uncertainty, I suppose.

Spirituality is another necessary element, to find joy in one's existence, regardless of daily pressures that sabotage one's spiritual well-being. An actor must find a way to remain calm, while in a pressured, professional situation. In my case, I challenged my habitual reaction to pressure and noticed the mental insecurity I'd been creating. I was forced to straighten that out by studying Eschatology, a spiritual science of how to think. This study provided the last stage of growth that enabled me to flourish both as an actor and as a man.

"There is nothing good or bad, but thinking makes it so."

How much more time is left? I smoke and doubt I shall stop. I do wish to stop, but some element of my personality wishes to be bad. I am bad, not to others but to myself. Something inside is screaming for release. That's why I must create characters, to quell that internal scream.

Finished a Job

November 6, 2014, 1:25 PM.

Flying in a plane from Canada to Los Angeles, after a day's work, acting a role in a television series called *'The Hundred'*. The actors were mostly young and naïve to the hazards of the profession, whereas, after all these years of doing it, I'm used to the twists and turns of my career, the emotional entanglements that come with each completed job. Lack of money at times, the needs of my children, schooling and such.

Meanwhile, a certain awareness comes from being outside of me, looking down upon myself, while living out daily tasks, the floating sensation of being here and not being here simultaneously, of being in two places at once, concerned but not concerned. It all unfolds without effort. All will continue without interruption, and I in the middle, pushed, pulled, moving in one direction and then another, always watching from above, while behaving down below.

The plane flies me to Los Angeles, and then driven by a limousine to my home. I am patient, no effort exerted. No, no effort necessary. I will arrive in due time. My destination will be reached, while watching from above, 'me' down below comfortably ensconced upon a cushioned seat in the back of a black limousine. No talk, only silence, the uniformed driver driving this way and that, stopping at an excess of lights, bewildered by numerous wrong turns. I say nothing to clarify the proper route. Explaining to the fellow doesn't seem necessary. The misinformed driver will bring my body home eventually to rest. There is no need to talk.

Fatigue is the result of a day's work; watching from up above, observing movement this way and that, and I in the middle, working in one Canadian city and living in another American city. Children to raise, mouths to feed, minds to educate, values to instill, until the next interlude in another city, living in a hotel, a hot dog for dinner, changes in the script to memorize in one night, a hurried sleep, up early in the morning, working then, acting a role on television for the masses to see that require me to react to a young and gifted actor, my partner in the scene, who cried repeatedly from one take to another, six hours of concentration and vivid focus upon the lad's flow of tears, not to mention remembering the words, then wishing for the best, hoping to do it right, a compliment from a stranger, flattery we all need, recognition for a job well done, a life well lived. The dream of being an actor, not quite the result imagined but fulfilled nonetheless; wisdom acquired through the aging process and a full life in a profession once imagined as a young man, a life with the least resistance in a world that offers satisfaction and no pushing or forcing but merely 'being,' while observing from above, hoping for the best below. Effort is required, the focus, the concentration, the mind occupied with what should happen next. My profession requires skill to make a living.

Calm is part of this day, even while residing in a hotel room miles from my home, away from my children, away from my wife. Home has been this hotel room for an entire week. I endured my sojourn in Canada. I did my job well, acted the character well, a calm man, who has arrived at a stable existence, after enduring unadulterated hardship during the formative years.

~~~

My condominium is dark when I arrive, the others sleeping in their beds soundly, a drink of water after a long journey, a swallow of cold noodles, a cigarette smoked upon the balcony that overlooks the city of Los Angeles, the city where I live and to which I flew an hour before; observance of quiet nightlife on the street below, as I smoke from above, casually, without effort. The clock must be set for five-thirty next morning. I shall sleep now, after another swallow of cold noodles, another swig of water. No shower tonight, only sleep from a long day's work and travel, after first executing a difficult scene, then riding in a limousine, flying a plane and another limousine to my domicile, where I lie next to my wife and little girl, who has crawled into our bed.

I hold gently her little arm that lingers beside my body. No effort required, only rest, interrupted in the middle of the night, awake then and urged by a pang of hunger, up again, tip-toeing to the refrigerator, buttering two pieces of bread swallowed hurriedly and back to bed next to the little girl, her little arm again held gently and finally deep sleep.

The alarm bell rings. Awake again, cold shower, walk the dog, followed by a bowl of oatmeal with banana cut up in it, check the e-mail and soon after, driving my automobile with the young son off to school. Then on to the gymnasium to enjoy a sweat and happenstance encounters with various healthy types, who exercise the toxins from their bodies and live out their awkward lives with dignity. The interchange of males, dealing with the onslaught that life brings; a musician black man gregarious and full of spirit, another one who writes, an actor whose son graduated from my son's school, conversations that connect me to the mundane problems of the world, telling me that we're all in this together, the world's dynamic acting upon us in unison; humanity in lockstep, wondering what it's all about and where this mishmash called 'life' is taking us.

~~~

Yesterday I received the 'Gasparilla Film Festival Lifetime Achievement Award'. I went up to the podium, and a glass trophy was given me, after which I gave a speech to the audience, describing my numerous part time jobs during the early years of my career; my labors on the night of Martin Luther King's assassination, as a longshoreman on Pier #28; the night an old college friend looked in a state of wonderment at the sight of me washing dishes at a Mexican restaurant; that job of 'bouncer' at the 'Broome Street Bar' in Manhattan or laying pipe with my plumber friend, Ken Whelan.

While I proudly held that glass trophy in my hand, my speech seemed relaxed and well executed. 'Truth' was my companion while I spoke, the 'truth' of my entire life. The words came easily with inexorable pride in what I described while being honored with a 'Lifetime Achievement Award'. With a glass trophy in hand, I had survived a lifetime struggle in the theater that I believed in my heart to be both spiritual and creative. The audience responded to my humor, and at the risk of braggadocio, the speech was, indeed, well received

Seldom am I stricken with fear of facing audiences today and a nice transition from the days of my early career, not to overlook my silent youth. Communicating what's on my mind has become grounded in what might be called well-earned confidence - such a comfortable state of mind, after so many years of silent isolation. Today I'm fully capable of speaking before an audience or giving a full, spontaneous film or stage performance. Career security has finally arrived. Self-imposed silence is a thing of the past. Theater has given me sociability, for which I am deeply grateful. Willingness to speak my mind has replaced a rigid, inhibited, repressed old self, who never quite knew his ass from his elbow but was willing to endure the years necessary to climb to personal freedom. Finally I can breathe, and thank you, God. Thank also all those who played a part in my personal quest for freedom.

~ ~ ~

Return Visit, Nuyorican Poets Café

Lower East Side, New York City, January 28, 2011

Miguel Algarin, Puerto Rican Playwrights' Workshop,

Nuyorican Poets' Café; Published originally by

'The Storyteller Anthology', 2020

January 28, 2011: Coldness bolstered by a strong wind that angrily freezes my shoulders, I break out into a bending stride and breathe deeply the sharp bite of fresh winter air, passing the dilapidated buildings that surround Tomkin's Square Park. The only exception to the general ramshackle look of the area is a neatly painted white church on East Ninth Street and Avenue B. My hands pull my overcoat tighter, and the wind nips at my face, as I walk downtown and east, far into the bowels of the New York City barrio where the bulk of a Puerto Rican population had settled long before I'd became one of its inhabitants.

Bucking the wind, I scurry down Avenue B and turn left on Third Street, aiming east to the *Nuyorican Poets' Café*, passing the Hell's Angel's building that looms before me with its array of motorcycles in front and numerous sinister, muscled fellows dressed in their leathers cut off at the shoulders to exhibit their large biceps. They must be cold in this weather. Of all neighborhoods, they occupied an abandoned building on East Third Street and settled in for the duration.

Tonight I'll visit my Puerto Rican, poet friend and colleague, Miguel Algarin; an educated Puerto Rican with an axe to grind in a white man's world. He will greet me, as he always has, with a broad smile and the familiar, "Ola," from his lips. A fully tenured professor at Rutgers University, the man has a Doctorate Degree in comparative literature and is a published poet. He's also the founding member of the notorious *'Nuyorican Poets' Café'*. We created theater during the seventies. He wrote, and I directed the *'Puerto Rican Playwright's Workshop'*, composed of a group of Latino actors, mostly Puerto Rican and one Cuban.

Miguel was in a predicament at the time. He'd already founded his company with a talented cast and had been given a rehearsal space by Joseph Papp, the artistic director of famed *'Public Theater'* that had provided a living for me with roles in numerous productions during the seventies and eighties. But Miguel's education was that of a writer, not that of a director. The complex world of theater was foreign to him. He hadn't the knowledge nor the experience necessary to propel the company of actors toward a finished production. After seeing my performance in the *Open Theater's* production of *'Nightwalk'*, Miguel asked for my assistance directing his company. Since I was familiar with an actor's creative process, the cast trusted me for guidance, but to repeat myself, it was Miguel's company and not mine. At times, confusion arose about who was running things, I or Miguel Algarin, who, as I say, had founded the company.

My theater acumen placed me at the helm of our rehearsals of both *'Olu Clemente'* and our follow-up production, *'Apartment 6-D'*, both plays featuring casts of Latino, Lower East Side barrio actors. No matter how diligently I tried to offset this dynamic of leadership between Miguel and me, I was always the outsider. I was white, and I was also conservative compared to the Latino men in the company. I didn't pack a gun, and my drug use was limited to marijuana and a little coke now and then.

~~~

I hit Avenue C where the cafe is in sight, my stride accelerating as my destination nears. As I walk further east, an acquaintance greets me, as if we're old friends, talking incessantly about, "Where you been? What you been doing, after you dropped through a hole in the ground?" Patiently listening for a few seconds on the run, after mentioning briefly that I'm making movies in Los Angeles, I politely extricate myself from the fellow with a friendly, "See you later," and continue on my way into the biting cold. Bending into the force of the wind, I continue toward Avenue D. A thick, criminal atmosphere describes the neighborhood with the pervading cry of drug dealers calling from the entrances of buildings, leaving the belfries of rowed tenements resounding with the universal lament of poverty. It is a poetic verse of a kind from partially hidden figures, hovering in the door-wells of buildings as I pass, offering their wares, if I dare look into their faces.

"You lookin', bro? You lookin'? Hey, bro, you lookin'?"

An emaciated bum approaches, homeless, dirty and strung out from severe heroin addiction; signs of immanent death. Drugs are everywhere, reminding me of my years of creating theater with doomed and damned Puerto Rican folk, who have long since died or moved out of the area for their safety. These are characters, who over a period of some ten years, affected me deeply before evaporating without a trace. One black woman in particular comes to mind, as I pass a building where she lived, remembering when I broke her window with an empty bottle. I was high on coke at the time and very much in love. I wonder how her life went - a fine lady with whom I was involved off and on for years. She is long since gone from the neighborhood, got out when the going was possible. I remember us together, as I pass her building with a longing look in my eye, the memory of that hellish relationship flavoring my already somber mood.

My mind drifts to balconies above, stumbling through this war-torn ghetto with my dear friend Miguel Algarin in mind. He has survived this outrage of a community, this humiliation of poverty that once both of us endured - he for a lifetime, I merely a voyeur, who happened to live here for its cheap rent. Idyllic forests once grew here, sprouting flowers and verdant fields in place of its present squalor. Fresh streams sparkled then, instead of the galvanized metal of garbage cans, but now, centuries later, the barrio's stink of poverty remains, featuring the walking sick, with skeleton torsos and thin faces that express the haunting look of ghetto hopelessness. They shuffle from one end of the block to the other and back again with nothing to fill their day but the desperate need of their addictions. Sitting on stoops in front of the same dilapidated hovels where they were raised from childhood, they are made to believe that they themselves are responsible for the talons of poverty that grip them in this slum.

The *'Nuyorican Poets' Café'* finally appears between Avenues C and D, landmark of the literary community, where William Burroughs and Alan Ginsberg often shared their poetry, along with Miguel Pinero and Zake Shange. I was the product of university life, a Brown graduate, contrary to the café's neighborhood clientele, and yet those Third World poets, educated in state penitentiaries, affected me profoundly with the expression of their souls, their tongues speaking a poetic street language that moved me to the core of my being.

Poetry seemed my destiny during that brief period, until eventually I came to my senses. Forcing myself to write long-hand in unlined sketch books, I slaved away to include myself among the local poets of New York's Lower East Side. Spiritual survival in that slum meant writing every day to uncover the alleged genius within. There had to be something brilliant inside, I reasoned, if only I could locate its whereabouts and write it down for posterity. But writing poetry wasn't enough for me. I was compelled to perform my words, the way real poets did. On the informal *'Nuyorican Poets Café'* stage, I imposed upon the Lower East Side community the dulled fruits of my labors, much to the dismay of those forced to watch such a spectacle. Obsessed with rhyming couplets and thinking erroneously that is what all poetry required by definition, I ranted incessantly to an audience captured by a cover-charge they'd already paid.

Before long, a select coterie of curious folks gathered regularly for the purpose of paying homage to my literary eloquence. Stage fright was the worst of it. Terror gripped my body to such a degree that with the microphone sticking into my face, I screamed the words at such a high decibel level that the audience, in the face of my histrionics, would invariably inch to the back of the room. I was plainly out of touch with them, as well as with myself. At best, I presented a somewhat absurd figure with my bombastic delivery, complete with extended arms and stomping feet to enhance the message of my vapid verse. My throat too would contract in the throes of my efforts, leaving a rasping tone that would bellow through the room like a bull elephant mating. It wasn't the pleasant sound of a beast in harmony with itself. The tension in its delivery, the labored pronunciation of each word left audiences in a state of wonder as to what I was trying to say. That, of course, was not clear to me.

The subsequent frustration that followed audiences' dismal reaction to my presentation was allayed by the theater work Miguel Algarin and I accomplished with the *'Puerto Rican Writers' Workshop'*. While creating plays with a company of gifted Puerto Rican actors, all of whom were imprisoned by the bonds of poverty and racism, Miguel and I formed an everlasting bond.

~~~

The familiar, dark interior of the Nuyorican Café greets me with a flood of my past. I haven't been here since I moved to California to embark upon a film career. The empty hall of the performing area looms with memories of when I frequented the place nightly during my early thirties, while directing the *'Puerto Rican Playwrights Workshop'* and trying my best to create something that might prove worthy to the world. Miguel and I ran two theater companies then, requiring most of our time. *'Quena Company'* was the other, composed of Caucasian actors, again with Miguel writing and I directing. At night, I earned a living by performing numerous plays at Joseph Papp's *'Public Theater'*, while Miguel dutifully prepared for his morning class at Rutgers University.

A black man reads a newspaper at the end of the long, wooden bar, reminding me of myself, when I was one of its clientele. I'm the only white man here, and my attraction to this environment still remains a mystery. Why my life veered so far off its middle-class path will always be a puzzle to me. On the opposite side of the cavernous room a few stragglers sit at a table where they observe two actresses rehearsing a play. So as not to disturb, I am careful to lower my voice during my inquiry as to Miguel's whereabouts to the bartender, who is surprisingly welcoming, as he suggests that I ask the secretary upstairs if my friend has arrived. Having just spoken to Miguel on the phone, I expect him soon, but I respectfully proceed to the floor above anyway, where a young girl tells me he seldom comes at this time of day. I know better. He'll be here within minutes.

Again I wait downstairs at the bar, smoke a cigarette and watch the rehearsal of the play, a drama between a mother and a gay daughter, who wants her lover to meet the parent. A brave subject, I think to myself, as I digest the plot, trying my best to appear attentive. There is something straight forward and honest about their acting that seems from the heart, in spite of occasional spurts of over-doing it. The sparse audience offers spontaneous bursts of laughter. The sincere involvement between players and the room's few spectators brings a focus to this space that I remember well from years ago; the seriousness of the work, as well as its innocence.

~~~

Miguel enters the café with hat cocked to one side, black eyes, rhythmic street strut, his friendly Puerto Rican face carried upon his familiar portly frame. He searches the darkened room, and upon locating me next to the bar, greets me with open arms. His approach is somewhat hesitating in his fragile state - overweight, a thirty year HIV infection that could easily prove fatal, swollen from the indulgences of the last three decades. Time may be short for him and we both know it. We embrace, a bit too aware that we are two males clutching with robust, backslapping hugs. The color of his dark skin that stands so sharply against the white of my own, white like a cumulus cloud that evaporates as soon as we poke our fingers into it. At the end of this ritual, he engages the customary, "Ola," then a Puerto Rican handshake that I manage to fumble with my thumb in the wrong spot and fingers gripped too woodenly, lacking the required Latin sensibility to coordinate the salutation easily. "I love you," escapes his lips, while looking unabashedly into my smiling face. I return the sentiment in my clumsy fashion. We are two men happy to express what is in our hearts, joyful to share our spirit of love, after years of my sojourn to Hollywood but now together again, expressing words that suit a special occasion.

During the excitement of our renewed bond, so many memories flow in one brushstroke; Miguel and I occasionally combating each other, at war with each other, jealous of each other's influence upon the *'Puerto Rican Playwright's Workshop'* and too immature to ameliorate the sheer blindness of our ways. We loved each other inexorably, which cemented our collaboration. My God, how foolish and young we were, but through our creative process, something permanent was born, the plays we made for one, *'Olu Clemente', 'Apartment 6D', 'Pablo Neruda', 'Blue Heaven', 'Technocracy', 'Strange Beast',* not to overlook our bond, our tenacity, our insistence that each man would continue his creative vision and would always be deeply influenced by our work together. Miguel is a genuine friend, after so much creative work together, long hours of rehearsal and absence of financial resources for services rendered. Lack of funds was taken for granted, not to overlook our fragile egos. As we grow older, I respect and care for him more than ever. Our bond is firmly cemented by the heroism required in the face of adversity when running our theater companies years ago.

Meanwhile the room whispers its response to Miguel's unexpected visit. He is an important figure of the barrio, proven by continuous, welcoming handshakes from the few lingering friends delighted to see him. Warm, quiet greetings abound, and Miguel gracefully proffers the proper degree of respect to all, the measure of which depends entirely upon the specific nature of each friendship. The café's activities of poetry and theater are possible only by Miguel's undying commitment to the community's spiritual welfare. This has brought utmost respect to the man. He is a seasoned warrior of the ghetto with an education to boot, providing the medicine of poetry to heal his beloved barrio's wounded spirit. His life is a productive one, far more so than many of the hopeless locals, who bide their time unemployed and devastated by drugs.

While my friend greets his comrades, I observe the performing space. The room represents Miguel's canvass; his brush and paint are its local poets who read their work. Their lives matter by means of written metaphor, describing the battleground in which they live. The man before me has provided an arena for their poetry and theater that will live on when he will be dead. The café encourages young and old alike to notice the world's struggle, to write their perceptions onto the white pages of their notebooks, in some cases to memorize the words they have written for the benefit of its audiences. 'The Nuyorican Poets Café' is a neighborhood university, where people are free to think and encouraged to study the puzzle of writing itself and finally to express the barrio's collective consciousness. This hall is a place of learning, a university of the streets, where local youth is encouraged to discover the full potential of their thinking minds.

Intellect is involved for writing of any kind. Thought is required, clear thinking and perception of what truly exists in their lives. These are the ingredients necessary for education of the

241

highest order, created by the steadfast will power of Miguel Algarin. He alone is this university's president for he predicted, in the beginning of the *'Nuyorican Café's'* history, the vision that exists today. He alone saw the whole picture of what is now possible among its artists. But at this moment in time, he is sick with HIV. Our loss would be devastating should he die, and my spirit is burdened with that possibility. Miguel and I mirror each other, and as I see it, his weakened immune system parallels what once tainted my future in this poverty-stricken area before I escaped to greener pastures. Upon my return, the intimacy of our friendship is what is left. Years later in this hall, we comfort ourselves with the gentle caressing of our souls, sending messages of love, heart to heart.

~~~

Finally he returns from his coterie of friends with humble apologies, his ego a bit swelled by the unabashed tide of love he has just received from them. This private room features barstools that rock back and forth, like sitting on a cloud. Miguel maneuvers a seat next to me, confirming our friendship to the bartender and others in the cafe. Being the odd man out, I am grateful for his gesture. "I count too," I think to myself within this small group of Latino men. The cushiony chair gives into my weight, rocking back and forth. Once his hand is firmly placed upon my shoulder I am met with his "You are my only real friend" expression that I know only too well. His eyes penetrate deeply into my own, as if to cement our bond. Miguel is a rascal after all is said and done. The approach is a familiar one, useful whenever he wishes to flatter me for some ulterior motive. Nonetheless, today his affection is genuine enough and my need strong enough to submit.

Although we are in good spirits, he complains about his diarrhea that forces him to be near a toilet, the result of his HIV infection. I notice him looking urgently at the bathroom door. He complains that his stomach has been bothering him, the disastrous effect of drinking with a friend, Julio Bracha. The night before, his buddy offered Miguel a joint that he stupidly smoked, after which an unexpected party lasted into the late hours, resulting in the price he is paying now. He says he couldn't resist celebrating for one night, aware that drinking would make him sick in the aftermath.

Meanwhile, what has been happening during my sojourn to Hollywood? He, of course, has published another book, while I, in my inimitable fashion have achieved little aside from playing a few roles in an assortment of films here and there. This meeting between us, whenever too much time has passed, is an uncommon event, during which my 'near-do-well' personality and his 'overachiever' status complement each other congruently. Our differences blend with relative ease. Miguel is a professor and poet full of ideas and energy, while I, in my own way, offer what I can. We assume ourselves successful and do so unequivocally, he in terms of his numerous published books and I my films and plays, all of which are published; slight pride in citing the name of my anthology that no one reads. *'Mother's Son and Other Plays'* is a collection of my work is all, and his books of poetry are signs of his existence on Earth as well. We are survivors, both of us, having weathered the storm of our lives, and after my long absence, sit before each other in the *'Nuyorican Poets Café'* where we used to perform our plays. We are in full form; our minds alert, our bodies still breathing.

This performance room, which in my memory, was always packed at night with bodies, is cold, moist and almost empty during the day. While our lonely figures sit upon two bar stools, I smoke, flicking the butts into a plastic cup. Miguel drinks beer. I drink Coke Cola; haven't drunk alcohol in thirty-two years. It's better that way. Back in the day, I drank beer and smoked weed, also did a little cocaine. None of it did much for me. I could have avoided all of it, but we were young then and felt the urge to experiment. I look at Miguel and notice how fragile his health has become, the toll HIV has taken, his bloated throat from the effects of medical prescriptions. None of it matters to me. He was always a little fat man to me, but I never paid much attention. His mind always took precedence beyond the flesh.

In the cavernous café hall, Miguel's voice is barely audible. He whispers into my ear the lowdown on the situation, giving me a sense of importance, as we lay back in our seats, floating together at eye level, as if on a reclining bed. Long silence then that shifts the mood to a sudden somber tone.

"Wilfredo Hernandez's wife might have had AIDS, when she died of pneumonia in Bellevue hospital a few years ago."

Wilfredo Hernandez was the handsomest of Puerto Rican men and probably could have made something of himself, if he hadn't been influenced by Miguel Pinero, a deceased poet himself, playwright and the kingpin of the barrio, who had been nominated for the Pulitzer Prize for his play, *'Short Eyes'*. After the latter received so much attention for his work, along with the numerous awards and fellowships that came his way, young Puerto Ricans like Wilfredo related to him as a paradigm of a successful Puerto Rican artist. In doing so, Wilfredo imitated his mentor's use of heroin, thinking it was the source of the playwright's genius. Nothing could be farther from the truth. Wilfredo became one of heroin's victims at the sacrifice of his talent, believing incorrectly that he could maintain a weekend habit and remain clean during the week. The drug killed him in the end. By chance, Miguel had seen him before he'd died from an overdose and describes what he'd become.

"That beautiful man was a sorry sight, skeleton thin, homeless dirty and strung out from heroin," he says. "He looked like he was going to die, as his wife had only a short time before. I said to Wilfredo's face that his wife was too young to die of pneumonia and might have had AIDS. Wilfredo punched me in the jaw, landing me on my ass, bleeding from the mouth. My comment infuriated him." Miguel explains, "He'd always been proudly masculine. The slightest association with anything homosexual was an insult. At that moment, our friendship was finished, and I still pay the price for that. You weren't there and a good thing too, as I know you loved him."

The mood has taken a markedly darker turn, the result not only of our memory of Wilfredo but also of the subject of AIDS. Miguel moves with an assertiveness that belies his precarious health and mentions his HIV condition without shame. He speaks of diarrhea, bouts of it that prevent him from living normally from

244

hour to hour, describes his medication to control the HIV infection that has weakened his body for decades. How difficult it is to adjust to a new life of sobriety that contrasts so fully with the old. In our sober state, it is all the same to me. Witnessing each other is our pleasure, not lecturing about the advantages of health. We both have an interest in death anyway. That is common knowledge, an unspoken realization that death is close at hand and what will it be like? Most of our friends have died decades before. We speak in terms of decades, not years that are too brief a passage of time in our long history with gaps taken off to fulfill our singular paradigms of success.

Surreptitiously, so as not to be heard, he whispers, "I feel like a killer," he says. "If my juices were to enter someone's body, they would die, a killer, who could take a life."

He whispers, "Twenty-five years ago I was infected with HIV under a bridge in the Bronx."

"What bridge?"

"I don't know what bridge," he says, "Just a big, city bridge where I was having sex with young Spanish boys under a bridge in the Bronx. I met kids on planned occasions, had sex with them and paid them afterwards."

As he describes the story, his voice lowers to a bare whisper.

"They were typical young, physically attractive Puerto Rican boys, who resorted to prostitution to survive in New York City, a common practice among Nuyorican youth without fathers, who barter their sexuality for money. It's a dangerous game in this day and age."

Miguel relates the story with vigor in the telling of it, the words prancing from his lips and his eyes brightening.

"Once, while I was being commemorated for achieving tenure at Rutgers University, I fled early from the ceremony to the bridge in the Bronx where the boys waited for me."

As I'm listening to the details of his story, I imagine a picturesque image of foliage and sand at the bottom of the bridge's enormous pillars with Miguel's body on top of a Puerto Rican boy under the cover of brush. I also envision cars whizzing by overhead at eighty miles an hour and the AIDS virus passing into his body from the bleeding anus of the same young boy whose torso bends like a supple fern.

"I suspect the virus infected my system during that insane period. Numerous trysts beneath Bronx bridges with Puerto Rican, macho youngsters, standing naked for my pleasure have taken their toll."

Miguel is indeed paying a heavy price for the life he has led, but we are made of the same ball of wax, he and I; our pleasures dance to the music of the same fiddle. We are scandalous men, even to ourselves, who would rather drown our souls in a nightmarish sea of lust in place of what might have been a normal way of life.

~~~

A young girl enters the hall. They greet each other without question. Obviously she knows Miguel and my association with him gives me an open invitation in this room. From the efficiency with which she deals with various stations of the bar, it is apparent that her job is precisely that, to tend bar when the evening audience arrives. She is Latino, probably Puerto Rican, a short brown-skinned girl barely out of high school and thrown into the work force in order to survive. Her apparent natural intelligence makes her suitable for bar work where money is handled continuously. She doesn't look the type to steal and probably isn't. Her obvious pride in her function manifests clearly, as she intently labors from station to station behind the bar.

I notice two new clientele, a couple of black men, physically strong and somewhat out of place. The men maneuver to the far corner of the room away from everybody else. Uncertainty hampers their natural grace. Reclining in our chairs, Miguel's whispering gives the illusion of closeness between us, facing me as he speaks quietly, looking into each other's eyes at the exclusion of all, giving the impression that we are sunning ourselves on some Caribbean beach. Miguel continues buzzing into my ears.

"This woman comes up to me in the café, and she's sobbing right into my face, and I ask her,

"What's the matter?" "And she tells me she knows of a couple who are going to have a baby. I ask her why she's crying, and she tells me she's crying because they are talking about throwing the baby into the East River."

"Wow, the East River," I say.

"Yeah, the East River; so I ask her why she is coming to me, as if I can do anything about it, because basically I can't do much, and I ask her how she knows this information, and she tells me she heard them talking about throwing the baby into the East River, because they didn't want it. So I asked her again, "What can I do about it?" I wouldn't call a cop. The baby hadn't been drowned yet, and I'm not one to call a cop anyway. I'm already having trouble with my landlord, who could possibly be paying the cops, so he can evict me from my apartment without any problem."

"Why does your landlord want to evict you?" I ask.

"They say I'm a nuisance," Miguel says quietly, so no one can hear. "I've looked around the neighborhood, and the cheapest place I can find is eighteen hundred dollars a month."

"I know," I say. "I own my place," said with a certain degree of pride from having escaped this predatory environment of New York City landlords. I escaped to Hollywood and made a decent living. Now I'm just visiting. You might call it slumming, but that's not what it is. There are human values here to pay attention to, values that one wouldn't find in a white, middle-class environment, where babies are not thrown into the East River, but on the other hand, not much is happening in Los Angeles suburbs by way of aiming for the jugular of life, the essence of one's existence. Vitality pervades the hall of the *'Nuyorican Poets Café'*. I am alive in this room, on this bar stool perched before a plastic glass of Coke Cola and speaking about what has taken place over the past thirty years, speaking about the important things, the necessary ingredients that compose a life.

Miguel's fragile presence forbids waste of precious time. All that is required here is for us to be who we really are. Truth takes precedence. Words are expressed easily between us, words and lack of pretense. No, we are not pretending. Miguel hides very little; his HIV infection, a baby about to be thrown into the East River. Nothing is held back by either of us.

A full hour has passed. My old face stares into Miguel's old face, bearing no sign of shame. Personal pride has exonerated mistakes along the way. I have learned through the process of trial and error how to roll with the punches, how to adjust to my errors, how to laugh at my stupidity in circumstances that might have been solved by stepping back for a moment and breathing deeply, rather than responding with rash impulse. I am calmer now, not calm, but calmer. The present moment with Miguel means more to me than the future at this late stage of my life. I prefer to take stock of the goodness of each circumstance, rather than to be mired in anxiety that comes with expecting more of something unknown. Life is basically good. Its goodness is visible, if one is willing to look for a second and surrender to the way things really are, which, of course, is the basic requirement for creating art. Miguel too has learned to appreciate 'what is' rather than pining over 'what should have been'.

"I miss Mike," I say.

Miguel looks off into the space and says nothing. 'Nothing' is enough to fill the moment. 'Nothing' is everything. We are rejuvenated by the mere mention of our friend's name. We were witnesses to Miguel Pinero's life when he lived on these streets, as we witnessed the lives of Lucky Cienfuegos, Wilfredo Hernandez, Tito Goya, Bimbo Rivas and Pedro Pietri, all of them dead from numerous hazards that come with living in the barrio. At first, I didn't realize that people die young here, fooled as I was by the prodigious vitality within the Third World community with its access to poetry, theatre, drugs, music and sex, not to mention potential killers thrown into the mix. Add the ingredient of readily available weaponry, and you wind up with a majority of them dying below the age of forty.

"The last time I saw him, Mike visited me in Los Angeles," I say to Miguel, after a pregnant silence. " *'Short Eyes'* was being performed at the Los Angeles Theater Center, and they'd flown him out to see the show. My acting career had taken a positive turn by then; I did a couple of films, and I made money for the first time in my life.

"Going to Los Angeles was a good thing for you," Miguel responds.

"Yeah, I've been working," I say proudly. My success in Miguel's eyes means a great deal to me. I don't know exactly why, aside from the fact that he knew me when I didn't have a pot to piss in. Silence then before I continue.

"Anyway, there's a knock on my door, and standing before me is Mikey Pinero with a white guy, whose name escapes me. He used to hang around the *'Nuyorican'*, and he never had that much going for him. I forget the guy's name. But he brought Mike to my apartment, and it was good to see him. He greeted me with his usual, "Heey, man," and he gave me a big hug. It was so good to see him."

"Mikey and I talked then for hours then, an old, close friendship re-ignited, after not seeing each other for such a long period of time, maybe two years or so. We talked about the old days in the barrio, the *'Nuyorican Poets Café'* and different characters we knew, some dead, some still living. By then, I was beginning to get my act together. But Mike sadly was on his way out, having already been hospitalized for sclerosis of the liver, probably from dirty needles. His body was betraying him. The life he'd led had taken a toll, and he didn't have much time left."

Miguel quietly listens. He and Pinero were very, very close.

"That was the last time I saw Miguel Pinero. I didn't care what he had done with his life. He was my close friend, and that would always be the case. We talked in my apartment for about four hours, had a wonderful conversation about our past and our present. Above all, no drugs. He did an imitation of me that day, I remember, of the way I walk. My daughter, Oona, was there and couldn't stop laughing. How close Miguel Pinero and I were during our last meeting. It saddens me to think of it. Subliminally there was an understanding that we might not see each other again. We knew intuitively our meeting was special for that reason. In our somewhat shy way, we were communicating without actually saying that we loved our history together. Our memories were a poignant part of our past, and mutual love and respect were certainly part of the mix."

Miguel listens silently, absorbing every detail.

"Pinero mentioned the times he used to visit my apartment to take a shower and refresh himself. I lived on East Tenth Street at the time on Tomkins Square Park, and every once in a while, I'd hear a knock and open the door. Mike Pinero would be standing before me, asking to take a shower or have coffee, smoke or talk, whatever. He would've been up all night, or he'd have crashed the night before at your apartment on East Third. We had a good chuckle over those visits."

"He used to come to my place for a shower too," Miguel says with a vague smile.

"He was one of those people who just . . . He didn't have to deal with phone bills, rent, electric bills. That was totally out of context to him."

A moment of silence then.

"Miguel Pinero died a month later. I didn't go to the memorial services in New York City, but I saw it on tape afterwards."

We leave the subject then, and talk for an hour more, remembering different characters of the barrio as they come up. Tito Goya was murdered in a Texas jail in retaliation for killing someone with a shotgun in a Miami discotheque. The Mexican mob put a contract out on him. He was a beautiful Puerto Rican man with light skin and green eyes, but the word was that you couldn't bring him into your home. He would steal to buy drugs. The man was a talented director and actor, as well as a confirmed junkie. He played the role of the original 'Cup Cakes' in Miguel Pinero's

250

'Short Eyes' at Lincoln Center and earlier at Joe Papp's *'Public Theater'*.

Lucky Cienfuegos was another gangster poet, playwright, shot to death in a drug deal, after he became a wealthy from selling heroin in large quantities. I'll never forget watching him sniff glue in an empty storefront on East Third Street. Chinamen were his specialty. They kept their savings on them in money belts or in their socks. Once he ripped off one of them for fifteen thousand dollars. He killed the guy to rob him, poor man.

There were others too. Lope De Vega who died of AIDS, either from the needle or from sex with boy prostitutes. A few of them preferred young boys, who by the very nature of their livelihood were infected themselves. There was always the threat of dirty needles. Marvin Camillio also died of AIDS. He was the brilliant director of *'Short Eyes'*, who had theatre companies in Newark, New York and in Paris. He went off to Paris to die of the disease. Few people knew he was gay, and he continued hiding that fact even after he became ill. Now Miguel Algarin is infected, the last of a long line of brilliant Latino artists.

In the distant past, these men composed Miguel Algarin's world, into which I was welcomed warmly; a world that educated me and forced me to grow as an artist and as a man. Sitting before my friend, we have survived with a fair share of optimism. Our lives have meaning in the face of the world's resistance that would have obliterated our creativity had we chosen a safer path.

~~~

When it's time to move on, Miguel and I scramble out to the street and stand on the curb in the freezing cold. Miguel insists we go to a Dominican restaurant for dinner but emphatically makes it clear that he isn't paying for it, cheap Miguel. This is too much for me to ignore. I have a field day with this one, first calling him a "cheap son of a bitch" and then listing chronologically the restaurants I've taken him to. I insist he must pay for dinner, or, "I will simply kill myself," dramatically overacting with feigned despair. Miguel is busting at the seams, as I swish around in the back seat of a rented cab, laughing my ass off and badgering Miguel, who refuses to part with his money. My relentless banter won't let him off the hook, reciting a litany of specific dinners I've fed him with a few fictitious ones thrown in the mix, which is met by the sound of great belly laughs from both of us. Miguel's cheapness has left a reputation for which he is well known. I call him "a tight assed professor" and promise to write a poem about the subject, when I return to Hollywood. Again we howl with laughter, while the cab hurls through Alphabet City. Chiding him unmercifully, shouting as if intoxicated, I conclude my onslaught with numerous slaps upon the man's shoulders, while expressing my appreciation for his inviting me to dinner.

"Thank you, thank you, Miguel, thank you, thank you for picking up the tab!"

Meanwhile Miguel is enjoying our banter as much as I am, while the car barely manages to avoid crashing into a pole. As our madcap ride hurls headway towards the Dominican Restaurant on Avenue A and Ninth, we are bound in uncontrollable convulsions of laughter. We trust the situation. Eager for more fun, various good natured jokes to please my irreverent audience are shouted at the top of my lungs, quips directed at both myself and Miguel for the duration of the short ride. Our warm friendship permits insulting one another in the company of our driver.

Our voices are loud, and at a strategic point I insist Miguel is treating me "naughtily" because I am white, using the word, "naughtily" to accentuate my feminine side that contradicts my loud, overbearing voice. It is such a dainty word for a man to be using, particularly a big man as I happen to be. Spanish males are overly sensitive to the issue of masculinity. Throwing them off guard with a word like, "naughtily," coming from the mouth of an ape like myself, is my unique talent. Quick quips and sharp barbs aimed at myself transform me into a lovable laughing stock for my audience of one. Miguel enjoys a white man, who doesn't take himself seriously, a man who is the brunt of his own jokes. This is a safe game when it comes to preserving the proper level of humbleness within a pair of egos such as ours. In fact, we are both being 'naughty' and having a grand time of it, heading towards that

Dominican restaurant that Miguel has recommended and he, still repeating along the way, "I won't pay for dinner so you'd better be prepared to shell out some money!"

By now he seems worried about it. The short drive is grand fun. Miguel assails me with a long monologue about my well-known character defects. This is a favorite pastime for both of us, to rail at each other in order to inflict feigned guilt, and while doing so, confirming our love for each other by overstepping boundaries. It is an odd game we play, but we understand its rules. My friend assails me unforgivingly, but not without a touch of affection. Now he imitates the self-righteous expression I hold on my face, while I in turn, chide him for being "porcine fat". Fits of laughter send our limbs in every direction. Within his babble at my expense, I ridicule his double chin that abruptly sends us off into more streams of uproarious giggling to the point of helplessness. He opens his coat to reveal his worn out body, similar to a circus clown, who exhibits his swollen stomach to an appreciative gallery, resulting in uncontrolled convulsions that leave us both doubled over in the back seat. Tears roll down our eyes by now. Our driver is laughing with us. When we recover to a point of sanity, it occurs to me that this might be the last laugh we'll have together, considering Miguel's illness, but I keep that sad fact to myself.

We enter the nearby Dominican restaurant, the owner of which is an attractive, gutsy-looking Dominican girl. When she leaves the table I whisper to Miguel, "She looks like she needs some guidance." We giggle like schoolboys, while the nearby clientele observes our private joke with an obvious wish to be included. The effort isn't made by either of us. Our joviality seems a bit forced with Miguel fading fast, to the point where eventually, as orders are taken and meals are served, he leaves his unseasoned pasta untouched. During our brilliant hour in the sun, I forgot entirely his diarrhea from HIV, but now my friend seems to be slipping away from me, at least for the night. In his weakened condition, the party wanes noticeably. We converse a bit more, trying our best to pretend the night is young, until it is apparent Miguel should return to the comfort of his apartment, not before he excuses himself for the bathroom with his stomach plaguing him. He has salvaged a few anguished, diarrhea-filled hours in my behalf, but the time for parting has come. He asks to be escorted to his door, which I do. A handshake and promise from him "to get in touch if I'm ever in Los Angeles" ends the evening. We both know from the sincere expression on our faces that will never happen.

~~~

Taking my exit, I plod through the piles of rustling leaves that have drifted onto the sidewalk from Tomkin's Square Park along Tenth Street. My head dips into the freezing wind, passing a few ambulatory, gray shapes as I head west. I stride to my destination, listening to the city's percussive symphony with its bombastic blare of car horns and shrill shouts of children playing in the streets. The syrup sky envelops me with its thick coat of cobalt blue at dusk, familiar urban blanket of azure when shadow replaces light and the yellow glare from store windows spills glowing shafts onto cement sidewalks. Spanish bodegas give Avenue C a cool webbing of crisscrossed neon beams, as if an aerial light show were entertaining each passerby.

The city roars with expectancy, screams in defiance, wailing a night sound. Anything can happen. It is the beginning of the weekend after dusk, and the locals will dress up, gather in crowds, flaunt their sexuality and sleep with each other through the early morning hours. Overlooking the festering Tomkins Square Park, the velvet night breathes sympathetically, emitting faint clouds of steam, as I shiver in the brisk, early evening cold. All is in harmony, passing crowds of street people hovered between lampposts in their ghetto jungle, murmuring in deep, throaty tones, broken by an occasional piercing scream, as if from a herd of primordial, furry, horned species that raises the hairs on my arms. Junkies shoot chemicals into their arms, their legs scarred from kicking garbage cans out of their way, the cornered, the trapped, and I one of them, loping from street to avenue, from coffee house to barroom, until their homes are found at last. They scream in defiance and moan in dark railroad apartments, wailing a night sound in the wee hours, rolling and tossing in their beds, their

254

covers thrown onto board floors and windows opened wide for neighbors to hear.

Police sirens chase drug addicts in wide-brimmed hats, and the city is in burning chaos. Lanky long-haired poets pretend to break the law, shouting their literary message to coffee-drinking neighbors, who pay their rent late and fight court battles against stingy landlords - trials run by publicity hungry judges, who cater to shifty lawyers, defending guilty clients, who claw at the spiritual coffers of mankind and who are bargained free, until the next rape offence takes place on another day. The poor are crushed by the weight of their ways and left to elbow each other with their noses running, sinuses bursting, each needing to be first, each needing to be noticed. Corporations are blind to the rest of us, while they push to get ahead, trained by a selfish system to kick and to shove, to kill or to be killed. Meanwhile faraway Texas lakes are polluted by waste matter from Aero Dynamic factories, employing large numbers of workers to build planes that will bomb countries that speak in strange tongues, indecipherable languages.

I move quickly through the passing crowds, a man with a purpose, heading definitively towards Saint Mark's Place and then to my rented room below Houston.

Arriving at the Ludlow Hotel, I climb the stairs and enter my rented space with the image of Miguel purging his guts out. I envision him in a fetal position, while musing about our day together, aware that we won't see each other for a while, maybe forever. I probably won't witness his deterioration for the next few years, during which time he could possibly contract a case of full blown AIDS. Apparently the diarrhea has to do with not being able to ward off bacteria with his weakened immunity. He knows he's dying, and I confess my fear of his pending death, admitting also that even though our friendship has been complicated, he is special to me. I actually love the man. For want of a better explanation, I speculate our connection is based upon both humor in the face of all that is grim and my absolute respect for him as an artist. We had our differences once, but that time is passed. When a man is going to die, how can one dwell upon the negative? What is to be gained by overlooking what we've meant to each other? It is up to us to respect our bond before time runs out.

~~~

Miguel, my dear friend, there will be a time in the hereafter when we shall meet again. Our playful souls will bounce together in a jolly game of spiritual volley ball. Quiet codes of communication will softly breathe into our molecular fusion with an extra wattage of love that will ignite the hemisphere with delightful implosions upon our union. I miss you, Miguel, when you are gone, but too much time together would benefit neither of us. You are my kind friend, who with a serpent's tongue, has so easily diminished me in the past, but fortunately we have arrived at that plateau where we can appreciate each other fully. No hero worship between us either. No, we do not worship our kind but rather simply discover the value of friendship at a time when you are about to leave us.

I accept that, my friend, expecting to meet again but not without telling you first that you are special to me. Such cliché', but, nonetheless, it is the best I can say, given that I am part beast, and you have brought out the best in my primitive way of doing things, my friend. Hopefully I have done the same for you in spite of my small jealousy of your gift, your poetry, your enthusiasm, your rhythmic syncopation with life that is so congruent with the beauty of expression. My envy is disguised by my retreat from the world. If I were honest, I too would be out there with you, shouting to the rafters my poetry. As I listen to your message, greed for self-expression overwhelms me, causing a lock upon my throat. A cry is confined to a choked muffle that I call my voice. Upon hearing its gurgle, side by side with the spouting fountainhead of your mellifluous melody, Miguel, your poetry, I am stricken by the meagerness of my parched attempt. But such talent is not for everyone, my friend, certainly not for me. No, I hover in dark corners, hidden from those who might notice my interpretations of existence on this planet. My choice has been to cramp them instead.

The best of me has already disappeared with years, unnoticed passage of days and nights that measure time, but somehow I have managed to remain alert in the face of death. My burning lungs remind me daily of death's tendency to lean gravely in my direction, but I am inclined to side step that ominous event, so as not to be smitten with its curse.

Curse? No, not a curse, more a blessing, that long slumber that finally terminates endless banging in one's belfry, giving way to more important considerations that drive me forward *(or is it backward)* toward more fertile terrain? Death, after all, might take the form of gentle caressing of our souls, sending messages of love, comforting each other, side to side, belly to belly and heart to heart. Meanwhile, I am listing like an old ship to the left and then to the right, sinking gradually, growing more decrepit with each passing day. I'm tired of the effort to survive but insist upon moving forward.

I want to live in spite of my complaints - something about facing the struggle that makes sense. The battle is what gives me pleasure. But a 'significant other' must witness that battle. That's where you come in, Miguel; to witness my struggle, as I have witnessed yours. Having not contracted AIDS is the only thing I can brag about at this point in my life. Admittedly, I am a self-centered fool for even thinking such a thing, when I realize what a loss Miguel will be.

Slowly I ready myself for bed.

You're an Actor, Aren't You?

August 30, 2011, 12:04 pm, yesterday, while waiting for an interview at the *Los Angeles Theater Center,* I sat, drinking my coffee, at an outside table on Spring Street in downtown Los Angeles. The surrounding architecture impressed me, the beautiful cornices on the monumental building across the street, interrupted occasionally by an interesting passerby strolling on the sidewalk. It was a peaceful part of my day, capping the opening of a new play I'd written, *'Once in Doubt'* for which I was about to be interviewed by the Los Angeles Times. The play had received exceptional reviews and a *'Los Angeles Drama Critics' Circle Award'.* No pressure was upon me. The scheduled interview would be simple and honest with a few questions fielded on camera for publicity purposes during the run of my play. I watched and waited, drinking my coffee.

A man passed by, and upon recognizing me, he pointed and said, "You're an actor, aren't you?" I answered, "Yes." His excitement mounted. "You're in *'Year of the Dragon'*, aren't you?"

"Yeah," I said appreciatively for being recognized. The exuberant fellow obviously meant no harm. Immediately I enjoyed his warm enthusiasm and didn't mind being accosted during my private moment in the sun.

"Shit, I've seen you in a lot of great stuff, a lot of great stuff, *'Year of the Dragon'*, *'Born on the Fourth of July'*, *'Walk Hard'*, *'Interview with the Assassin'*. I saw you in *'The Hundred'* the other day on Netflix and *'The Ref'* too. You were in *'The Ref'*, weren't you?"

"Yeah," I said.

"You been acting a long time."

258

"Yeah, I been doing it for fifty years now, just finished the television series *'Justified'*."

"Oh, yeah, you were in that too with that other actor. What was his name?"

"Timothy Olafant", I answered.

"Oh, yeah, that's the guy."

He reached out and we shook hands. The man was beside himself. He was dark, with a pony tail and wore a black, well-fitted suit. He spoke very fast and was full of compliments about my work.

"You're a character actor," he said. "You can play anything. I've seen you in a lotta stuff. You'll always work. You're a character actor. You're a great actor. Boy, I love your work. You're great! You'll work forever. Oh, man, wait till I tell my brother. Oh, man. Thanks, man. I'm gonna tell my brother I met you. Oh, man, wow!"

"Thank you," I said. "Thank you."

"I'm so glad to meet you," he said. "It's great meeting you. I hope to see you again. Good luck," he said. "This is great. I'm gonna tell my brother. Wow, this is great."

He walked off, leaving me to my coffee. I felt good at having been recognized. His enthusiasm was genuine, and I was moved by his reaction to my work. He didn't know my name. It wasn't as if I were famous, but he respected me. Being recognized in public is life-affirming. My struggle to be an actor has offered a measure of worth to audiences I have affected. Today, my performances in some sixty films and numerous television shows provide visible proof that I am worthy as an artist and as a man.

But the notion of self-worth is still elusive today; to feel worthy, to feel confidence that there is intrinsic value in my being alive on this planet. Granted, people are affected by characters I've created for directors like Tim Robbins, Neil Burger, Jake Kasdan, Michael Cimino and Oliver Stone. But I'm still left with a lingering question, having to do with what public recognition really means on a personal level. Yes, I am recognized and have achieved that which I once pursued. This recent encounter with a total stranger gave me momentary pleasure, but after we parted ways, I was left with the question of "who am I really?" "And what does this experience of 'living the life' amount to"? Oh, yes, I am proud of the struggle I endured in bringing my career to its logical finishing point, although, at age fifty, I'm not dead yet, and I'm still working, so the journey not over. In fact, I'll be shooting a film next week, entitled *'Made in Chinatown'*.

Still, the goal I've been pursuing for some thirty years still leaves me in a state of wonder. I am still searching for something more spiritual than pleasing strangers who flatter me with a few words and are gone forever. Momentary satisfaction is too often followed by a spiritual void. Their enthusiasm, of course, is appreciated, but at one time I believed attention from audiences might solve the condition of angst with which I live daily. That belief no longer holds true.

Today I am not completely at peace with myself. Public approval alone, although enjoyable, does not fulfil me. After overcoming so many obstacles, some unknown element is missing in the end. Recognition for my work at a turning point of my career did encourage me to continue, but today my greatest satisfaction stems from a number of fronts, one of which is pride from never having surrendered to failure, but something more is necessary, my children's education and their personal satisfaction for one; creating beauty in the form of paintings, perhaps, which I do on a daily basis and, of course, my love for my wife, Robyn.

The truth is that, in spite of my success, which is fragile at best, I am left with a longing of sorts, a pang in my stomach for something large in the human spirit, the nature of God perhaps, something 'bigger' that represents the very best in humanity, the spiritual, more human part that even now, after struggling to achieve in my profession, has been only partly fulfilled. I am still troubled in the aftermath of a lifetime of acting, still searching to assuage anxiety about what it all sums up to. Universal love perhaps? Both to give it and to receive it? My children and my wife again come to mind, the love I feel for and receive from them. What could be more meaningful? Something more? No, nothing. Perhaps the 'search' itself has offered what might be called momentary 'happiness'. I'll take it for what it's worth and continue searching.

~~~

A slight haze comes upon me, like billowing clouds, soft as they graze my cheek, revealing the cherubic face of Oona, my green eyed daughter, dancing as a little girl and how I love her so. My daughter managed to grow up happily, and that is a small miracle. Nonetheless, it is true. She was an unrehearsed product of my too often planned life. How could she have managed to come from her father's loins, alive and so well in spirit, considering the whacks I have given myself along the way? Something I rehearsed beforehand, perhaps, but then, no, I attribute it rather to the guile of nature that does things so well. In addition to nature's scheme of things, I'm also taken by a somewhat dreamy quality of pure joy *(I say this earnestly)*, when faced with her graceful presence, her eyes big and clear, full woman's body, tall and radiant to behold. I've never been jealous of her admirers. She's always provided a respite from the looming, dark world that aimed itself at me during my youth. I love her for being a personification of peace, an island of calm, a month of weekends in the country that her luminous face provides, along with her love for her dad and, yes, even her dependence upon me for a few bucks once in a while. In the end, my beautiful daughter allowed me to overcome the shadow of my youth. I am so very thankful for her presence in my life.

I had a Meeting Then with my Agents

2018

I am an actor in need of a job, sitting before my agents, dressed in beige Dockers with a green silk shirt, polished shoes that fit like the boxes they came in. I am the center of attention, aiming to please. Selling my talent is my sole purpose in this office. Two of these good people are in their twenties; Cornelius, an articulate African-American, who speaks with a pleasant, educated, British accent and Christina, both unmarried without children. Sarah, a mother of two, appears to be in her early fifties. They've never acted on stage, nor will they ever do so. I forgive them for that. It is an impossible profession for most. Battle scars left from living 'the life' will never be imprinted upon their faces; the inherent insecurities performing life brings, lack of income, difficulty supporting one's children, not to mention nagging inhibition that blocks full expression on stage. My agents' healthy appearance sharply contrasts with my frayed figure, earnestly looking for work, seeking my next buck. They understand, I'm sure, the plight of an actor's survival, the precariousness of such a life.

I'm safe in their presence.

Calmness defines my comportment. The meeting is going well. My prodigious gift of gab allows conversation to progress smoothly. I smile often, as if I were confident, which oddly I am, entertaining with pleasant anecdotes about my children. The mention of children is particularly useful. The notion that I, of all people, could possibly raise four young ones suggests I'm somewhat civilized. Taking my children to soccer and basketball games and making sure their homework is done properly is not for the meek of heart. Only a functioning human being takes care of his kids, a man responsible enough to maintain a house of dependents with a wife of thirty years and willing to stay.

Surely I mention that too, but in a subtle way, so as not to exaggerate the normality of my daily existence, which might suggest I am too bourgeois to be a truly creative artist. Perhaps it would be more impressive to present myself in the same light as the very talented Robert Downey Jr. with his erratic drug-induced off-screen behavior or possibly the eccentric genius of Marlon Brando would be a suitable paradigm. But there is something to be said for normality. Being a somewhat boring person, I abstain from drink nor do I take drugs, but I assume that shows on my face, after forty years of abstinence. This subject I avoid, and prefer elaborating upon my son's basketball games to affirm the image of a family man.

My agents respond favorably. I manage to slip in a few of my films at suitable intervals, with special emphasis upon my recurring role of *'Arlo'* in the TV series *'Justified' (There's a money-maker for you)*; films and television that define me as a professional, not to overlook twenty-three years on the New York stage, during which time dozens of plays were performed. But careful not to boast, I'm overdoing it a bit, listing credits of all things. No, best to be modest - personal tidbits describing periods of dysfunctionality could possibly be revealed, if only for the humor of it, events that have pushed me to the edge when a lighter touch might have served me better. At least the past has offered a measure of emotional depth, both as an actor and as a human being.

As I say, the meeting is going well with a few anecdotes offered to lighten the mood - my false beard falling halfway off during Mark Anthony's "Friends, Romans, countrymen . . ." speech while playing a plebeian in Shakespeare's *'Julius Caesar'*.

"I tripped over a flat while running across the stage towards Anthony, falling flat on my face and my beard hanging loose from my chin; the cast and the audience doubled over with convulsions of laughter and the sixty-year-old actor, playing twenty-year-old Mark Anthony, furious weeks afterward for ruining his so-called 'brilliant performance'."

My agents laugh loudly. Humor serves a purpose here, releasing tension in the room. The manner in which I carry on suggests 'sitcoms' as a career possibility. Yes, I am indeed a funny man; that is, when I put my mind to it. Goodness, how far I've come since my youth; describing my false beard falling off on stage would've been impossible once. My, my, how I've matured, so willing to admit foolish blunders on stage. We all are fragile fools in the end, even these kind agents, sitting before me, allowing the time spent to amuse them. Yes, things are going very well with my agents. Decades ago, not a word of this would be mentioned, but today honesty is a full-fledged commitment for me. I'm even willing to reveal what a fool I've been for much of my career. Nothing to fear in the telling of it; we've all fallen on our faces at one time or another. All of us have failed. Failure is part of life and nothing to hide.

Meanwhile there is no conflict between us to speak of, no suspicion detected in the light patter of our conversation. Pleasant expressions are plastered upon our faces. They trust me on the basis of my varied fifty-eight year career, only parts of which I dare reveal, avoiding most of the mishaps along the way, the emotional road blocks and various hazards that briefly held me at bay. No, I needn't mention those to my agents.

Sarah inquires what has happened to my hand. Two of its fingers are covered with white tape. She asks jokingly if I've been boxing. I pause for a second before answering.

"Yeah, I have been boxing," I exclaim. "I punch a heavy bag for exercise and lost one of my hand wraps," I add. "The inside of my boxing glove rubbed against my bare skin and burned my knuckle. It's nothing."

Again, the whole truth; I do punch a heavy bag, and I did lose my hand wrap. I wonder whether this sounds odd, to be violently punching a leather bag at my age, whacking it to the point of oblivion - the physicality of it, the force of my blows against its surface, the exertion of muscles in the throes of a feigned battle against a deadened heavy bag that cannot fight back. The pleasure of physicality is foreign to them, I suspect, the clean fun of bashing my gloved fists against a dead weight, as if it were a real person. "Is he violent?" they must ask themselves - strange sport, boxing, especially for a sixty-year-old man not in the least interested in combat. They seem to accept my explanation. I'm safe for the moment.

My violent youth of breaking noses and jaws won't be suitable subject matter, nor my job as a bouncer in a New York bar some thirty-five years earlier. None of it is revealed, the jealous rages, the fights, sucker punches to anonymous faces, when I was a young, insecure, teenage boy, the havoc I imposed upon others and upon myself, when inadequacy was felt so deeply that the only recourse was to strike out at the nearest male. Jealousy over a girl was always involved. My father was my model then; "Like father like son", the barroom brawler, a man who dealt with the world with fists. Men fought in the fifties with fists. Violence was more accepted before the Vietnam War. Men were men, if they were willing to fight, a sign of alleged manhood. Drugs changed all that, along with the unwinnable Vietnam War, which gave birth to the 'flower children,' not to mention common sense.

Much has changed since then. There was never an easy choice along the way. It was always harsh and difficult, always teetering on a tightrope about to fall, until success finally came my way. Roles in *'Walk Hard'*, *'Dead Man Walking'* or *'Interview with the Assassin'*, *'The Ref'*, *'Year of the Dragon'* and *'Born on the Fourth of July'* brought long delayed acceptance among my critics. I was in my forties by then, after twenty years of hand to mouth living, bordering on poverty. My wayward behavior changed for the better with success, thank God. Today rational thought is my model, not violence, but I needn't explain to my agents. Violence toward a heavy bag is not violence at all, rather pure exercise to keep myself fit; biceps, back and chest, firm and taut, the body of an aged boxer but not quite.

Sitting before my agents, dressed in my Dockers and green silk shirt, polished shoes, aforementioned bandages on one hand, eager to please, ready to serve. "Please, please represent me, find me a film. I'm a normal, peaceful guy," is the underlying theme of my comportment. "I won't smash anyone in the mouth, the way I do a heavy bag," is my tacit promise. "I'm a professional actor, a pro's pro and yours for the taking. I only punch heavy bags" with a

265

placid smile on my face. In truth, I pose little threat to the world. Violence is out of the question. If my agents do reject me, I certainly won't retaliate.

The urge to entertain again overtakes me. Yes, it's important to be funny in this office. My description of forgetting my lines in a production of *'Julius Caesar'* produces huge belly laughs from all of them, as does a detailed description of my late entrance in a Broadway musical, *'Zoot Suit'* that left the cast in an absolute frenzy, finally walking onto the stage with a full-sized American flag in my hands and a dumb expression on my face, as if nothing were unusual.

"Oh, Ray, you are too, too funny!" Cornelius begs, "Please, you're killing me."

At which point, I embark upon a description of my first television venture, rising from my chair, as I imitate myself in a state of total panic.

"How petrified I was during my first television series, *'The Oldest Rookie',* how tense and to the point of absolute distraction! Such self-doubt controlled my every move those days, so daunted I was of being discovered a charlatan."

"A charlatan? What's a charlatan?" Cornelius asks, barely able to speak through a spasm of laughter.

"A charlatan is a phony, a fake actor," I say, "like me!"

They all chuckle at that one.

"That pompous British director of 'K-2' was a charlatan! That guy I worked for back in 1990. He'd never directed anything more than some 'cooking show' in England and never a full length feature film. Remember him? Frank . . . something was his name. He suspected I didn't care enough about the project we were filming. Which I absolutely did not! The script was abominable! My failure to attend a cast dinner on the first night on a barren, Canadian glacier caused an unspoken rift between us for the entire month on that God-forbidden tundra!"

Now I'm laughing at myself in the company of these professionals. The darker periods of my career I freely describe, obstacles I thought I'd forgotten, the outright blunders that become a joke between us. For three years during my mid-twenties, I left the acting business and turned to sculpting and painting. No, I won't get into that; no purpose in revealing that anxious chapter of my life.

My agents have fought their own internal battles in the so-called 'business' on a scale perhaps equal to mine. Credit is due for their struggle, although their demons are less visible than mine, another shade of gray in an otherwise somber palette. Their survival instincts are no doubt more intact than mine, especially in the case of Sarah, both older and also a caring parent. At any rate, working behind the scenes seems to suit all three of my agents very well.

"Good, honest people," I say, and a suitable criterion for our collaboration.

Again I smile. They return my smile. I speak of the current goodness of my life, and they respond with approval. Sarah, the agent boss, speaks of her twelve-year-old son, a safe subject, expanding the importance of our careers to something far more significant, namely our children. On the basis of tenure in the business, Sarah is the most important voice in the room. The complexity of rearing a child establishes an unspoken bond between us. She trusts me as a parent, as she trusts her own parenthood. Our commonality separates us from the other two.

"My oldest son recently graduated from Amherst College," I proudly say.

"That's wonderful," she says. "My kids will be going to college in the next few years."

"My youngest son, Liam, has been accepted to Sara Lawrence College with a thirty thousand dollar Merit Scholarship. He just finished his freshman year."

"Wow!" she exclaims. "That's wonderful!"

Her response is genuine. Our bond is based upon our offspring. We both care about our children more than ourselves, two adults, having lived, lost ground, regained our composure and onward to the next. Sarah and I respect each other. She's never said as much, but I sense her respect. The woman's eyes suggest the struggle she has endured in this harsh show-business world. We are two adults poignantly aware of what hardship means to survive.

If these good people were to be inflicted with bouts of fear, common sense would steer them away from its cause. "Rightfully so," I say. Fleeing from personal demons I recommend whole-heartedly; that is, under normal circumstances. But the profession of acting is not normal. Performing involves both confrontation with one's self, while doing the business of escaping into a character's psyche. One has to "face the music", so to speak, before an audience. This is, of course, confrontation at its extreme. Looking back on my past that almost sunk me more than once, yes, I forgive anyone for avoiding that which they fear. Flight for safer ground is a human tendency, when floods of anxiety become unmanageable. Escape would be expected for any normal soul.

Small talk is best in this office. I cleverly focus upon subjects amusing to them, highlighting the traumas, the road blocks, the empty holes, hazardous mental terrain that precipitated numerous blunders in my career. Laughter continues; the mood has become irreverent. I can say anything at this point, and my agents respond with uncontrolled bursts of laughter. In the same breath, I mention being fired from a job at the 'White Barn Theater'.

"Age twenty-eight and so inadequate in the role, mostly from nerves, not to mention I couldn't act to save myself. Absolutely petrified during dress rehearsal, skipping out to New York City with my heart in my mouth, forlorn from a breakup with a girlfriend and so depressed I could barely speak the lines. With the help of a friend I did return and opened the play. My shaky performance made it through the evening, but the audience must have wondered why I was hired for the role. In my weakened state, I did manage to complete the play's short run, but they refused to use me in the New York production, understandably so. My exclusion was mutual, the daunting costume changes were impossible. The play closed in a week to bad reviews. The lead actor, 'Kevin' was his name, has since been silenced by a fatal brain tumor, a fine actor too. The uninspired, female lead, who wrote the play as a vehicle to enhance her career and whose name I've forgotten, has dropped off the face of the planet as well. She probably left the business, as well I might have done, had I common sense, which I sorely lacked at the time."

Again, my agents giggle throughout my self-effacing scenario. So far they've responded with gales of laughter. The mood here is richly warm. Things are going well with my agents. My stories are good for another laugh or two. Encouraged by their response, I continue.

"What, he, an actor?" I shout, imitating my peers' impression of me when I first began my career.

My fellow football teammates at Brown University ridiculed my early attempts, sitting in the back row of the college theater, smirking at my alleged 'performance'. I certainly gave them something to laugh about; couldn't act to save myself and still can't!" exclaimed with unabashed bravura.

But humor at my expense has run its course. Their laughter is beginning to feel strained. Humor is useful to be sure, but time to switch the mood. A shy confidence seems the best strategy, rather than bluster, a conscious effort to focus upon my current, rewarding and sane life. I prefer to appear calm and confident. My agents are on my side by now; no need to panic. Common sense must prevail. It is so very important to be liked by my agents; so important for these people to find work for me. Projecting my natural charm is the best tact and, above all, avoid trying too much to please. Earning a living in film is my imperative in this office and not tooting my horn nor overdoing it with tedious jokes that require an endless and tiring response.

Meanwhile, my agents seem so very trusting of my dependability. If only they knew the whole of it. Christine shifts the discussion to some of my films, describing some of my proudest portrayals of fathers whose children have been murdered or paralyzed from the waist down by the perils of war, as in the case

269

of *'Born on the Fourth of July'* and *'Dead Man Walking'* - mentioning in the same breath how adept I am at playing menacing gangsters or killers of Presidents, as in *'Interview with the Assassin'*, pathological men with that 'thousand mile stare,' who have a propensity for injuring people or bullying them unmercifully to have their way, not to overlook neurotic poets and half-crazed artist painters hopelessly in love, as in my play, *'Once in Doubt'*, the main character of which carries a weight so great that accommodating the normal requirements of society is not an alternative. They are unaware that each and every one of these characters could easily have been I, had my life taken a different turn, pushed, as they were, by psychological forces beyond the boundaries of social acceptability and maybe the reason I played them so well. Demonstrating the proper degree of restraint, I avoid commenting and simply listen to her flattery with a humble expression planted on my face.

I seem so seasoned, sitting before my agents, a bit old, but healthy and wise; the wisdom that comes from experience, toughness of mind from surviving numerous obstacles along the way. In fact, my obstacles have been my education, the platform upon which is built a sane existence and a career that has enjoyed decades of success. If only they knew the whole of it. No, better they don't. As far as my agents can surmise, I'm a solid performer, a confident man as well. They would never believe how many auditions I've bungled or my state of panic, when under pressure of seeking a job. Nor would they believe I once crumpled to the stage floor, as if I'd been wounded, after forgetting my lines during the aforementioned performance of Shakespeare's *'Julius Caesar'*. No, I seem so healthy and wise. Such a mishap could never have happened to such a professional. To avoid alienating the three agents before me, the fears, anxiety and tension I once carried into work situations are excluded from our conversation.

Yes, all is good. My agents will submit me for roles; that is, if I keep an even keel when the waves become inordinately rough. I am a dependable, working actor, and for all intents and purposes, things are going quite well, small miracle. How did that happen? Is it because somewhere deep inside I am confident that each and every mishap was not a true reading of who I am? A core of strength within me will never, ever give up. Undaunted toughness has established a willful, although somewhat blind longevity that refuses to bend to this day.

"I like what I do," I suddenly exclaim and meaning every word of it. "My career has been good to me."

I cannot for the life of me stop myself.

"Strangers sometimes shake my hand, offering enthusiastic congratulations for my work! I'm proud of my career!"

This momentary outburst is a bit much both to them and to me. I've promised myself not to boast. Bragging never serves a purpose. Their eyes widen in surprise and a worried look appears on their faces when I speak.

"Yes, you've done very well, Ray" followed by an uncomfortable silence.

A line has been crossed. My excitement got the better of me. Goodness, what came over me, the bragging part that is? Within a few seconds, I calm down, realizing I've shot my wad, realizing also that success has often been the result of pure accident; once by coming to tears, while the cameras were rolling, for reasons having nothing to do with the story-line of the film I was shooting. The audience never knew the difference. I was feeling bad was all, after being chastised by Oliver Stone for taking too many pauses while shooting a scene in *'Born on the Fourth of July'* and immediately after his scolding, it rained, forcing a schedule change to the scene with Tom Cruise returning home from Vietnam paralyzed from the waist down. My vulnerability in that scene, although accurate to the tragic situation between father and son, was a happy accident, having more to do with Oliver's manipulation, rather than any skill on my behalf. The scene, I might add, was performed brilliantly, again the result of a happy accident, but nonetheless, these kind agents attribute the emotional fullness of my character to my acting skill. Surely that was not the case. Oliver Stone's disapproval was the stimulus for my excellent work on that day and not Tom Cruise's paralyzed body.

271

But the truth would serve no purpose here.

I bid them goodbye and warn them that I won't be available during the twenty-seventh through the thirtieth of September. "A high school reunion," I explain.

"What year?" Sarah asks, then a slight pause, long enough for the other two to perk up their ears. My age will be revealed at last and probably a detail they've been wondering, since I walked into the room. "He's well-preserved," followed by the underlying question, "But is he older than he looks?" "My forty-eighth," I say, knocking off two years a bit defiantly as if, "What are you going to do about it." Sarah says, "No!" as if that's shockingly old for a man in my profession, but I quickly sidetrack the subject by mentioning a teacher, who will attend my reunion, a 'surrogate father' of sorts. Now they all know my age. God forbid. The bottom has been taken out of everything.

I am a bit tongue-tied with my agents fully cognizant of how much time it has taken to arrive at this level in my career, until success balanced the equation. Decades have passed and fewer possibilities are available, but on the more positive side, I am able finally to settle for "what is" rather then what "should have been". I am me, old and still confident enough to make a go of it, determined enough to bring quality to my career, even at this last stage of my life. Yes, my silk shirt and beige Dockers have served me well. I'm going places with my widening girth that suggests a degree of comfort that at long last has come my way; quite a contrast to the days when I slept on a mattress on the floor on Manhattan's East Tenth Street and washed out of a small sink. Much goodness has happened since then, but never an easy choice along the way. It has always been difficult; always teetering and about to fall. But I did finally find my place in the world, thank God, but needn't explain it to my agents.

My relationship with them is that of an elder statesman, enjoying respect that is due me. We all shake hands. They know little about me, and I know little about them. Perhaps that is best. Our pasts are irrelevant to the present. We say goodbye, and I leave my agents' office, make my entrance into the elevator, whose mirrored walls reveal the bald spot on the back of my head.

~ ~ ~

Los Angeles, California

November 1, 2016, 11:41 am

~ ~ ~

The sun shines through my brain, swooping ideas like birds. Images strike me continuously, a mental fluidity of sorts, images lying at my fingertips, moments of life itself, like swooping cranes with wing spans, reaching with far-reaching girths, spanning continents. My wings have not been clipped at age eighty-one. I am still able to fly, while stationed here on Earth. Metaphor is expressed by writing words or painting pictures, the struggle to tap into rich, creative terrain that might approach the truth during a work session in my studio.

My mother warned me that a day would come when work would end.

"You'll see," she said, as she lay in bed, waiting to die at age ninety-four. She wanted death in the end, lying in bed, watching television aimlessly, empty of ambition to do anything, wanting death, welcoming it, even hastening death by doing nothing with no willpower left to fulfill life's demands. For that old woman, who had accomplished so much with her life, nothing was left to do.

Dare I lie in bed like my mother did before she died? Upon contemplating that prospect, one more cigarette smoked. One more and closer to death, that long sleep uninterrupted. Life wasted? No, I shall move forward and make something of so little time left. My little girl Manon urges me onward with her little kisses to my cheeks. I must move forward for her, if for nothing else, an existential choice to live on and dig further into life's potential and accept all that comes with that choice. I will live on. I will. I will.

There must be a reason to continue creating; a remnant of salvation perhaps, a reason to live with goals still intact, goals to achieve. Internally, I gasp aimlessly for a handle to hold, for a solid reason to continue and to contend with all obstacles along the way.

At table upon which to work, yes, upon which to rest my elbows as I write or draw. Visible tools with which to work - work at something, anything, simply to work. My hands need to be busy, need to be active. Out of cigarettes now. I shall continue. Thoughts are grounded at low altitude. Wandering through the neighborhood of memory, like a vagabond, a bum, a near-do-well, who tried so earnestly to be an actor, finally doing it, followed by an actor's success and then what? Writing or a painting? And succeeding at those activities? What then? Beating the odds? Winning against all odds? What would winning involve? Peace of mind? Years invested undoing the fear, the anxiety, the self-inflicted terror that once gripped forward momentum to a halt. A few victories here and there, money in the bank to pay the bills, to provide food and a roof for my family's survival, striving, always striving for a little piece of the pie.

On! On! I can't go on! I will go on! Yes, I will go on!

Unsettled urgency - a longing within me wishes to be healed at the end of my life, to escape the usual concerns of the day and to smooth out the bumps along the way. Another part of me wishes to do nothing. Nothingness has its appeal, a blank slate, perhaps a bottomless pit, assuaged by a cigarette here and there, smoked to its filter. I write and paint in the interim. I write and act in the interim. I attempt to make a creation. I work for breath, for purpose, for life itself, regardless of the product. I find satisfaction in words. What words? This sunny Los Angeles day? A premier on Wednesday? Voting for a new President on Tuesday? Attempting to make sense of it all, when there is no sense. Creative work for the sake of equilibrium, for the sake of forward movement to the next level of awareness in a string of associations derived from day by day existence.

I exist, yes, but it is up to me to make something of living a life. What gives a life meaning? Thoughts that are common? Ordinary people go to jobs that too often dull one's existence. But thankfully I do not have a mundane job. This writing is my job, the writing down of thoughts define time spent, the arduous labor of personal expression that might fulfill this ache in me, this longing to consolidate my spirit and provide personal celebration, when so

275

much of life seems repetitive. A sense of wholeness comes my way by placing words upon paper, by dripping paint upon canvass, by playing roles and by continuing on a straight, creative path to make something beautiful out of nothing.

Alone, again; my eyes absorb color in my studio. I see shape. I see form. I hear the quiet whirr of a heater blowing warm air into the room. What will this day sum up to? 'Beauty' alone and no more than that, simply 'beauty', born from intuition alone and not so much from logic. 'Beauty' alone makes sense of it all, when a kind of 'nothingness' prevails. I might believe in God, but for me that would be a conscious choice, rather than an organic, natural truth. Truth wavers when pursued. Might as well not think about it.

"Continue" is the rule of thumb here, and no more than that. Beckett said it best.

"I can't go on! I must go on! On! On! Yes, I must go on!'

Made in the USA
Middletown, DE
25 June 2020